Evidence
Concentrate

Maureen Spencer

Principal Lecturer in Law
Middlesex University

John Spencer

Barrister, Law Reporter, and Visiting Senior Lecturer in Law
Middlesex University

OXFORD
UNIVERSITY PRESS

OXFORD

UNIVERSITY PRESS

Great Clarendon Street, Oxford OX2 6DP

Oxford University Press is a department of the University of Oxford.
It furthers the University's objective of excellence in research, scholarship,
and education by publishing worldwide in

Oxford New York

Auckland Cape Town Dar es Salaam Hong Kong Karachi
Kuala Lumpur Madrid Melbourne Mexico City Nairobi
New Delhi Shanghai Taipei Toronto

With offices in

Argentina Austria Brazil Chile Czech Republic France Greece
Guatemala Hungary Italy Japan Poland Portugal Singapore
South Korea Switzerland Thailand Turkey Ukraine Vietnam

Oxford is a registered trade mark of Oxford University Press
in the UK and in certain other countries

Published in the United States
by Oxford University Press Inc., New York

© Oxford University Press 2010

The moral rights of the authors have been asserted
Database right Oxford University Press (maker)

Crown copyright material is reproduced under Class Licence
Number C01P0000148 with the permission of OPSI
and the Queen's Printer for Scotland

First published 2010

British Library Cataloguing in Publication Data

Data available

Library of Congress Cataloging in Publication Data
Spencer, Maureen, 1941–
    Evidence concentrate / Maureen Spencer, John Spencer.
        p. cm.
    Includes bibliographical references and index.
    ISBN 978-0-19-955156-9
1. Evidence (Law)—England.   I. Spencer, John, 1942 June 2–   II. Title.
    KD7499.6.S685 2009
    347.42'06—dc22

                                                    2009024663

Typeset by Macmillan Publishing Solutions
Printed in Great Britain on acid-free paper by
Ashford Colour Press Ltd., Gosport, Hampshire

ISBN 978-0-19-955156-9

10 9 8 7 6 5 4 3 2 1

Contents

#1

Introduction, principles, and key concepts

Due process, fair procedure, the rule of law, and natural justice are interrelated principles which are fundamental to a civilised society. Achieving them in practice however involves complex considerations. This book examines the way that the law of evidence protects the right to a fair trial. This right applies of course to the participants in the trial but also to society as a whole. We all have an interest in justice being done and also being seen to be done. Achieving the correct outcome of the trial whether civil or criminal is crucial, otherwise resentment, disaffection, and agitation may follow.

Law of evidence

Murphy (2008, p1) draws a distinction between the law of evidence and evidence itself. The latter is defined (at p2) 'as any material which has the potential to change the state of a fact-finder's belief with respect to any factual proposition which is to be decided and which is in dispute'. It is the material out of which the events which led to the trial will be reconstructed in court and may consist for example of eyewitness accounts, forensic samples or objects such as weapons. The law of evidence is the system of rules and judicial discretionary practice which regulates how such material may be presented at the trial. This system is largely concerned with exclusion of evidence at trial. One reason for this was that a lay jury would not be able to evaluate certain types of evidence such as hearsay. At an extreme level evidence may be excluded because its admissibility would undermine the integrity of the system such as evidence obtained by torture. Evidence law is based on several underlying assumptions including the need for trials to be fair, to uphold standards of a civilised society and to achieve as accurate an outcome as possible, given that the truth of what happened may be elusive. The adversarial nature of the common law system is important also in determining the shape of evidence law since the parties aim to convince the court of the justice of their case and the law acts to control their submissions which might otherwise be overlong or reflect superior or inferior resources. The rules differ according to whether the case is a civil or a criminal one, in part of course because the consequences of a wrong outcome in the case of the latter are more serious.

In this book we concentrate primarily on criminal evidence because that is where the most complex issues in evidence law lie. Civil law will also be examined where appropriate.

Lack of fairness might involve wrongful acquittals as well as wrongful convictions. For example, the failure to secure convictions for the murder of Stephen Lawrence formed part of the background to proposals to remove the rule on **double jeopardy** whereby acquitted defendants could not be prosecuted again for the same offence (see *Macpherson Report* (1999) Cm 4262-1). In recent years, the thrust of government policy has been to redress the balance of the criminal justice system to be more advantageous to victims and less so to defendants. This has been one of the main objectives of the Criminal Justice Act 2003.

Evidence law could be seen as a mass of rules, but it is better, at least to start with, to look at its underlying principles, traditionally derived largely from case law, but in modern times increasingly flowing from statute.

ECHR and fair trial procedures

A good starting point in understanding what is meant by a fair trial is Article 6 European Convention on Human Rights (ECHR), now part of English law as a result of the Human Rights Act 1998.

The common law equivalent is the doctrine of natural justice which, like Article 6 ECHR, applies in both a civil and a criminal law context. Article 6 is a natural progression from Article 5, which sets out the procedure under which a person may lawfully be deprived of personal liberty, in many cases in anticipation or as a result of a civil or criminal hearing. The provisions of the two Articles, therefore, to some extent overlap. The wording of Article 6 is complex and some of the terminology needs to be analysed carefully before transposing into English law. Article 6(1) applies to both civil and criminal proceedings and calls for 'fair and public hearing within a reasonable time by an independent and impartial tribunal established by law'. Articles 6(2) and 6(3) apply only to criminal proceedings. These latter two are supplementary and give some specific but not exhaustive instances of requirements of a fair criminal trial. These provisions apply to the law of civil and criminal procedure with which the law of evidence is closely associated. Procedural and evidence law are known as 'adjectival law' to distinguish them from the substantive law of crime, tort, land, equity, and so on which form the basis of a prosecution or a suit in civil law.

Criminal and civil procedure

Procedural law is a separate area of study from evidence and will not be covered in this book although you should be aware of the importance of the Civil Procedure Rules 1998 and Criminal Procedure Rules 2005. The latter sets out the practices the parties should follow as well as proclaiming the 'overriding objective' of the Rules. Paragraph 1.1(2)(a) states that this includes ' acquitting the innocent and convicting the guilty'. It refers (para 1.1.(2)(c)) to 'recognising the rights of a defendant, particularly those under Article 6 of the European Convention on Human Rights' and also (para 1.1(2)(d)) to 'respecting the interests of witnesses, victims, and jurors and keeping them informed of the progress of the case'. It is important to recognise also that Article 6 applies to pre-trial as well as trial procedures and therefore influences the way the police gather evidence at the investigative stage.

Key concepts

The following are the main provisions, explicit and implicit, which are likely to occur in your study of evidence.

Foundational principles

The presumption of innocence

A fundamental aspect of a fair criminal trial is the requirement of the state to prove its case against the defendant. The state should run the risk of losing. However, presumptions of law or fact in favour of the prosecution, such as the principle of strict liability, are acceptable 'within reasonable limits'. Parliament may expressly shift the burden of proof. See Chapter 2.

Privilege against self-incrimination

This is a very broad concept of which the right to silence is just one part. It includes the question of how far a citizen should be required to cooperate with the state in the investigation of crime. However, the right not to incriminate oneself is not specifically included in the Convention. See Chapters 3 and 11.

The right to examine witnesses

This right is intimately related to the equality of arms principle which is enshrined in Article 6. In some cases the court has found a violation where the testimony of anonymous witnesses was permitted, such witnesses being unavailable for questioning by the defence. However, this is a difficult area particularly in view of the need to protect vulnerable witnesses, particularly victims. See Chapter 7.

Admissibility of evidence: covert surveillance

Sometimes the investigatory authorities, including the police, resort to undercover methods. The case law suggests that the provisions of the Article require similar considerations to be raised as in the operation of s78 PACE which provides discretion to exclude prosecution evidence. The Strasbourg court stresses that the admissibility of evidence is essentially a matter of national law. See Chapter 4.

Key concepts

✳✳✳✳✳✳✳✳✳✳

Admissibility of evidence: entrapment

If it is difficult to catch offenders the police may set traps or even encourage the committing of offences. They here may act as 'agent provocateurs'.

English law does not allow a defence of entrapment but in principle such evidence may be excluded under s78 PACE or alternatively the prosecution could be stayed. The key element is causation – has the accused been persuaded to do something he would not otherwise have done? See Chapter 4.

Admissibility of evidence: disclosure

In order for a trial to be fair it is necessary for evidence to be exchanged between the parties. This is particularly important in an adversarial trial because evidence is only gathered by the parties themselves. There is no investigating magistrate.

See Chapter 10 for some aspects of this complex area. It is not covered in detail in this book.

Revision tip

You are unlikely to be asked a question about fairness in general. However, in assessing, for example, whether the rules on hearsay or character are fair it is useful to have in your mind academic comment on the matter. Roberts and Zuckerman identify (2004, p18) 'five foundational principles of criminal evidence'. They are listed as:

- promoting factual accuracy;
- protecting the innocent from wrongful conviction;
- the principle of liberty or minimum state intervention;
- the principle of humane treatment; and
- the principle of maintaining high standards of propriety in the criminal process.

They argue that these provide a framework for an understanding of fair trial procedures. It would be a useful exercise for you to consider whether the current operation of the law of evidence meets these standards or indeed whether you would add to or subtract from this list.

Relevance

The above account has introduced the key legal concepts which make up the expectations of a fair trial. However, equally important for achieving a just outcome is the presentation of the facts of the case in a rational, logical, and intelligible way. As Twining (1990, p23) put it:

> The serious study of reasoning in regard to disputed matters of fact is at least as important and can be at least as intellectually demanding as the study of reasoning in respect of disputed questions of law.

A crucial concept is that of relevance. Which of the facts are relevant to the case as presented by the prosecution or claimant or the defence?

> Relevant evidence means evidence having any tendency to make the existence of any fact that is of consequence to the determination of the action more probable or less probable than it would be without the evidence. *(Rule 401 US Federal Rules of Evidence)*

Although not all relevant evidence is admitted, in order to be admissible all evidence must be relevant. Relevance is largely a matter of logic and common sense while admissibility is a matter of law. Thus, some relevant evidence may be excluded because it is more prejudicial than probative or because it would undermine the integrity of the trial to admit it. Thus there are competing issues of fairness and relevance:

> Although relevant, evidence may be excluded if its probative value is substantially outweighed by the danger of unfair prejudice, confusion of the issues, or misleading the jury, or by considerations of undue delay, waste of time or needless presentation of cumulative evidence. *(Rule 403 US Federal Rules of Evidence)*

Law and facts

All legal disputes involve a mixture of fact and law. The parties may disagree over:

- what happened;
- what are the relevant facts;
- what inference(s) can be drawn from even agreed facts; and
- how the law should be applied to the facts.

The evidence has to be relevant to a matter at issue in the trial. This means it must shed light on at least one of the following:

Facts in issue

These are based on the substantive law and in a criminal case are:

- those which the prosecution must establish to prove the defendant committed the offence which include for example the *actus reus* and *mens rea* of murder; and
- those which the defendant denies which might include issues such as lack of intent.

Facts relevant to facts in issue/collateral facts

These are side issues, eg those relating to the admissibility of evidence relevant to a fact in issue such as a confession and those relating to the credibility or the competence of a witness.

What is relevant, however, is sometimes a matter of subjective assessment and thus dispute. However, it is important to approach the matter in a rational way, starting with generalisations based on experience. Take this example from the case of Barry George who was first convicted and then acquitted on a retrial of murdering the television presenter Jill Dando.

Premise/generalisation

Part of the prosecution case was based on the following arguably questionable reasoning:

- People who obsessively collect large quantities of photographs of celebrities are more likely to be involved in their murder than those who do not collect such photographs.
- BG collected such photographs.
- BG is therefore more likely to have committed the murder than someone who did not collect such photographs.

The prosecution argument was that this evidence was relevant in that it increased, albeit minimally, the likelihood that BG was involved in the murder. The jury in the retrial was not persuaded to convict the reasoning from this generalisation.

Forms of evidence

Evidence may be categorised in a number of different ways:

Direct and circumstantial evidence

Direct evidence is based on first hand knowledge, eg A saw Y shoot Z.

Circumstantial evidence falls short of directly establishing a fact in issue, eg A saw Y running away from the scene of the shooting of Z, or Y was seen to buy a shotgun the day before the shooting of Z.

Real and testimonial evidence

Real evidence is an object, such as the gun in the above example or Barry George's photographs. Difficulties arise when the object may include a piece of writing such as a ticket. This may bring into play the rule against hearsay evidence because it then becomes a piece of documentary evidence. Testimonial evidence is the spoken evidence of a witness at trial.

Admissibility

Once the evidence is judged to be relevant then the court has to decide if there is any bar to its admissibility. This may be a rule of exclusion such as legal professional privilege or the rule against hearsay or it may be based on the exercise of judicial, common law, or statutory discretion to exclude evidence **adduced** by the prosecution. There is no common law inclusionary discretion although there is statutory inclusionary discretion for hearsay. If there is a dispute over admissibility the judge will decide the issue after hearing submissions in trial within a trial known as a *voir dire* where the jury will not be present.

Weight

Obviously, the judge is to a certain extent considering the strength or weight of the evidence when he decides on admissibility but once evidence is admitted it is for the jury to decide whether they believe it or not, ie what weight to attach to it. In a civil trial the judge performs both functions. The matter is often expressed as that it is for the judge to decide on the law and the jury to decide on the facts. Obviously, in a *voir dire* the judge is deciding on both law and facts in assessing whether there is sufficient evidence and a case to answer to go to trial. The prosecution might be halted if, for example, the only evidence presented at trial is weak identification evidence or tainted hearsay evidence.

Truth seeking versus process values

There is currently much scholarly debate on whether the current practice of evidence law is concerned too much with values other than getting at the truth. The American author Larry Laudan (2008) argues that some rules such as the standard of proof are overly concerned with making it more difficult to convict the innocent than with the overall establishment of truth. Yet other rules, such as spousal privilege, are based on protecting certain relationships rather than seeking the truth. What is clear at least is that the law has no one single objective.

Rules versus discretion

The sources of the law of evidence are to be found in common law precedents and increasingly in statute. The law is a mixture of rules and the exercise of judicial discretion either under the common law or authorised by statute, particularly **s78 Police and Criminal Evidence Act 1984 (PACE)**. The difference between the two is largely marked by the approach of the Court of Appeal. It is more likely to overturn a decision which is based on a breach of a rule than one based on judicial discretion to exclude evidence. There is no common law. Discretion to include evidence but the **Criminal Justice Act 2003 (CJA)** does introduce an inclusionary discretion for hearsay evidence (see Chapter 6).

✅ *Looking for extra marks?*

A pervasive theme in the following chapters is the relationship between the Strasbourg jurisprudence and that of the national courts. At times they seem to be at odds – see, for example, Chapter 6 on whether a conviction can be founded on hearsay evidence alone. It is useful to cite in such cases the House of Lords judgment in a housing case which has implications for the doctrine of precedence. In *Kay and others v Lambeth BC* (2006) the House of Lord held that English courts are not strictly bound by Strasbourg decisions save in an 'extreme' case where the decision of a superior court could not survive the introduction of the 1998 Act.

Conclusion

✳✳✳✳✳✳✳✳✳✳

① Conclusion

The following ten chapters aim to give you the leading principles which govern the specific areas of evidence law and also try to demonstrate the relationship between the topics covered. Textbooks and undergraduate evidence courses vary in the order in which they cover these topics. Chapter 2 covers the foundational issue at a trial, namely who has the burden of proving the case. Chapters 3 and 4 review evidence gathering during the investigation before trial particularly in relation to police undercover activity and interrogation of suspects. Chapters 5 and 6 cover hearsay and character. These are the two of the four traditional common law exclusionary rules of evidence now largely modified and codified in the **Criminal Justice Act 2003**. Chapters 7 and 8 cover various areas concerned with treatment of witnesses at trial and the final three chapters cover the remaining common law exclusionary rule, opinion evidence, and public interest immunity/privilege, the latter embracing the privilege against self incrimination and legal professional privilege.

At the end of the material in each chapter you will find a summary of the leading cases which have been examined in the text. The chapters end with Exam Questions, with some Answers at the back of the book, providing a succinct guide to success in problem-based and essay assessments which are covered in more detail in the companion volume Spencer and Spencer (2009).

❳❳ Key debate

Topic	How evidence law has been affected by the implementation of the Human Rights Act.
Authors	A L-T Choo and S Nash
Viewpoint	Reviews the impact of the Act in selected areas and concludes that it has had the most impact on the reverse burdens of proof, calls for the courts to develop a more principled, and 'English/Welsh approach' to Article 6 provisions.
Source	'Evidence Law in England and Wales: The Impact of the Human Rights Act 1998' 7 (2003) *International Journal of Evidence and Proof* 31–61.

#2
Burden of proof and presumptions

Key Facts

In criminal cases

- The presumption of innocence is specifically enshrined in **Art 6 European Convention Human Rights (ECHR)** but it is not recognised as an absolute since legislatures may **reverse the burden** of proof within reasonable limits which take account of the importance of what is at stake and of maintaining the rights of the defendant.

- In English law the principle of placing the burden of proof on the prosecution was acknowledged under the common law although it was not until *Woolmington v DPP* (1935) that the courts fully acknowledged that this applied to the *mens rea* as well as the *actus reus*.

- A criminal offence may contain several elements and there may be therefore several different allocations of the burden of proof.

- Where the prosecution bears the burden of proof, the standard is beyond reasonable doubt. If the defence bears the burden the standard is the balance of probabilities.

- The term burden of proof should be reserved for the legal or persuasive burden which is determined at the end of the trial when the jury decides whether to convict or not. The party that has the legal burden usually has the evidential burden, that is the burden of adducing sufficient evidence to make the issue a live one at the trial. It is also known as the burden of passing the judge. Exceptions to this are certain common law defences where the defendant will have to present material grounds for their consideration, before the judge will allow them to be considered by the jury.

- Misdirection by the judge on burden or standard of proof is likely to lead to an appeal.

Key facts

✳✳✳✳✳✳✳✳✳

- The **Human Rights Act 1998** has had considerable influence in this area. **Reverse burdens** will only be acceptable if they are proportionate and preserve the interest of the defendant. The court may read down a statutory provision in order to comply with Art 6.

In civil cases

- The principle in civil cases is he who asserts must prove. The placing of the burden of proof would therefore be apparent from the statement of claim and any counterclaim or specific defence, such as reference to an exclusion clause in contract or to contributory negligence.

Presumptions

- Presumptions work on occasion to remove the need for proof. They are mostly of significance in relation to civil cases.
- Factual presumptions are common sense logical inferences from a state of affairs.
- Irrebuttable presumptions of law are provisions of the substantive law, such as the provision that a child of ten and over has criminal liability.
- Rebuttable presumptions of law cover situations where once foundational facts have been proved by a party a particular state of affairs will be assumed to exist.

Related areas

The allocation of the burden of proof is intrinsic to all trials, criminal and civil. It has particular resonances with the privilege against self-incrimination in that it could be argued that the undermining of the right to silence impacts on the allocation of burden of proof. Under statute may now be a permissible presumption of guilt for failure to respond to questions or failure to testify. More specifically, it has been argued that placing the legal burden or even the evidential burden on the accused violates the privilege against self-incrimination in that the accused is at a disadvantage if he does not testify. This is, however, probably an untenable argument since the presumption of innocence in itself does not specify that obtaining proof of guilt in any particular way is prohibited activity. The debate on this involves quite sophisticated doctrinal argument. At a more concrete level you will see that references to the burden and standard of proof occur throughout your consideration of the production of evidence at trial. Note, for example, in the discussion in Chapter 3 on confessions that there are differing rules for the standard of proof for the prosecution and for the co-defendant under ss76 and 76A.

The assessment: key points

This is primarily a case law subject and you should be familiar with the details of the argument in the leading cases which are set out in the tables below. The issue of the allocation of the burden of proof in criminal cases raises both principled constitutional questions and practical problem-solving ones. As far as the former is concerned, you need to have read widely on what has been a fertile area for academic comment of late. As for the latter, you may specifically be asked to advise on the burden and standard of proof or you may assume that it forms an indispensable part of any question which gives you a scenario and asks you to 'Advise on evidence'. A common feature of such questions is to give you an imaginary statute which includes an apparent reverse burden and to ask you how the courts will approach this. Watch out also for references to common law defences, such as self-defence. They give you an opportunity to display your knowledge of evidential burdens.

Questions on civil trials are likely to concentrate on two areas. These are the question of whether the standard of proof ever approaches the criminal standard and also the shifting of the burden as claimant and defendant put claim and counter claim such as relying on an exclusion clause in a contract.

Revision tip

You need to refresh your memory about the meaning of key terms which you will have also studied in criminal law. These include: the elements of an offence, *actus reus* and *mens rea,* common law and statutory defences.

Key features and principles

This topic is really about who will bear the risk of losing a trial. A simple example from civil trials explains the point. Suppose that the claimant, C sues the defendant, D on the grounds that he failed to perform a contractual obligation to deliver some goods. D claims he did deliver. C is not able to provide proof to convince the court on the balance of probabilities that the goods were not delivered. Should the court:

Decide in favour of C

OR

Decide in favour of D

OR

Split any award between C and D?

In fact it will decide in favour of D here since in civil cases, 'He who asserts must prove' is the principle. It was C who initiated the case so he bears the risk of losing if he cannot produce proof to the required standard, the balance of probabilities. In a criminal case of course the 'presumption of innocence' has the effect of placing the burden of proof on the prosecution, who also of course initiate proceedings. This is a principle of the common law enshrined specifically also in **Art 6 European Convention on Human Rights**. If the prosecution cannot prove the case against the defendant to the standard of beyond reasonable doubt the defendant is acquitted. Legally he does not have to produce proof of innocence although tactically he will be well advised to do so.

There are three particularly problematic areas in relation to the burden of proof which will be reviewed in this chapter; the first two relate specifically to criminal trials. Firstly, the terminology, particularly the difference between the legal and the evidential burdens; secondly, the rationale behind reverse burdens; and thirdly, the contentious subject of the standard of proof in civil cases where the allegation by the claimant is of a quasi criminal act such as fraud. The standard of proof in criminal cases is more straightforward and will be covered in outline. The chapter concludes with an examination of presumptions.

Legal and evidential burdens

You must be careful how you use language in this area which is a terminological minefield. You need to understand clearly the difference between the legal and evidential burdens. In particular bear in mind that it is best to reserve the term 'burden of proof' for the legal (or persuasive) burden.

Legal/persuasive burden of proof: This is the burden which is discharged at the end of the trial when the jury gives its verdict or the civil court makes a decision.

Evidential burden: This is the burden of adducing sufficient evidence to convince the judge there is an issue to put before the court. Chronologically, it occurs at an earlier stage of the trial than the discharging of the legal burden.

Note that Lord Bingham in *Sheldrake v DPP; Attorney-Gerneral's Reference (No 4 of 2002)* (2005) stated (at p289):

> An evidential burden is not a burden of proof. It is a burden of raising, on the evidence in the case, an issue as to the matter in question fit for consideration by the tribunal of fact. If an issue is properly raised, it is for the prosecutor to prove, beyond reasonable doubt, that that ground of exoneration does not avail the defendant.

There are two preliminary keys to understanding this area which some students take time to grasp:

- firstly, be aware that there may not be one burden of proof in a trial but several according to the various elements of the offence and any statutory or common law defences; and

- secondly, it may help to consider how the burdens may shift over time as the trial progresses.

The prosecution initiate the case and they have the initial evidential burden of 'passing the judge' ie convincing the court that there is enough evidence on which a trial can go ahead in the sense that there is a case to answer. The prosecution also have the legal burden of convincing the jury of the defendant's guilt on the charge.

The defendant legally at this stage does not have any burden. A not guilty plea is enough to make every matter a fact in issue, including the identity of the defendant. Tactically, of course, it would be wise for the defendant to produce some evidence which might raise a reasonable doubt in the mind of the jury but legally there is no requirement to do so. The general rule is that the party which has the legal burden has the evidential burden but there are a number of exceptions. The situation changes if the defendant plans to raise a particular defence or if the statute purports to reverse a burden. In such situations the defendant may have only an evidential burden, or, if the court consider it reasonable and proportionate in the light of the provision of Art 6(2), the evidential AND the legal burden. How the courts decide is reviewed in the next section.

Placing the burden in criminal cases

Generally, the party which has a legal burden also has the evidential burden. There are two situations where the legal and the evidential burden may be split:

Common law defences

You will have come across the details of these leading cases in your criminal law course and most evidence courses will require that you can cite an authority for the placing of the evidential burden of a common law defence on the defence. Remember that the defence of accident is not a common law defence. As *Woolmington* (1935) decided, it acts to negative *mens rea*. See Fig 2.1. Remember that the legal burden in these cases is on the prosecution.

Legal and evidential burdens

✳✳✳✳✳✳✳✳✳✳

Figure 2.1 Evidential burden and common law defences

Common law defence	Burden	Authority
Self defence	Evidential burden on D	R v Lobell (1957)
Duress	Evidential burden on D	R v Gill (1963)
Non-insane automatism	Evidential burden on D	Bratty v A-G for Northern Ireland (1961)
Provocation	Evidential burden on D	Mancini v DPP (1942)

Statutory defences or elements of the offence

See the discussion below for a consideration of the principles on this.

The legal burden and the golden thread

Every law student will know by heart the passage from *Woolmington v DPP* (1935) referring in reverential terms to the golden thread while even then acknowledging two sets of exceptions, one, the defence of insanity, based on common law and the other based on statute, either by express or implied expression.

Reggie Woolmington was convicted of the murder of his wife by shooting. He claimed the gun had been fired accidentally. The trial judge and the Court of Appeal had held that the defence of proving lack of *mens rea* was on W. The House of Lords allowed the appeal and stated that at common law in criminal proceedings the burden of proving, beyond reasonable doubt, the *actus reus* and the *mens rea* is on the prosecution. The only two exceptions to this rule were the defence of insanity and statutory provisions. Viscount Sankey stated (at p 481–482):

> Throughout the web of English criminal law one golden thread is always to be seen, that it is the duty of the prosecution to prove the prisoner's guilt ... No matter what the charge or where the trial, the principle that the prosecution must prove the guilt of the prisoner is part of the common law of England and no attempt to whittle it down can be entertained.

Revision tip

Woolmington recognised one common law exception to placing the burden of proof (legal and evidential) on the prosecution, namely the defence of insanity, see *McNaghton's Case* (1843). In such cases remember that the standard is the balance of probabilities (see further below). This is a controversial requirement since, in effect, the accused is asked to prove the absence of *mens rea*. You should demonstrate in any question on this that the case raises questions about two presumptions, that of innocence and that of sanity. In *H v United Kingdom* (1990), the European Court of Human Rights ruled that the insanity exception did not breach Art 6(2) since the rule did 'not concern the presumption of innocence, as such, but the presumption of sanity'.

The common law approach to the burden of proof continued after *Woolmington* with the flurry of academic commentary arising from the two cases *R v Edwards* (1974) and *R v Hunt* (1986). Most evidence courses still include a review of the reasoning in these cases which is still pertinent in relation to regulatory offences. This reasoning was much criticised by academics as marking a retreat from principle to public policy considerations which were very loosely expressed.

R v Edwards [1975] QB 27

E was convicted of selling alcohol without a licence. He appealed on the grounds that the prosecution had not produced evidence that he had not been granted a licence. His appeal was dismissed. The Court of Appeal held that under the common law, where a statute prohibited an act save in specified circumstances, the court could construe the statute such that the burden of proving the existence of the circumstances, including the granting of a licence, could lie on the defendant.

R v Hunt [1987] AC 352

H was convicted of being in unlawful possession of a Class A drug, morphine. One issue at the trial was the composition of the alleged drug. The statute provided that if the proportion of morphine was not more than 0.2 per cent the substance was not unlawful under the regulations. The prosecution had not adduced evidence on the proportion of morphine; the judge would not allow a defence submission of no case to answer. The applicant pleaded guilty. The Court of Appeal upheld the conviction but the House of Lords allowed the appeal. On the facts, the composition of the morphine was an essential element of the offence, which it was for the prosecution to prove.

It could be argued that *Hunt* and *Edwards* are of mainly historical interest and have been overtaken by the enactment of the **Human Rights Act 1998**. On the other hand some leading academics such as Dennis see a re-appearance of the factors discussed in *Hunt* in the current preliminary approach under the **Human Rights Act 1998** (see 'Reverse Onuses and the Presumption of Innocence' in [2005] Crim LR 901). The cases are also cited in recent leading judgments such as *R v Lambert, Ali and Jordan* (2002). It is therefore useful for you to have some knowledge of them. *Hunt* primarily concerns the interpretive approach in the case of implied statutory exceptions. It is not applicable in cases where the burden has been expressly shifted by statute.

In essence the decision in *Edwards* attempted to address how to interpret the precursor of what became **s101 Magistrates' Courts Act 1980**. This covers the situation where an otherwise unlawful act may become lawful if the perpetrator falls within a category of persons 'with an exception, exemption, proviso, excuse or qualification'. Thus it is an offence to drive unless the driver has a licence. Following *Edwards*, it was for the accused to prove he fell

Figure 2.2 Key aspects of judgments in *Hunt* and in *Edwards*

Edwards [1974] (approved in *Hunt*)	Hunt [1986]
• Examine the wording of the statute to see if it creates an exception, exemption etc • The approach should be the same whether the offence is tried summarily or on indictment • Where the legal burden is on D the standard of proof is the balance of probabilities	• Examine what the **mischief** was that the statute was addressing • Examine the practical problems in allocating the burden of proof, including who would find it easier to discharge • Examine the seriousness of the offence which could resolve ambiguity in favour of the defence

within these categories, ie had a licence etc. The difficulty still existed, however, of distinguishing such specific defences and the elements of the offence where the burden remained on the prosecution. *Hunt* added additional factors to statutory interpretation, to be considered whether, in cases where the statute was unclear, Parliament had intended the burden to be on the defence. Both cases referred to an earlier civil case, *Nimmo v Alexander* (1968), which is still extensively cited as authority in criminal cases involving health and safety issues particularly.

Fig 2.2 summarises the combined aspects of the rulings in *Hunt* and *Edwards*.

Human Rights Act and burden of proof

There is probably no area of evidence law which has been more affected by the implementation of the **Human Rights Act 1998** than that of the allocation of the burden of proof in criminal cases. The presumption of innocence is specifically enshrined in **Art 6(2)** but the Strasbourg Court has not taken it to be an absolute principle. In *Salabiaku v France* (1988) the European Court of Human Rights found there was no principled objection to the imposition of strict liability in a criminal case involving violation of customs regulations. This should be applied 'within reasonable limits' and subject to the test of proportionality in that the courts should balance the interests of the community and the rights of the individual.

The Convention and English law

At first it seemed that the English courts in applying the Convention were adopting a more robust approach to upholding the presumption of innocence. In *R v DPP, ex p Kebilene* (2002) the House of Lords considered whether the reverse burden provisions in the

Prevention of Terrorism (Temporary Provisions) Act 1989 violated **Art 6(2)**. In the Divisional Court Lord Bingham had stated that the provisions blatantly undermined the presumption of innocence. In the event the House did not have to decide the issue since it was held that the issue in the hearing was not reviewable. However, in *R v Lambert, Ali and Jordan* (2002), the House in a majority decision held that it was not justifiable to use **s28 Misuse of Drugs Act 1971** so as to transfer the legal burden on the accused and to require him to prove that he did not know the bag he was carrying contained a controlled drug. The section should be read down to impose only an evidential burden. Lord Hutton dissented stating (at para 194) that 'it is not unprincipled to have regard to the practical realities where the issue relates to knowledge in a drugs case'.

There are to date four House of Lords cases on the subject, a number of them reversing decisions of the Court of Appeal. It is significant of the controversial nature of this area of law that a number of the decisions are majority decisions suggesting the fluid state of the law. The Court of Appeal in *A-G's Ref (No 1 of 2004)* (2004) identified a conflict between the House of Lords decisions of *Johnstone* (2003) and *Lambert* (2002). This was held not to be the case, however, in *Sheldrake v DPP; A-G's Ref (No 4 of 2002)* (2005) where the House stated that both *Lambert* and *Johnstone* were the primary domestic authorities and *Johnstone* did not depart from *Lambert*.

Navigating your way through this conflicting scenario therefore is not easy. The following account will act as a compass. You will be tempted in addressing a problem to repeat the mantra that each decision is made on its own facts and that it is impossible to derive principles to apply to the problem. This will not get you many marks. Rather, you should familiarise yourself with the judgments and their nuances and consider them in the context of the question you have to address.

✔️ *Looking for extra marks?*

In order to perform well in your assessment you should show evidence of wider reading than the standard texts and the notes you have taken from lectures. You should keep up to date with the academic discussions in key journals such as the *Criminal Law Review* and the *International Journal of Evidence and Proof*. The article by Dennis (2005) cited above provides an excellent framework with which to approach either an essay or a problem question in this area. In particular, it contains an extremely helpful table examining the key features of the leading cases. A very useful exercise would be for you to add the additional judgments which have been pronounced since the article was written.

Reverse burdens and statute

Consider the following provisions of the **Health and Safety at Work Act 1974**:

- s2(1) It shall be the duty of every employer to ensure, so far as is reasonably practicable, the health, safety and welfare at work of all his employees.

Reverse burdens and statute

****

- s3(1) It shall be the duty of every employer to conduct his undertaking in such a way as to ensure, so far as is reasonably practicable, that persons not in his employment who may be affected thereby are not thereby exposed to risks to their health or safety.

- s37 Where an offence under any of the relevant statutory provisions committed by a body corporate is proved to have been committed with the consent or connivance of, or to have been attributable to any neglect on the part of, any director, manager, secretary or other similar officer of the body corporate or a person who was purporting to act in any such capacity, he, as well as the body corporate, shall be guilty of that offence and shall be liable to be proceeded against and punished accordingly.

These provisions place on the defendant, an employer, or a corporation, a duty to provide a safe place of work, the breach of which is a criminal offence. A separate section gives the defendant employer a possible defence:

- s40 In any proceedings for an offence under any of the relevant statutory provisions consisting of a failure to comply with a duty or requirement to do something so far as is practicable or so far as is reasonably practicable, or to use the best practicable means to do something, it shall be for the accused to prove (as the case may be) that it was not practicable or not reasonably practicable to do more than was in fact done to satisfy the duty or requirement, or that there was no better practicable means than was in fact used to satisfy the duty or requirement.

In *R v Chargot Ltd* (2009) Chargot was charged with breaching this statute following an accident in which an employee who was driving a dumper truck was killed when the lorry load fell on him. The House of Lords considered where the burden of proving the defence under s40 lay. It held that the legal burden was on the defendant to prove that it was not reasonably practicable to provide the safe conditions. The employer was convicted.

Contrast this with the decision in *Sheldrake v DPP; A-G's Ref (No 4 of 2002)* (2005). The contested statutory provisions in the second of the conjoined appeals were contained in the Terrorism Act 2000. Section 11 covers membership of organisations which are listed as **proscribed** by the government as having terrorist associations:

(1) A person commits an offence if he belongs or professes to belong to a proscribed organisation.

(2) It is a defence for a person charged with an offence under subsection (1) to prove –

    (a) that the organisation was not proscribed on the last (or only) occasion on which he became a member or began to profess to be a member, and

    (b) that he has not taken part in the organisation since it was proscribed.

The defendant was charged with belonging to the proscribed organisation Hamas. He relied on s11(2) in his defence. The House held that (by a majority judgment on this point)

Figure 2.3 Outcome of *Sheldrake v DPP; Attorney-General's Reference (No 4 of 2002)* (2005)

Element of offence/statutory defence under Terrorism Act 2000	Evidential burden	Legal burden	Standard of proof of the legal burden
Belonging to a proscribed organisation; s11(1)	P	P	Beyond reasonable doubt
Proof that the organisation was not proscribed at the time of joining; s11(2)(a)	D	P	Beyond reasonable doubt
Proof that has not taken part in organisation since it was proscribed; s11(2)(b)	D	P	Beyond reasonable doubt

Figure 2.4 Outcome of *R v Chargot Ltd* (2009)

Element of offence/statutory defence under HSWA 1974	Evidential burden	Legal burden	Standard of proof of legal burden
Employee harmed by exposure to risks to health and safety	P	P	Beyond reasonable doubt
Not reasonably practicable for employer to do more than was done; s40	D	D	Balance of probabilities

notwithstanding that it was Parliament's intention to impose a legal burden on the defendant he should only bear the evidential burden. It is worth quoting part of the headnote (p 264) in full:

> ... the justifiability and fairness of provisions which imposed a burden of proof on a defendant in a criminal trial had to be judged in the particular context of each case, and the court's task was to decide whether Parliament had unjustifiably infringed the presumption of innocence; that the over-riding concern was that a trial should be fair, and the presumption of innocence was a fundamental right directed to that end; that the Convention did not outlaw presumptions of fact or law but required that they should be kept within reasonable limits and should not be arbitrary; that it was open to states to define the constituent elements of a criminal offence, excluding the requirement of *mens rea*; but that the substance and effect of any presumption adverse to a defendant had to be examined on all the facts and circumstances of a particular provision and had to be reasonable ...

The outcome of these cases is set out in Figs 2.3 and 2.4.

Applying the Human Rights Act on burden of proof

This section will try to expand on the jurisprudential considerations which underpin these two contrasting judgments. Dennis's penetrating 2005 article, cited above p 15, is the basis of the following account. He identifies several stages in the court's deliberations on whether a reverse burden should apply. First of all, there is the question of statutory interpretation and it is here that *Edwards* and *Hunt* could be applied. Then the courts move on to considering whether a reverse burden is justified as proportionate. It is here that the policy considerations in *Hunt* may be developed. At this stage Dennis considers that there are six factors which can be derived from the cases.

Factors to consider, according to Dennis (pp 908–916):

1. Judicial deference
2. Classification of offences
3. Construction of criminal liability: element of offences and defences
4. Significance of maximum penalties
5. Ease of proof and **peculiar knowledge**
6. Presumption of innocence

We have based the following tables (Figs 2.5–2.11) on the account in Dennis's article and added comment as some of the cases have been decided since its publication.

Judicial deference

Figure 2.5 The courts and the will of Parliament

Cases cited by Dennis	Comment
For a deferential stance see Lord Hope's judgment in *Kebilene* (2002), Lord Nicholls in *Johnstone* (2003) and Lord Woolf CJ in *A-G Ref (No 1 of 2004)* (2004). But contrast this with Lord Bingham in *Sheldrake* (2004) who argued that this approach might result in too little consideration of the presumption of innocence.	Dennis (p 909) distinguishes between legitimate aim, which it is the task of Parliament to pronounce on when making an enactment, and proportionality. The latter is a procedural not a substantive issue and therefore the courts should be more robust here in challenging provisions.

Classification of offences

Figure 2.6 Can the courts distinguish truly criminal and regulatory offences?

Cases cited by Dennis	Comment and additional cases
See Lord Clyde in *Lambert* (2001)	Dennis (p 911) points out the difficulty in determining the moral quality of criminal offences and in particular that it does not necessarily follow that a statutory defence to a regulatory defence will be any easier for a defendant to prove.
	See now *R v Chargot* (2009) applying *R v Davies* [2002] in placing a legal burden on the defendant employer for breach of health and safety law leading to the death of a worker.

Construction of criminal liability: element of offences and defences

Figure 2.7 Can the courts distinguish elements of offences from defences?

Cases cited by Dennis	Comment and additional cases
Lord Hope in *Lambert* (2001), referring to *Edwards* [1974] and Lord Rodger in *Sheldrake* (2004) suggested that the courts can distinguish between the elements of the offence and any defences. Lord Steyn in *Lambert* and the Court of Appeal in *A-G's Ref (No 4 of 2002)* (2005) suggested that discovering the '**gravamen**' of the offence may blur the distinction. It is better to concentrate on the nature of the moral blameworthiness.	The burden should more properly be on the prosecution for an element of the offence. However, Dennis (p 913) observes that it may be acceptable on occasion to place a reverse burden for an element of the offence in the sense that not having a licence is an essential element of the offence of unlicensed driving. Note that in *R v G (Secretary of State for the Home Department)* [2008] the House of Lords upheld the presumption of strict liability in the offence of having sex with a minor. The Strasbourg case *Salabiaku v France* (1991) on that point was disregarded. The content of the substantive law did not engage Art 6.

Significance of maximum penalties

Figure 2.8 The relevance of the penalty

Cases cited by Dennis	Comment
See Lord Steyn in *Lambert* (2001), *Sheldrake* (2004), and *A-G (No 4 of 2002)* (2005). But contrast *Johnstone* (2003) where a reverse burden was approved where the maximum penalty was ten years.	Dennis (p 914) writes that the application of this principle has been 'patchy to say the least'.

Ease of proof and **peculiar knowledge**

Figure 2.9 Ease of proof, peculiar knowledge and *mens rea*

Cases cited by Dennis	Comment and additional cases
Lord Hope in *ex parte Kebilene* (1999), Lord Nicholls in *Johnstone* (2003), Lord Clyde in *Lambert* (2001) and the Court of Appeal in *A-G's Ref (No 1 of 2004)* (2004) all referred to peculiar knowledge.	'Peculiar/special knowledge' relates to state of mind. Dennis (p 915) points out that *Edwards* (1974) had rejected the approach to peculiar knowledge which had earlier been a feature of the common law allowing reversal of the burden of proof. The current common law position is that peculiar knowledge in relation to certain common law defences places an evidential burden only. Note that in *R v Keogh* (2007) the Court of Appeal 'read down' the reverse onus defences in **ss2(3) and 3(4) Official Secrets Act 1989** because they related to *mens rea*.

Reverse burdens and statute

✳✳✳✳✳✳✳✳✳✳

Presumption of innocence

Figure 2.10 Procedural and substantive aspects of the presumption of innocence

Cases cited by Dennis	Comment
Lord Steyn in *Lambert* (2001) and Lord Bingham in *Sheldrake* [2004] identified substantive as well as procedural aspects to the principle of the presumption of innocence. Lord Bingham in *A-G's Ref (No 4 of 2002)* (2005) identified the risk of a wrongful conviction.	Dennis (p 917) points out that concentration on outcomes rather than processes is a feature of the approach of the UK courts.

Dennis continues his analysis by identifying additional principles which he argues should be considered. A more structured approach, he suggests (p 919), would be achieved by elevating ease of production of proof which, following *Edwards*, would 'require a defendant to prove a formal qualification to do an act that is otherwise prohibited by legislation'. However, questions of moral blameworthiness, particularly questions of *mens rea*, should be on the prosecution. Dennis's analysis on this point in some ways has been confirmed by the decision in *Keogh* (2007) where the court was not prepared to shift the burden on *mens rea* in a case concerning the Official Secrets Act.

The exception to the 'foundational principle' (p 920) that in cases involving moral blame the burden should be on the prosecution is to be seen in cases such as *Johnstone* (2003) and the health and safety cases such as *Davies* (2002). In these cases the perpetrator engaged in a regulated activity but one which arguably involved moral blameworthiness, such as breaching the Trade Marks Act 1994. However since in such cases the alleged offender obtained a benefit he and not the prosecution should prove exculpation from the apparently wrongful acts. Dennis (p 920) calls this the 'voluntary acceptance of risk' principle and likens it to what Roberts and Zuckerman call 'the duties of citizenship' (2004, p 348).

Sheldrake (2004)

Finally, Dennis turns to Lord Bingham's speech in *Sheldrake* (2004) and calls for an examination of not only of moral blameworthiness in the definition of the offence in question but of how far the alleged conduct itself is properly criminal. He refers (p 922) to Lord Bingham's observation in *A-G's Ref (No 4 of 2002)* [2005] 'that the definition of the offence under s11(1) Terrorism Act 2000 was sufficiently wide and uncertain as to include persons whose conduct could not reasonably be regarded as "blameworthy or such as should properly attract criminal sanctions"' namely belonging to an organisation which was not at that time **proscribed**. If the only defence available to the defendant was s11(2), to show that he had not taken part in the activities at any time while it was proscribed, he should only have an evidential burden.

As Dennis himself acknowledges (p 923), it is difficult to overcome problems even in this structured approach. The nature of moral blameworthiness is historically and socially conditioned. Dennis points out that (p 925) allowing reverse burdens for statutory defences to actions which are presumptively morally blameworthy, under the 'voluntary acceptance of risk' principle, contrasts with common law defences to serious crimes. There the burden is only evidential.

These first two stages of judicial decision-making, according to Dennis (p 927), establish whether a reverse onus is 'justified as proportionate to a legitimate aim'. If it is not so justified the courts move on to the third stage and examine whether the section can be 'read down' to impose only an evidential burden (see pp 925–927). Dennis comments (p 927), 'On the basis of Sheldrake it seems that it will almost always be possible to do this... Accordingly a declaration of incompatibility of a reverse onus will almost never be necessary.'

We have set out as a flow chart, Fig 2.11, the three-stage process identified by Dennis.

Revision tip

Identify the facts in issue in a problem scenario. This may include all the elements of the offence and also any statutory or common law defences. It is a useful exercise to do this in the form of a table since it makes it clear that there may be a number of burdens in any one case (see Spencer and Spencer 2009, p 91).

Burden of proof in civil cases

With regard to civil common law cases the allocation of the burden is apparent from the statement of claim. If the claimant fails to prove any essential element of his claim, such as for example duty of care in a negligence suit, the defendant will be entitled to judgment. Some statutes specify where the burden of proof should lie in civil cases such as unfair dismissal.

Of course, there may be difficulties in determining who bears the legal burden if it is not clear whether the defendant's denial is simply negativing an essential element of the claim or takes the form of putting forward new information. The position will depend on the construction of the contract and the legal burden may shift with each claim or counterclaim.

In *Joseph Constantine Steamship Line Limited v Imperial Smelting Corporation* (1942) the plaintiff corporation (P) claimed damages for breach of contract when the shipowners could not carry out a charter voyage because the ship was damaged by an explosion. The shipowners (D) claimed frustration in their defence. The question arose as to whether the shipowners had to prove that the frustrating event was not caused by negligence. The House of Lords decided the case as follows:

- legal and evidential burden of proving breach of contract on P;
- legal and evidential burden of proving defence of frustration on D; and
- legal and evidential burden of proving negligence which obviated the frustration on P.

Reverse burdens and statute in criminal cases

✳✳✳✳✳✳✳✳✳✳

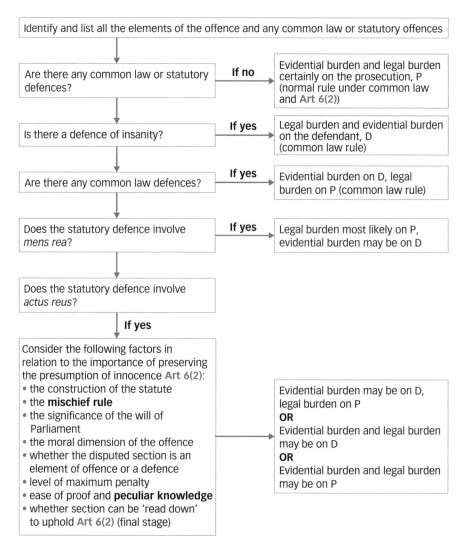

Figure 2.11 Diagram based on the analysis in Dennis (2005)

✅ *Looking for extra marks?*

Knowledge of the case of **Rhesa Shipping Co SA v Edmunds** (1985) will enhance your answers on civil cases. This case demonstrates the crucial significance in civil cases of deciding to initiate proceedings or not. On some, admittedly rare occasions, the outcome can be decided by the allocation of the burden of proof. The case involved the sinking of a cargo ship where the insurance policies required proof that the loss was caused by perils at sea. The plaintiff shipowners claimed the cause was a collision with an unidentified submarine. The defendant insurers argued the cause was wear and tear. The House of Lords held that the shipowners had the task of proving that their explanation was more probable than not rather than more probable than that of the defendant. The court did not have to decide which of the explanations was the least improbable.

Standard of proof

Criminal cases where legal burden is on the prosecution

An incorrect direction may give grounds for appeal. There are a number of cases which give guidance on the form of words to be used to convey the meaning of beyond reasonable doubt. One example is that of *Miller v Minister of Pensions* (1947). This was a civil case but Lord Denning's words (at p 372) have been often cited: 'If the evidence against a man is so strong as to leave only a remote possibility in his favour, which can be dismissed with the sentence "of course it is possible but not in the least probable", the case is proved beyond reasonable doubt'.

Revision tip

Note the miscarriage of justice case of *R v Bentley* (2001) on the importance of judicial directions on the burden of proof. In a posthumous appeal the court criticised the trial judge's summing up and, referring also to Bentley's co-defendant, Craig, stated (per Lord Bingham at p 326):

> By stressing the abundant evidence calling for an answer in support of the prosecution case, and by suggesting that that case had been 'established' and by suggesting that there was a burden on Craig to satisfy the jury that the killing had been accidental (however little, on the facts of the case, the injustice caused to Craig thereby) the jury in our view could well have been left with the impression that the case against the appellant was proved and that they should convict him unless he had satisfied them of his innocence.

Criminal cases where legal burden is on the defence

The case law clearly establishes that here the standard is the lower civil one of the balance of probabilities. The evidential burden does not require proof, simply adducing sufficient evidence to convince the judge to allow the matter to be raised at trial, see *Jayesena v R* (1970).

Civil cases

Here again Lord Denning's *dictum*, this time on the civil standard in *Miller v Minister of Pensions* (1947) (at p 372) is worth memorising: 'If the evidence is such that the tribunal can say, "we think it more probable than not", the burden is discharged, but, if the probabilities are equal, it is not'.

Standard of proof

There has been considerable controversy over whether there are, however, differing standards in civil cases, in particular those where the allegation is a quasi-criminal one, such as fraud or assault on a child. The issue seems to have been conclusively settled by the House of Lords in two cases namely *Re Docherty* (2008) and in *Re B (Children) (FC)* (2008). It is worth quoting Lord Hoffman (at para 5) in the latter case in some detail:

> Some confusion has however been caused by dicta which suggest that the standard of proof may vary with the gravity of the misconduct alleged or even the seriousness of the consequences for the person concerned. The cases in which such statements have been made fall into three categories. First, there are cases in which the court has for one purpose classified the proceedings as civil (for example, for the purposes of article 6 of the European Convention) but nevertheless thought that, because of the serious consequences of the proceedings, the criminal standard of proof or something like it should be applied. Secondly, there are cases in which it has been observed that when some event is inherently improbable, strong evidence may be needed to persuade a tribunal that it more probably happened than not. Thirdly, there are cases in which judges are simply confused about whether they are talking about the standard of proof or about the role of inherent probabilities in deciding whether the burden of proving a fact to a given standard has been discharged.
>
> My Lords, I would invite your Lordships fully to approve these observations. I think that the time has come to say, once and for all, that there is only one civil standard of proof and that is proof that the fact in issue more probably occurred than not . . . I agree . . . that clarity would be greatly enhanced if the courts said simply that although the proceedings were civil, the nature of the particular issue involved made it appropriate to apply the criminal standard.

In *Re Docherty* (2008) also the House reaffirmed that there was one civil standard but applied with some flexibility according to the seriousness of the allegations such as sexual abuse. Lord Carswell (at p1509) referred to 'the application of good sense'.

Revision tip

It is possible that you will have an essay question on the debate on the civil standard of proof. You should be aware of examples where although the form of the offence is civil in essence it has a criminal dimension. Thus in *R v Chief Constable of Avon and Somerset* (2001) Lord Bingham stated (p 354) that the proof of conditions for making a sex offender order under s2 Crime and Disorder Act 1998 should be to 'a civil standard of proof which will for all practical circumstances be indistinguishable from the criminal standard'.

✅ Looking for extra marks?

The first class and upper second class student will demonstrate more than an outline knowledge of the key cases. Thus for example, although it is true to say that the Human Rights Act has had a profound impact on the approach of the English courts to the allocation of the burden of proof, a more scholarly approach would be to show the significance in the judgments of Commonwealth as well as Strasbourg cases. See for example the citation of South African cases in *Lambert*.

In addition, you should read the commentaries by leading academics and be aware of the nuances of the arguments. Thus, Ashworth (2001) in his article in the Criminal Law Review, 'Criminal Proceedings after the Human Rights Act: the First Year' is critical of the judgment in *Salabiaku v France* (1988). Commenting on the differing approaches to the presumption of innocence he has written (p 865) that it 'must be said that the Strasbourg jurisprudence on art 6(2) is underdeveloped, not to say flaccid, and it is British judges, taking their cue from Commonwealth constitutional courts, who have sought to give greater sharpness to the right and any exceptions'.

Presumptions

Not all evidence courses include a review of this topic and those that do tend to concentrate on rebuttable presumptions of law. They can take two forms in civil cases, namely persuasive presumptions, which place a legal burden on the party relying on them and evidential presumptions which place an evidential burden.

Rebuttable presumptions of law:

- derive their authority from common law and statute; and

- place on the party relying on the presumption, the burden of presenting the basis facts which will then be presumed unless the other party presents some countervailing facts.

Fig 2.12 summarises the main features of presumptions.

✅ *Looking for extra marks?*

In a question on **res ipsa loquitur** you should be aware that the existence of the doctrine is contested. In *Fryer v Pearson* (2000) the Court of Appeal stated that 'one should take care not to use unhelpful Latin phrases whose meaning does not express a defined principle'. Negligence could not be inferred in that case. See also Witting (2001).

Figure 2.12 Legal and evidential presumptions

Name of presumption and type	Conditions
Legitimacy: legal	Once it is established that the woman was married at the time the child was born or conceived, the child is presumed to be fathered by the husband. The party challenging the presumption will have to convince the court to the standard of beyond reasonable doubt.
	s25 Family Law Reform Act 1969
	Cases: *S v S* [1972]

Presumptions

Name of presumption and type	Conditions
Marriage: legal	There are three aspects to this presumption: i) if a marriage has been celebrated there is a presumption that legal formalities have been followed. Applies to foreign as well as UK marriages; ii) the marriage is presumed to have essential validity in that the parties have the capacity to marry and their consent is genuine; and iii) if a couple have cohabited they did so as man and wife. The party challenging the presumption has the burden of proof to the high standard of beyond reasonable doubt in i) but to the lower standard of the balance of probabilities in ii) and iii). Cases: *Mahadervan v Mahadervan* (1964)
Regularity: evidential	There are two aspects to the concept of 'regularity': 1. public acts have been properly performed and public officials have been properly appointed; and 2. mechanical devices are working properly. Cases: 1. *Campbell v Wallsend Slipway & Engineering* (1978). This concerned the actions of a health and safety inspector. (NB in a criminal case the prosecution may not be able to rely on the presumption to establish facts in issue, eg that escaped prisoners had been lawfully in a police officer's custody: see *Dillon v R* (1982)). 2. *Nicholas v Penny* (1950). This involved the operation of a police speedometer.
Death: evidential	If someone is not heard of for seven years, by people who might be expected to have heard of him during that period, he will be presumed to have died. NB there is no presumption about the date of death. Cases: *Bullock v Bullock* (1960)
***Res ipsa loquitur*: evidential**	Applies in a civil case where a state of affairs is under the control of the defendant and an accident occurred which would not normally happen in the absence of negligence on the part of the defendant. There is a presumption of negligence on the part of the defendant if there is no other plausible explanation. Current approach is that it is an evidential presumption, see *Ng Chun Pui Lee Chuen Tat* (1988) and *Royal Bank of Scotland v Etridge* (2001). See also *Scott v London and St Katherine Docks Co* (1865) and *Widdowson v Newgate Meat Corp* (1988).

(✳) *Key cases*

Case	Facts	Principle and comment
Woolmington v DPP [1935] AC 462	W was convicted of the murder of his wife by shooting. He claimed the gun had been fired accidentally. The trial judge and the Court of Appeal had held that the defence of proving lack of *mens rea* was on W. The House of Lords allowed the appeal.	At common law in criminal proceedings the burden of proving, beyond reasonable doubt, the *actus reus* and the *mens rea* is on the prosecution. The two exceptions to this rule were the defence of insanity and statutory provisions.
R v Lobell [1957] 1 QB 547	On a charge of wounding with intent to cause grievous bodily harm, the accused argued that he was acting in self-defence. The trial judge held that the burden of proving this lay on him. The Court of Appeal allowed the appeal.	The prosecution had the legal burden of disproving self-defence. The issue should only be put to the jury if the accused produced sufficient evidence to make it possible for a reasonable jury to acquit. This is an instance of what are known as common law defences where the accused has the task of producing sufficient evidence to make the issue a live one before the jury but the legal burden remains on the accused.
Nimmo v Alexander Cowan & Sons Ltd [1968] AC 107	The House of Lords held that in a prosecution under s29(1) of the Factories Act 1961 the burden of proving that it was not reasonably practicable to make and keep a place of work safe rested upon the defendant employer.	Where the text of a statute did not make clear where the burden of proof lay, the court should take into account the **mischief** at which the statute was directed and the ease or difficulty that the different parties would face in discharging the burden of proof.
R v Edwards [1975] QB 27	E was convicted of selling alcohol without a licence. He appealed on the grounds that the prosecution had not produced evidence that he had not been granted a licence. His appeal was dismissed.	Under the common law where a statute prohibited an act, save in specified circumstances, the court could construe the statute such that the burden of proving the existence of the circumstances, including the granting of a licence, could lie on the defendant.
R v Hunt [1987] AC 352	H was convicted of being in unlawful possession of a Class A drug, morphine. One issue at the trial was the composition of the alleged drug. The statute provided that if the proportion of morphine was not more than 0.2 per cent the substance was not unlawful under the regulations. The prosecution had not **adduced** evidence on the proportion of morphine, the judge would not	The House acknowledged the principle that the burden of proof on an element of the defence could be placed on the defendant. Courts should examine the linguistic construction of the statute and if that is ambiguous take into account policy considerations and also the relative ease with which defence or prosecution could discharge the burden. The same approach should be

Key cases

✳✳✳✳✳✳✳✳✳✳

Case	Facts	Principle and comment
continued	allow a defence submission of no case to answer.	taken whether the offence was a summary one or a trial on indictment. *Edwards* was approved. *Hunt* and *Edwards* have been largely overtaken by the post-HRA cases such as *Lambert*.
R v Bentley (Derek) (2001) 1 Cr App R 307	B (19 yrs), and C (16 yrs), were cornered by police on the roof of a warehouse. B was held by police on the roof. C produced a pistol and shot one of the policemen. It was alleged that B had shouted 'Let him have it, Chris' before the fatal shot was fired. Both were convicted of murder and B was sentenced to death and executed in 1953 despite widespread pleas for clemency. In 1993 he was posthumously pardoned.	A clear and unambiguous direction on the burden of proof was a cardinal requirement of a properly conducted trial. The direction in this case was not satisfactory. By stressing the abundant evidence calling for an answer in support of the prosecution case and by suggesting that that case had been 'established' and that there was a burden on C to satisfy the jury that the killing had been accidental (however little, on the facts of the case, the injustice caused to C thereby) the jury could well have been left with the impression that the case against Bentley was proved and that they should convict him unless he had satisfied them of his innocence.
R v Lambert [2002] 2 AC 545	L was convicted of being in possession of a controlled drug. The judge directed the jury that the prosecution had to prove that L knew he had the bag in his possession and that the bag contained the controlled drug. If L wanted to rely on the defence in s28(3)(b)(i) that he did not believe or suspect or have reason to suspect that he was in possession of a controlled drug he had to prove on the balance of probabilities that he did not know the bag contained a controlled drug. His conviction was upheld by the Court of Appeal and the House of Lords. L could not rely on the HRA since it was not in force at the time of trial. When the HRA was in force, s28 of the 1971 Act should be read as imposing an evidential burden.	In order to comply with s3(1) HRA it may be necessary to read down a statutory provision which imposes a legal burden of proof on the defendant. Given the seriousness of the offence, if the HRA had been in force, the court should have imposed only a evidential burden on the accused in relation to s28(3)(b)(i).
R v Johnstone [2003] 1 WLR 1736	J was convicted of violations of the Trade Marks Act 1994. He had relied on s92(5) whereby it was a defence for the accused to show he believed on reasonable grounds that the use	Art 6(2) ECHR permitted **reverse burdens** provided they were kept within reasonable limits which took account of the importance of what was at stake and maintained the

Case	Facts	Principle and comment
continued	of the sign in question did not infringe the statute. The Court of Appeal, upholding the conviction, had not made it clear where the burden of proof on this section lay. The House of Lords refused the appeal and pronounced on the burden of proof.	rights of the defence. In this instance there were compelling policy reasons to place the legal burden of the specific defence on the accused to the standard of the balance of probabilities.
Sheldrake v DPP, A-G's Ref (No 4 of 2002) [2005] 1 AC 264	The House of Lords considered two conjoined appeals. One concerned s5 (1)(b) Road Traffic Act 2000 and the other s5(2) Terrorism Act 2000. Both provisions imposed **reverse burdens** on the accused. The House held that the task of the court was not that of deciding whether a reverse burden should be imposed on the defendant but whether a burden that Parliament had enacted unjustifiably infringed Art 6(2). The Road Traffic Act provision imposing the burden was justifiable but not in the case of the Terrorism Act provision.	The House acknowledged that the decision in relation to the Terrorism Act meant flouting the clear will of Parliament in relation to the allocation of the burden of proof.
R v Keogh [2007] EWCA Crim 528	A civil servant was charged under the Official Secrets Act 1989, having handed to an MP's researcher a copy of a letter from the PM to the US President. The Act required the defendant to prove that he did not know and had no reasonable cause to believe the disclosure of the secret information would be damaging. The judge concluded that the Act infringed the presumption of innocence but this was justified in the circumstances. The Appeal Court allowed the defendant's appeal.	The Act could operate effectively without obliging the defendant to prove that he did not have a guilty state of mind. Given its natural meaning, the Act was incompatible with Art 6 ECHR, and the relevant sections should be 'read down' by applying a similar interpretation to that achieved by s118 of the Terrorism Act 2000. That provides: If the person **adduces** evidence which is sufficient to raise an issue with respect to the matter the court or jury shall assume that the defence is satisfied unless the prosecution proves beyond reasonable doubt that it is not.'
R v Chargot Ltd [2009] 1 WLR 1	C was convicted of health and safety breaches following a dumper truck accident in which an employee died. Their appeal was dismissed in the Court of Appeal and they appealed to the House of Lords.	The prosecution had to prove that C had not ensured the employee's health and safety or prevented exposure to risk. This established breach, unless the defendant could establish that it had not been reasonably practicable to do so. The prosecution did not have to identify and prove specific breaches of duty; the overriding test was whether or not defendants had been given fair notice of the claim against them.

Key debates

✱✱✱✱✱✱✱✱✱✱

99) *Key debates*

Topic	**Should there be a third standard of proof in civil cases?'**
Author	Ian Dennis
Viewpoint	Criticises the decision in *Re H (Minors)* [1996] and argues that rejection of a third standard 'was perhaps over-hasty'.
Source	*The Law of Evidence* (3rd edn, 2008) pp482–486

Topic	**Is it a satisfactory response to the placing of a reverse burden in regulatory offences to decriminalise such activity?**
Author	Nicola Padfield
Viewpoint	Argues for a category of administrative regulations which would carry little stigma and for which strict liability or reversing the burden of proof would be acceptable.
Source	'The Burden of Proof Unresolved' [2005] *Cambridge Law Journal* 17

?) *Exam questions*

Essay question

Is it ever permissible to place the burden of proof on the defendant in a criminal trial?

An outline answer is available online at http://www.oxfordtextbooks.co.uk/orc/concentrate/

Problem question

a) Harold is facing prosecution under the (imaginary) Pest Eradication Act 2008. Under s1 of PEA 'It is an offence for householders to use traps to kill rats if there is a risk that a human being will be harmed'. Harold set a trap in his front yard. He wishes to argue that there was no risk to humans since his yard was fully protected from access by others. The penalty for the offence is six months' imprisonment. The offence is triable either way. Advise Harold on the burden and standard of proof.

b) Jane is charged under the (imaginary) National Security Act 2008 Act. A Manual detailing how the Vietnamese Liberation Army targeted bridges to blow up was found in a suitcase in her loft, in folder marked 'War Memories'. Under s5 of this Act 'It is an offence to knowingly possess material which may be used for terrorist purposes'. Under s6 'It is a defence for the defendant to prove that he did not know the material in his possession could be used for terrorist purposes.' Jane plans to argue that the suitcase was left by a former lodger and she did not know that the folder contained the material it did. The maximum penalty for this indictable offence is seven years' imprisonment. Advise Jane on the burden and standard of proof.

An outline answer is available at the end of the book.

#3
Confessions and the defendant's silence

Key Facts

Confessions

- A defendant may be convicted on the evidence of a confession alone.
- The definition of a confession is contained in s82(1) Police and Criminal Evidence Act 1984 (PACE).
- A confession proferred by the prosecution may be excluded by rule under s76(2)(a) and (b) PACE.
- A confession that has been proferred by the prosecution may be excluded by operation of statutory discretion under s78 PACE.
- Section 82(2) PACE preserves the common law discretion to exclude evidence.
- PACE Codes of Practice C, E and F govern the procedure for police interrogation of suspects.

Pre-trial silence

- A suspect's failure to give an explanation when questioned by a constable under **caution** may allow the jury at trial to draw an inference of guilt under ss34, 36, 37 Criminal Justice and Public Order Act 1994 (CJPOA).
- Sections 4, 36, 37 CJPOA only apply if the suspect is questioned at an authorised place of detention and has been allowed an opportunity to consult a solicitor prior to being questioned, charged or officially informed he might be prosecuted.
- The fact that the suspect relied on legal advice to remain silent does not in itself prevent adverse inferences being drawn at trial.

Key facts

✳✳✳✳✳✳✳✳✳✳

- **Article 6 European Convention on Human Rights (ECHR)** does not specifically include the right to silence or the privilege against self-incrimination. These have been recognised as international standards which lay at the heart of the notion of fair procedures but not as absolutes.

- Inferences of guilt permissible under **ss34, 36, 37** are not sufficient without additional evidence to establish a case to answer or a finding of guilt.

- If the suspect and interrogator are on 'even terms', silence on the part of the former may amount to an admissible confession under the common law.

Related areas

There are aspects to this complex area in a number of other chapters. In Chapter 4 we look at the law relating to improperly obtained evidence other than confessions. There is considerable overlap with this area, particularly because the discretionary exclusion of evidence plays a large part in both. The law on privilege is discussed in Chapter 10 where the broader aspects of the privilege against self-incrimination, of which the right to silence is part, are discussed. Note the importance of legal professional privilege which may be called into question if a suspect claims that he or she has failed to respond to questioning by a constable on legal advice. The effect of the accused's failure to testify is covered in Chapter 7. Finally, it should be stressed that confessions form arguably the biggest exception to the rule against hearsay, see Chapter 6. In that chapter you will find an examination of the conditions under which confessions by third parties may be admitted (p 86).

The assessment: key points

This large area remains one of considerable debate and case law and must obviously form a key part of your revision plan. Since it raises principled questions about the relationship between the individual and the state, it is likely to form the subject of researched essay questions as well as problem-based questions. There is a considerable amount of case law to get to grips with, including a number of important European Court of Human Rights' decisions. The key statutory sections are:

Police and Criminal Evidence Act 1984

- s76: inadmissibility of confession by rule
- s77: confessions by mentally handicapped persons
- s78: exclusion of unfair evidence, including confessions and silence, by judicial discretion
- s82: definition of confession

Criminal Justice and Public Order Act 1994

- s34: effect of accused's failure to mention facts when questioned or charged
- s36: effect of accused's failure to account for objects, substances, or marks
- s37: effect of accused's failure to account for presence at a particular place
- s38: interpretation and safeguards

Key features and principles

This chapter covers two areas which are closely related but which have developed their own body of case law. They are confession evidence and the evidential consequences which may arise for the defendant arising from a failure to respond to pre-trial questioning. There are two main assumptions underpinning the law.

- *People do not as a rule make statements which are against their own interests.*

✳✳✳✳✳✳✳✳✳✳

It follows that an out of court confession to involvement in an offence should in principle be admitted at trial even if the suspect then wants to retract the confession and plead not guilty.

- *The law should protect the individual from intrusive and oppressive questioning which might lead to unreliable evidence being obtained.*

To do otherwise would violate individual autonomy and jeopardise the moral integrity of the trial and the verdict. Thus, confessions have historically been regarded as powerful evidence of guilt and they have played an influential role in the development of Western criminal justice culture since the late Middle Ages, influenced in part by religious models. It was also recognised that official interrogation may be abusive and thus controls were needed. Following the exposure of a number of miscarriages of justice in the 1970s arising from the admission of false confessions obtained by the police, a Royal Commission was established which recommended the introduction of an elaborate set of legislative controls on the obtaining of confessions, replacing the system which had operated under non-statutory Judges Rules. The outcome was the PACE 1984.

Defendant's silence

The privilege against self-incrimination, of which the right to silence is a part, has been acknowledged since the excesses of the Court of Star Chamber in the seventeenth century to be vital to protect the individual from an abuse of state power. Pressure mounted in the 1980s to limit the right to silence under certain conditions; the argument being that it was being abused by career criminals. The CJPOA 1994 has eroded this long-standing principle to the extent that, although a suspect is not compelled by law to respond to questioning under official interrogation, he or she may face adverse evidential consequences from such a failure under certain circumstances.

Note the distinction between the weight of evidence of a pre-trial confession and of pre-trial silence. Under the common law the former does not need corroborative evidence, on which see criticisms by Pattenden (1991) who argues that some of the most notorious miscarriages of justice might have been avoided if there had been a requirement to corroborate confessions. By contrast, silence alone is not sufficient to found a conviction, see s38 CJPOA.

Human Rights Act 1998

The Human Rights Act has had considerable influence on the application of ss34–38 CJPOA but less so in relation to confessions. One exception is *R v Mushtaq* [2005] where the House of Lords considered the application of Art 6 in a situation where a the judge had ruled that a confession had not been obtained in violation of s76(2) PACE. It was open to the jury to reconsider this and if they judged s76(2) had been violated they should disregard the confession.

Definition and content of a confession

Note the key aspects of the definition of a confession in **s82(1) PACE**:

> ... confession includes any statement wholly or partly adverse to the person who made it, whether made to a person in authority or not and whether made in words or otherwise.

This definition follows that of the common law so many of the earlier cases will still be good law. It is important to determine whether the proffered or disputed statement falls within this definition for two reasons: to determine if i) it will be admissible by the prosecution as an exception to the rule against hearsay or ii) if it is inadmissible against the defendant since, if it is a confession, he or she would be entitled to protective measures, the absence of which could affect the inadmissibility of the statement.

Points to note:

- 'wholly or partly adverse' means 'adverse' at the time it was made *not* at the time of trial – see *R v Hasan* (2005) where a defendant whose statement was **exculpatory** at the time it was made could not be protected by the PACE safeguards when the prosecution proffered the statement at trial; and

- mixed statements are those that are partly incriminatory and partly exculpatory. They may be admissible and the **fact-finder** may treat both aspects as evidence of truth – see *R v Sharp* (1988).

How do the safeguards operate?

The tests for inadmissibility under s76(2) and discretionary exclusion under s78 and s82(1)

The statute sets out four tests whereby a confession may be held inadmissible. In order to understand them it is necessary i) to have a knowledge of the specifications set out for a properly constituted interrogation since breaches of these *may* lead to exclusion; ii) to understand what the tests are. These will be discussed in more detail below but they have to be understood as an integral system.

PACE s76(2)(a): the oppression test

The test for oppression is included in **s76(2)(a) PACE** and a partial definition of oppression is given in **s76(8)**: '... "oppression" includes torture, inhuman or degrading treatment, and the use or threat of violence (whether or not amounting to torture)."

The key elements of this test are:

- the confession is obtained by oppression; ie there is a causal connection between the action complained of and the confession;

- "oppression' should be given its ordinary dictionary meaning; see *R v Fulling* (1987);

How do the safeguards operate?

- there would generally need to be bad faith on the part of the investigating authorities;. see *R v Fulling* (1987);
- verbal as well as physical abuse may amount to oppression; see *R v Paris, R v Abdullahi, R v Miller* (1994);
- the particular characteristics of the suspect will be taken into account in deciding if the questioning had been oppressive; *R v Spens* (1991);
- a confession may be excluded 'notwithstanding that it may be true'; and
- the burden of proof is on the prosecution to prove beyond reasonable doubt that the confession was not obtained by oppression.

PACE s76(2)(b): the reliability test

The test for unreliability is s76(2)(b) PACE. A confession may be inadmissible if it is represented to the court that it was obtained 'in consequence of anything said or done which was likely, in the circumstances existing at the time, to render unreliable any confession which might be made by him in consequence thereof'.

The key elements of this test are:

- there is no need for bad faith on the part of the police; see *R v Harvey* (1998);
- the 'something said or done' must be done by someone, not necessarily the police, other than the suspect; see *R v Goldenberg* (1989);
- the section has been restrictively interpreted by the courts so that the provision 'circumstances existing at the time' has usually meant that the defendant must have been in a vulnerable mental or emotional state; see *R v Harvey*;
- see *R v Barry* (1991) where the court set out the reasoning which must be applied in s76(2)(b);
- a confession may be excluded 'notwithstanding that it may be true';
- the test relates to 'any confession' that may have been obtained in this way; the truth of the actual confession is a matter for the jury; and
- the burden of proof is on the prosecution to prove beyond reasonable doubt that the confession was not obtained by this means.

PACE s78: the fairness test

The discretionary test for fairness is in s78(1) PACE whereby 'In any proceedings the court may refuse to allow evidence on which the prosecution proposes to rely to be given if it appears to the court that, having regard to all the circumstances, including the circumstances in which the evidence was obtained, the admission of the evidence would have such an adverse effect on the fairness of the proceedings that the court ought not to admit it.'

The key elements of the operation of this test are derived from the case law. You should be aware that there are many possible situations where the judge could exercise discretion to exclude prosecution evidence, including a confession under this section:

- breaches of the Code or s58 PACE particularly if accompanied by bad faith on the part of the police are the most common causes;
- again there must be a causal connection between the breach or impropriety and the making of the confession;
- evidence will not be excluded by virtue of the breaches only but there must be such an adverse effect on the fairness of the proceedings that justice required exclusion; see *R v Walsh* (1989); and
- the importance the courts attach to the exercise of bad faith on the part of the police is illustrated by the use of trickery in *R v Mason* (1988).

PACE s82(2): the common law test

This will apply if evidence is held to have been wrongly admitted at trial and the judge directs the jury not to take account of it.

Think of these tests as providing a series of filters whereby the disputed confession is to be screened. In order for them to apply, there has to be some flaw in the operation of the interrogation. Most often this involves a breach of the statute or accompanying Codes. To some extent the tests overlap and cases which fall under s76(2)(a) or (b) might also fall under s78. It would be more advisable to seek inadmissibility of a confession under s76 rather than exclusion under s78 if the conditions suggest both, since the misapplication of a rule of law by the trial judge is more likely to give grounds of appeal than the operation of discretion. Note that if the question facing the court is whether the confession was made or not, rather than whether it was improperly obtained, that is a question of fact which it is for the jury to decide. See *Thongai v R* (1998) where the Privy Council held that if the proof that the confession was made is difficult because of police impropriety then that may be a question of admissibility and a *voir dire* needed.

Access to legal advice

Section 58 PACE and PACE Code C para 6 relate to an accused's right of access to legal advice *but* note that the statute provides that it may be lawfully delayed under certain circumstances in cases involving indictable offences. Thus, a confession is not necessarily inadmissible if it had been obtained in the absence of a solicitor, a contrast to the position in relation to pre-trial silence under CJPOA (see below).

Revision tip

Questions in this area will often ask you to assess the consequences of wrongly denying the suspect access to a solicitor under s58 PACE. It is important to appreciate that the court will be looking for a causal connection between the wrongful denial and the obtaining of a confession. Thus, in ➡

How do the safeguards operate?

✴✴✴✴✴✴✴✴✴✴

➡ *R v Alladice* (1988) the court declined to exclude the confession on the grounds that the defendant had been improperly denied access to a solicitor. The police had been concerned that the solicitor might advise A to remain silent. A made a number of admissions at the interview. There was no ground for inadmissibility under s76(2)(b) since, as the suspect had a criminal record the presence of a solicitor would have made no difference. By contrast, in *R v Samuel* (1988), the Court of Appeal considered that the right to legal advice was 'one of the most important and fundamental rights of a citizen' and denial led to exclusion under s78.

The Codes

PACE Code C: this contains detailed guidance on how a properly conducted police interview should take place. It ranges from elementary provisions such as adequate food and rest and significant information such as the need to **caution** suspects. It needs to be read in conjunction with the statute. Thus, for example, Part IV PACE deals with periods of detention before charge as does the whole of Code C.

PACE Code D: tape recording of interviews.

PACE Code F: visual recording with sound of interview with suspects.

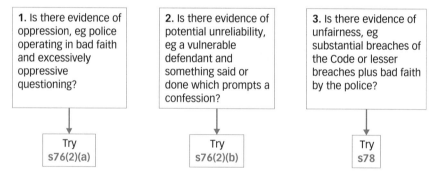

1. Is there evidence of oppression, eg police operating in bad faith and excessively oppressive questioning?	**2.** Is there evidence of potential unreliability, eg a vulnerable defendant and something said or done which prompts a confession?	**3.** Is there evidence of unfairness, eg substantial breaches of the Code or lesser breaches plus bad faith by the police?
Try s76(2)(a)	Try s76(2)(b)	Try s78

Figure 3.1 Statutory rules governing inadmissibility of a confession

Revision tip

You may be asked about the admissibility of confessions where the defendant has made more than one. Remember that if an earlier confession is ruled inadmissible under s76(2)(a) or (b), then even a later properly obtained confession may be inadmissible since there may be a causal link between the earlier tainted confession and the making of the subsequent one. See *R v McGovern* (1990) where the defendant was a pregnant young women with a low IQ. She was improperly denied access to a solicitor and confessed to the charge of murder. In a subsequent, properly conducted interview she again confessed. Both sets of statements should have been excluded since the later admissions may have been made in consequence of the earlier ones.

Fruit of the poisoned tree

This is an area where you need to be very familiar with the details of the statute. Some questions on confessions may slip in a reference to real evidence being found as a result of information being given in a confession where the problem sets out the circumstances in which the confession was obtained. You are expected then to consider not only whether the confession is admissible but whether the finding of the real evidence may be divulged at trial if the confession is inadmissible. Thus, for example, D confesses to murder and says he hid the murder weapon, a gun, on Hampstead Heath. His confession is ruled inadmissible under s76(2)(b); can the jury know about the finding of the gun? Answer yes, but they must not be told *how* the police came to know it was there. See s76(4)–(6). It would probably impress the examiners if you referred to *A v Secretary of State for the Home Department* (No 2) (2005) where the House of Lords ruled that, although a confession obtained by torture was inadmissible, this did not affect the admissibility of real evidence obtained as a result of the confession.

Revision tip

It is worth making sure that you have fully understood the complexities of the law relating to confessions by drug addicts. In order to avoid too simplistic an interpretation of the decision in *Goldenberg* (1989) it should not be taken to mean that the effects of drug withdrawal can be discounted in deciding on the admissibility of a confession. You could argue that such effects were a relevant circumstance in the same way that the defendant's mental or emotional state was a factor to be considered. An example is *McGovern* (1990) where the accused's pregnancy should have been taken into account in determining her vulnerability.

Confessions and co-defendants

This is an area which has been subject recently to both statutory change and case law so it is a likely assessment topic. You need to be aware of the following scenarios where there are two co-defendants (D1 and D2) and both plead not guilty.

- *Question: D2 confesses and exonerates D1 but the confession is inadmissible under s76(2)(b). Can the statement be presented as evidence in defence of D1?*

Answer: Yes, if it is relevant to his defence and D1 can prove on the balance of probabilities that it was not obtained as a result of something said or done that was likely in the circumstances existing at the time to render unreliable any confession which might be made by D2 as a consequence.

Source: s76(A) PACE, as amended by CJA 2003. Note that the same approach would apply if the confession had been excluded under s76(2)(a).

- *Question: D2 confesses and exonerates D1 but the confession is excluded under s78 PACE. Can the statement be presented as evidence in defence of D1?*

Answer: Yes, if it relevant to his defence.

Authority: *R v Myers* (1997).

• *Question: D1 confesses and implicates D2. Can the prosecution rely on the confession as part of the case against D2?*

Answer: The confession is only evidence against D1 (see s76(1) PACE) but the jury, if they find D1 guilty, may use that finding as evidence of the guilt of D2.

Authority: *R v Hayter* (2005).

Revision tip

It is important to be aware who is covered by the PACE Code. Many examiners allow statute books to be taken into the examination but this will only be of use to you if you know your way around in advance. Note that although a confession may be made informally to a person not in authority, the statutory provisions and Codes C and D only apply to police interrogation. On the other hand, the tests for exclusion and non admissibility apply to all confessions. If the police have used underhand methods to avoid the statutory and Code requirements, this may lead to the application of s78. This applies for example to cell confessions. See *Allan v UK* (2002) p 63.

Silence as evidence

The right to silence is an aspect of the privilege against self-incrimination whereby a suspect who is being interrogated by a state official is not forced to respond to questions. The principle is thus applied to protect the individual from the power of the state. It was and remains the case that at common law, where two individuals are on 'even terms', silence in the face of an accusation of guilt may amount to an admission and is thus admissible as evidence of guilt. *Parkes v R* (1976) illustrates the point. The Criminal Justice and Public Order Act 1994 (as amended) has made considerable inroads into what was the common law principle of the right to silence. In essence, under certain conditions, a suspect's failure to respond to police questions may be used as supportive evidence of guilt. The key sections are ss34, 36, 37.

Section 34 CJPOA 1994: effect of accused's failure to mention facts when questioned or charged. Before such failure may be used as evidence the pre-conditions shown in Fig 3.2 should apply.

Note the particularly complex question of how the courts have approached legal advice as an explanation for the suspect's silence; see the cases cited in Fig 2.2 and the Key Debates below.

Other key sections of CJPOA 1994 are ss36 and 37. These deal with specific circumstances and failure to give an account. The police interview under these two sections may form part of the primary case against the defendant even if he does not give an explanation at trial. Section 36 covers failure to account for objects, substances, or marks, and s37 with the suspect's failure to account for his presence in a particular place. Like s34, these only apply if the suspect has had an opportunity to consult a solicitor.

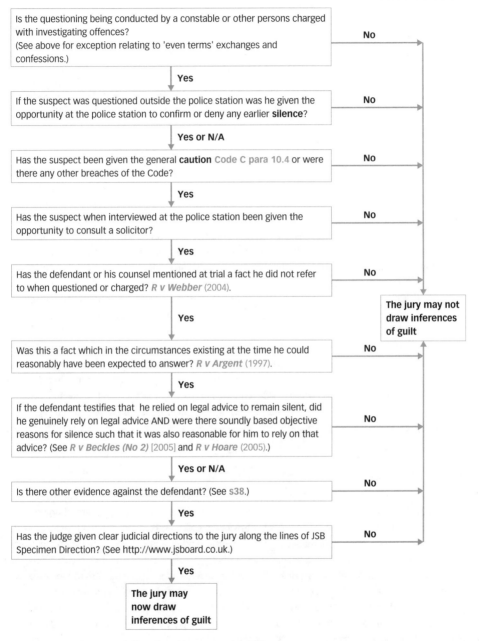

Figure 3.2 Inferences of guilt and s34 CJPOA 1994

Silence as evidence

✳✳✳✳✳✳✳✳✳✳

Revision tip

In answering questions on the evidential value of silence at the police station it is not enough to be familiar with the complex wording of the statute. You need also to have at your finger tips the growing body of interpretive case law particularly on **s34**. An important case on the meaning of responding to police questions is *R v Knight* (2004) which establishes that a prepared written statement given to police at interview, and from which he did not depart at trial, meant that **s34** did not apply.

The ECHR and ss34–38

A number of Strasbourg cases have covered the complex question of whether **s34** complies with the provisions of **Art 6**. As you will be aware, the right to silence is not specifically referred to in **Art 6** but its importance as a fundamental, if not an absolute, principle was made clear in *Murray John v UK* (1996). The court, going further than the UK statute, stated that a conviction should not be based solely or mainly on inferences of guilt from silence. The judgment also stressed the importance of access to legal advice. The case led to an amendment of the statute to provide that the silence provisions would only apply if the suspect had access to legal advice.

Again, in *Condron v UK* (2001) the court stressed that **s34** was compatible with the ECHR and that it was not a violation of the Convention to permit inferences to be drawn if the accused claimed he had remained silent on legal advice. However, the court indicated the crucial importance of carefully worded judicial directions to the jury on the permissibility of drawing inferences from silence. One controversial area which the Strasbourg court has not yet pronounced on is that of legal professional privilege. (See further Chapter 11) English courts have held that where a defendant claims legal advice as the reason for his silence at interview and gives the content of that advice, he has waived his legal professional privilege; see *R v Bowden* (1999).

✅ Looking for extra marks?

There is considerable case law on what amounts to a 'fact' given at trial under **s34 CJPOA**. A resourceful examiner may ask you to consider the following scenario: A and B are charged with conspiracy to murder. A gave a 'no comment' interview to police and did not testify. At trial B gave an innocent explanation of the whereabouts of both himself and A, and in his submission A's counsel adopted that explanation. Is the counsel's submission a 'fact' relied upon by the accused but not given earlier? In other words, does a defendant risk an adverse inference under **s34** as well as **s35** if he does not give evidence but his counsel introduces a fact in his defence. The answer is Yes; see the House of Lords decision *R v Webber* (2004). In that case, the defendant did not give evidence but his counsel put facts to prosecution witnesses which the defendant had not referred to at the police interview. The House of Lords held that **s34** applied.

✳ Key cases

Case	Facts	Principle and comment
Confessions: definition		
R v Sharp [1988] 1 WLR 7	S was spotted running away from the site of a burglary. He admitted being near the scene of the crime but gave an exculpatory reason to the police for this.	His statement was 'mixed', ie both **inculpatory** and **exculpatory**, and was admissible as a whole as evidence going to the truth of its contents.
R v Hasan [2005] 2 AC 467	H was charged with aggravated burglary. In an 'off-the-record' statement to police not carried out under **caution** or, tape-recorded, he claimed duress. There were inconsistencies between this statement and his evidence at trial. The Court of Appeal held that the off-the-record statement was a confession and fell to be excluded under s76(2)(b) since when it was sought to admit it at trial it was inculpatory.	The House of Lords reversed the Court of Appeal. To fulfil the definition of an out of court confession, the statement must be wholly or partly adverse to the maker at the time it was made.
Confessions: inadmissibility and exclusion		
R v Fulling [1987] QB 426	F confessed after being told by police that her lover's mistress was in the next cell. She claimed her distress had been caused by police oppression which led to her confession. The Court of Appeal rejected her submission.	Oppression in s76(2)(a) PACE must be given its ordinary dictionary meaning, which connotes 'detestable wickedness'. Ordinarily, oppression would entail impropriety on the part of the interrogator. Contrast with *R v Paris, R v Abdullahi, R v Miller* (1994) where bullying questioning, even with a solicitor present, was held to amount to oppression and the confession should be excluded.
R v Mason [1988] 1 WLR 139	M was suspected of involvement in an arson attack. Police pretended to both him and his solicitor that his fingerprints had been found at the scene. His subsequent confession should have been excluded because of the police deceit.	Deliberate and serious malpractice on the part of the police may lead to a confession being excluded under s78.
R v Goldenberg (1989) 88 Cr App R 285	G, who was a heroin addict, gave admissions to police about his supplier. At trial he argued that he had confessed in order to get more drugs. The trial judge had correctly admitted the confession.	The test set out in s76(2)(b) required that things said or done were extraneous to the maker of the confession.

Key cases

✳✳✳✳✳✳✳✳✳✳

Case	Facts	Principle and comment
R v Walsh (1989) 91 Cr App R 161	Breaches of the Code and statute which occurred during interview included denial of a solicitor and failure to record the interview or give the suspect a chance to check it.	Serious and significant breaches of the statute and the Code may lead to exclusion of a confession under s78 PACE in the absence of bad faith on the part of the police.
R v Barry (1991) 95 Cr App R 384	B was charged with conspiracy to steal. He was anxious to obtain bail because he had custody of his young son. In interviews held in breach of Code C para 16.8 he offered assistance in return for bail. In a later recorded interview where he had not been offered legal advice he confessed. He argued that the confession had been induced by offer of bail. The Court of Appeal held the trial judge had erred in admitting the confession. The conviction was overturned.	The courts set out the steps which should be taken when a defendant alleges that his confession was unreliable within s 76(2)(b) PACE. First, identify the thing said or done, which requires the trial judge to take into account everything said or done by the police. Second, ask whether what was said or done was likely in the circumstances to render unreliable a confession made in consequence. The test is objective, taking into account all the circumstances. The last step is to ask whether the prosecution have proved beyond reasonable doubt that the confession was not obtained in consequence of the thing said or done, which is a question of fact to be approached in a common-sense way.
R v Spens [1991] 1 WLR 624	S was charged, along with others, with insider dealing. They had made adverse statements to inspectors appointed by the Trade and Industry Secretary which were admitted at trial. It was claimed that they ought to have been excluded under s76(2)(a) since it was not explained to them that they could be used in evidence at trial under the Companies Act 1985. It was held that the questioning was not oppressive since S was intelligent and sophisticated.	The particular characteristics and mental state of the accused are relevant in considering whether the confession was a result of oppression.
R v Harvey [1998] Crim LR 241	The police, acting without evidence of bad faith, had made H aware of lesbian lover's confession to a murder. H, who was psychopathic and of low intelligence subsequently also confessed. H's confession should have been excluded.	There is no need for police impropriety for s76(2)(b) to apply.

Case	Facts	Principle and comment
Confessions and third parties		
R v Myers [1997] 3 WLR 552	M was tried along with Q for murder. M had confessed prior to trial but her confession was excluded under s78 PACE because of breaches of Code C para 10.1. At trial she blamed M who wished to **adduce** her confession in his defence. The confession was admissible.	In a joint trial D1 was entitled to adduce D2's confession to prove the truth of its contents even if it had been excluded as prosecution evidence under s78(1) PACE. The conditions for such admissibility were that (1) the confession was relevant to D1's defence and (2) was made voluntarily in the sense that it was not made in consequence of oppression or anything said or done that was likely in the circumstances to render it unreliable. **(See now s76A PACE, following the amendment made in CJA 2003.)**
R v Hayter [2005] 1 WLR 605	There were two other co-defendants, B and R, as well as H, to a charge of murder. The prosecution case was that B wanted to arrange the murder of her husband and H recruited R as contract killer. At trial R's confession was admitted.	The rule that a confession is only evidence against the person who made (see s76(1)) does not mean that where there are co-defendants, the jury cannot use one defendant's confession in establishing his guilt and use that finding of guilt in deciding the guilt of the co-defendant.
Silence of the accused at pre-trial questioning		
Parkes v R [1976] 1 WLR 1251 (PC)	P was confronted by the mother of a woman bleeding from stab wounds. She asked P, who was holding a knife, why he had stabbed her daughter. P made no reply but when the mother tried to get hold of him tried to stab her. The PC held that the jury had been entitled to take into account P's silence and his reaction as evidence of guilt.	At common law where the parties are on even terms, silence in the face of an accusation may amount to a confession. Preserved by s34(5) CJPOA 1994.
Argent v R [1997] 2 Cr App R27	The defendant gave no comment in interviews but at trial claimed he had left the scene before the crime occurred.	The reference to 'fact' in s34(a) and (b) means a fact that the accused could reasonably be expected to mention in the circumstances. The judge should direct that the personal characteristics and circumstances of the accused should be taken into account.

Key debates

✳✳✳✳✳✳✳✳✳✳

Case	Facts	Principle and comment
Condron v UK (2001) 31 EHRR 1	Two drug addicts were advised by their solicitor, who considered they were suffering withdrawal symptoms, not to answer police questions. The judge did not direct the jury that they could only draw adverse inferences if they were satisfied that their silence could only sensibly be attributed to their having no explanation which would stand up to scrutiny.	Section 34 did not violate Art 6 ECHR. Legal advice to remain silent under questioning did not, in itself, mean that the jury could not draw an inference of guilt but the judge must direct the jury on how to assess the effect of this legal advice.
R v Knight [2004] 1 WLR 340	K was charged with indecent assault on a child. At the start of a police interview his solicitor gave a written statement and K failed to answer further questions. His evidence at trial was consistent with the content of the statement.	Adverse inferences could not be drawn when a pre-trial written statement was comprehensive and new material was not raised at trial.
R v Hoare [2005] 1 WLR 1804	H manufactured illegal drugs as a by-product of his glassware company. On legal advice he failed to respond to police questions and at trial claimed he believed the drugs were for cancer research.	The judge must direct the jury to consider whether, regardless of legal advice genuinely given and genuinely accepted, an accused has remained silent not because of that advice but because he had no, or no satisfactory, explanation to give.

⑨⑨ Key debates

Topic	**Is the test for allowing inferences to be drawn from silence on legal advice too harsh?**
Author	B Malik
Viewpoint	Reviews the differing approaches of the court of appeal in *R v Betts and Hall* (2001) and *R v Howell* (2005). In the latter the court held that genuine reliance on legal advice, as accepted in *Betts and Hall*, was not sufficient; it had also to be reasonable. Suggests that consequently the suspect is having to 'second guess' the jury and calculate whether it will believe that reliance on legal advice was the true reason for his/her silence.
Source	'Silence on Legal Advice: Clarity but Not Justice?: *R v Beckles*' [2005] E&AP 211

Topic	**'Defensive Use of a Co-accused's Confession and the Criminal Justice Act 2003'**
Author	John Hartshorne
Viewpoint	Section 76(2) PACE, following the amendments in the CJA 2003 is unsatisfactory, in particular since it allows a co-defendant's confession to be excluded, not withstanding that it may be true. The author suggests an amendment which, it is argued, would make the provision compliant with Art 6 ECHR.
Source	[2004] E&P 165

(?) Exam questions

Essay question

Is the current law on drawing inferences from silence a violation of the right to a fair trial?

An outline answer is available at the end of the book.

Problem question

Dorrit and Nell are accused of murdering Pip. Dorrit is confronted by Pip's friend David when he is discovered with the body. David accuses him of having killed Pip and Dorrit makes no reply. Nell is arrested, cautioned, and taken to the police station. She is offered access to a solicitor but declines it on the grounds that she cannot afford it. She is pregnant, has a low IQ, and is in a highly emotional state. She tells the investigating officer they did poison Pip and that Dorrit had nothing to do with it. She also tells him that the poison is in her kitchen. At a later interview where she is given access to a solicitor she repeats the confession and also exonerates Dorrit. The police find poison in Nell's kitchen.

Advise on evidence.

An outline answer is available online at http://www.oxfordtextbooks.co.uk/orc/concentrate/

#4

Improperly obtained evidence, other than confessions

Key Facts

- There is no rule of law requiring the exclusion of evidence simply because it has been improperly obtained. There is a judicial discretion to exclude such evidence under both common law and statute.

- Section 78 Police and Criminal Evidence Act 1984 (PACE) applies to the exclusion of non-confession as well as confession evidence on which the prosecution proposes to rely.

- The most common area of exclusion, other than confession evidence, relates to undercover police activity which might arguably involve impropriety such as obtaining evidence by **entrapment** or illegality such as trespass and evasion of PACE and the Codes of Practice.

- The court may elect to stay the prosecution rather than exercise discretion to exclude evidence; the Court of Appeal will interfere with a trial judge's exercise of his discretion to exclude evidence only for unreasonableness by the *Wednesbury* test but the appellate court will review the grounds for stay of prosecution more robustly.

- The common law discretion, retained in s82(3) PACE, may still be employed, in particular if the evidence has already been admitted, to guide judicial directions to the jury.

- The relationship between the common law and s78 PACE has not been clearly set out but it is arguable that the latter allows a more extensive discretion.

- The European Court of Human Rights (ECtHR) has held that s78 enshrines the relevant principles of Art 6 European Convention on Human Rights (ECHR).

Related areas

In Chapter 3 we looked at the way reference to silence on the part of the defendant and also confession evidence may on occasion be excluded by judicial discretion. In this chapter we examine how other evidence, which might be considered relevant, may be excluded because of flaws in the way it was obtained. In other words there are considerations other than the accuracy of fact finding which must be taken into account. We consider specifically the exclusionary discretion contained within s78 PACE. Common law and statutory exclusionary discretion may also be exercised in relation to other areas of evidence in particular character evidence (see Chapter 5) and hearsay evidence (see Chapter 6).

The assessment: key points

The question of improperly or illegally obtained evidence is causing much debate. Current concerns stretch from the propriety of undercover police activities to the admissibility of evidence obtained by torture. It is an area that is likely, therefore, to appear in assessments either in the form of an essay where you would review the ethical and human rights issues or a problem on the likelihood of the admissibility of evidence at trial. You need to be clear also on the conditions in which a stay of prosecution might be ordered.

Key features and principles

Trials have a factual and a moral dimension. It is vital that the right person is convicted and the innocent acquitted. It is also crucial that the outcome is arrived at in a way which satisfies standards of propriety and integrity and that evidence is not tainted by being collected in a morally dubious way or is so prejudicial that it clouds the fact finder's judgement. In this chapter we will be looking exclusively at criminal trials since the same requirement of moral probity is not so crucial in civil law. The question posed in this chapter is why should apparently relevant evidence be excluded from criminal trials?

Historically, English law has been reluctant to exclude evidence, other than confession evidence, on the grounds that there was some impropriety in the way it was obtained. The exception for confession evidence was based on the acknowledgment that this involved subverting the will of the suspect in some way. Two subsequent changes to the law have impacted on this area. Firstly, s78 PACE allows the discretionary exclusion of evidence. Secondly, the Human Rights Act has led to a more jurisprudential approach in this area, although the House of Lords has concluded that the requirements of Art 6 ECHR are compatible with the pre-existing s78 (see *R v Looseley; A-G's Ref (No 3 of 2000)* (2001)).

The general rule and the common law background

The traditional rule of English law is that the impropriety of the method by which evidence is obtained is irrelevant to its admissibility. There were exceptions, however, for confession evidence and evidence which undermined the defendant's privilege against self-incrimination. The view of the English courts (as opposed to those of the United States and other jurisdictions) has traditionally been that if evidence is relevant to issues in the trial, it is admissible no matter how obtained. An often quoted (*obiter*) comment is that by Crompton J in *R v Leatham* (1861) (at p501): 'it matters not how you get it; if you steal it even, it would be admissible in evidence'.

R v Sang (1980) is the leading case before PACE.

. . . .

R v Sang [1980] AC 402

The defendant was charged with conspiracy to issue forged bank notes. He sought to exclude evidence obtained, he claimed, due to the activities of an ***agent provocateur***. The trial judge refused the application and he pleaded guilty. The House of Lords acknowledged that there was a general discretion to exclude evidence on the grounds that its prejudicial effect exceeded its probative value. There was also discretion to exclude evidence obtained after the commission of the offence if it had been obtained unfairly or by trickery in violation of the privilege against self-incrimination. Lord Diplock (at p436) explained it as follows: 'That is why there is no discretion to exclude evidence discovered as a result of an illegal search but there is discretion to exclude evidence which the accused has been induced to produce voluntarily if the method of inducement was unfair.' The House also stated that there was no defence of **entrapment** known to English law.

. . . .

Recent case law although not overruling *Sang* (1980) indicates that the courts now take a more robust stance in excluding evidence obtained improperly.

Developing a principled approach: s78 PACE

Academic commentators have debated whether it is possible to derive from the case law a coherent set of principles which the courts apply in excluding improperly obtained evidence. It is arguable that the narrow stance of *Sang* marks the lowest point of a principled approach. The common law test for exclusion is whether the probative value of the evidence is less than its prejudicial effect. Following *Sang*, save in the case of evidence akin to a confession obtained after the commission of the offence, there was no discretion to exclude evidence on the grounds that it was improperly or unfairly obtained. The approach was based on the principle that it was not the task of the courts to discipline the police. PACE marked a departure from that narrow stance.

Section 78(1) PACE gives a discretionary power to judges and magistrates to exclude evidence on which the prosecution proposes to rely if it appears that 'having regard to all the circumstances, including the circumstances in which the evidence was obtained, the admission of the evidence would have such an adverse effect on the fairness of the proceedings that the court ought not to admit it'. The statute also preserves the common law discretion.

As you read the case law and in particular the apparent retreat from *Sang* in the post-PACE cases keep in mind the various criteria which have been put forward to justify exclusion of improperly obtained evidence. You will be able to find *dicta* in the cases to justify each of the reasons set out below but it is arguable that there is no overall coherent judicial stance. The debate ranges between those who argue that if relevant evidence exists it defies common sense not to admit to others who protest that the moral authority of the verdict may be undermined if the court admits apparently reliable evidence that has been obtained unfairly. The following reasons have been put forward to justify excluding evidence on the grounds that there is some illegality or impropriety in the way it has been obtained:

- to ensure that only potentially reliable evidence is admitted?
- to deter the police from wrongdoing?
- to uphold the reputation of the criminal justice process?
- to compensate the defendant for the wrongdoing of the investigators? and
- to provide a fair balance between the powers of the state officials including the police and those of the defendant?

Reliability and fair process considerations

An early decision under PACE in the Divisional Court seemed to herald a disciplinary approach to exclusion of evidence under s78 PACE. In *Matto v DPP* (1987) the court held that the police had acted in bad faith and beyond their powers in trespassing in order to obtain a breath specimen from a suspect. Subsequent cases have shown that it is difficult to derive clear principles for exclusion. Thus, in *R v Khan* (2000), even though the police had committed trespass and criminal damage in planting a listening device on premises used by a suspect, the House held that the evidence should not be excluded. Dennis points out (2007, p 320): 'It seems that the House of Lords attached importance to the probative value of the evidence and to the fact that its use did not make the trail unfair in the sense prejudicing the rights of the defence.' The Strasbourg court held that there had been no violation of Art 6 but there had been a violation of Art 8.

Post HRA 1998

A more jurisprudential approach appears to have followed the implementation of the Human Rights Act. Evidence obtained by torture in any jurisdiction is indisputably inadmissible. In a landmark decision, the House of Lords, reversing the Court of Appeal, has ruled that evidence obtained by torture abroad is not admissible in English courts, *A v Secretary of State for the Home Department (No 2)* (2006). The appeal was granted on the basis of the common law prohibition on torture, on Arts 3 and 6 ECHR and on general principles of public international law. The case of course raises far wider issues than those of the admissibility of evidence. As Lord Bingham (at para 51) put it,

> It trivialises the issue before the House to treat it as an argument about the law of evidence. The issue is one of constitutional principle, whether evidence obtained by torturing another human being may be admitted to proceedings in a British court, irrespective of where, or by whom, or on whose authority the torture was inflicted. To that question I would give a very clear negative answer.

Revision tip

The common law discretion has largely been overtaken by **s78 PACE** but you will gain credit in a question on improperly obtained evidence for knowing some recent cases where judges have drawn on it. A good example is *R v Stagg* (*Colin*) (1994). Ognall J relied on the common law as well as **s78** to exclude evidence obtained by an undercover policewoman and then subsequently stayed the prosecution.

   The following table (Fig 4.1) gives a picture of the contrasting approaches taken by the courts to the acceptance of improperly or illegally obtained evidence under the common law and PACE.

Figure 4.1 Contrasting judicial approaches to excluding improperly obtained evidence

Cases tending to show a more restrictive approach to exclusion, eg emphasis on reliability of the evidence, crime control, deference to investigative authorities	Cases tending to show a more robust approach to exclusion, eg emphasis on human rights, due process, criticism of authorities
R v Leatham (1861)	*Matto v DPP* (1987)
R v Sang (1980)	*Teixeira de Castro v Portugal* (1998)
Williams and O'Hare v DPP (1993)	*R v Looseley; A-G's Ref (No 3 of 2000)* [2001]
R v Chalkley [1998]	*Allan v UK* (2002)
R v Khan [1997]	*R v Grant* (2005)
Nottingham City Council v Amin [2001]	*A v Sec State Home Department (No 2)* (2005)
R v Button [2005]	

PACE and unfairly obtained evidence
Discretionary exclusion under PACE

The following points should be noted:

- the judge has to consider fairness to the proceedings in considering whether to exercise discretion to exclude evidence; this includes fairness to the prosecution as well as fairness to the defendant;

- it is not sufficient for exclusion that the admission of the evidence will have some adverse effect it must have such an adverse effect that the fairness of the proceedings is at risk;

- fairness to the proceedings means proceedings in court;

- the Court of Appeal will interfere with a trial judge's exercise of his discretion to exclude evidence under this section only for unreasonableness by the *Wednesbury* test; and

- a breach of the Code of Practice or a provision of the statute may help to get the evidence excluded (most cases on the exclusion of confessions are decided under this section).

There has been considerable debate as to how far, if at all, the statutory discretion extends the common law discretion. On the one hand it has been held in *R v Mason* (1988), (p 144) that s78(1) 'does no more than to re-state the power which the judges had at common law'. In that case, the defendant was arrested for setting fire to a motor car. During questioning police officers lied in telling him that his fingerprints had been found on glass fragments in the car. The police also lied to his solicitor. The solicitor advised him to explain his involvement and the defendant confessed. The confession should have been excluded since the judge had failed to take account of the deception practised on the defendant's solicitor whose duty it was to advise the defendant unfettered by false information from the police. On the other hand, as the discussion on **entrapment** reveals below, the courts are now prepared to consider excluding evidence obtained by entrapment thus extending the discretion identified in *Sang*.

Several cases have shown that the reliability of the evidence is a key factor in determining admissibility. In *R v Chalkley* (1998) the Court of Appeal took a very narrow view of s78 and considered that it did not enlarge the common law. The trial judge had admitted evidence of secret tape recordings obtained in breach of PACE and the civil law of trespass and in violation of Art 8 ECHR. Auld LJ in the Court of Appeal held that 'save in the case of admissions and confessions and generally as to evidence obtained from the accused after the commission of the offence there is no discretion to exclude evidence unless its quality was or might have been affected by the way in which it was obtained'. The tape recordings were highly probative of guilt and not affected by the improper police activity.

On the other hand in *Allan v UK* (2003) there had been direct psychological pressure applied to the defendant and the evidence should have been excluded. The police coached an informant to question A, who was on remand, in a prison cell about his involvement in a murder. The conversation was recorded and admitted at trial. The Court of Appeal subsequently accepted the Strasbourg court's analysis that the evidence should not have been admitted (see *Allan v R* (2004)). Hooper J stated (at para 122) that, 'Allowing an agent of the state to interrogate a suspect in the circumstances of this case bypasses any necessary protections developed over the last twenty years.'

Revision Tip

The examiners will be impressed if you demonstrate that you are aware of some exceptions to the general reluctance of the courts to exclude evidence in these circumstances. One contentious area is intercept evidence. Under s17 Regulation of Investigatory Powers Act 2000 the admission of evidence of an 'intercepted communication' is not permitted if it might reveal the existence or absence of a warrant. The purpose is to protect the secrecy of such surveillance operations. See *R v P* (2001).

Entrapment

Consider the following case of *Teixeira de Castro v Portugal* (1999). Two plain-clothes police officers had asked a known petty drug trafficker to obtain heroin. He mentioned the name of the applicant who eventually obtained packets of the drug for the undercover officers. The applicant was arrested, charged, and convicted. He claimed breaches of Arts 3, 6, and 8. He claimed that the officers had engaged in immoral conduct since he had supplied the drug solely at the officer's request. They had not been carrying out drug trafficking searches to a court order. The ECtHR held that there was a violation of Art 6 and it was not necessary to consider violations of Arts 3 and 8. The officers had instigated and incited the offence and there was nothing to suggest that but for their intervention it would have been committed. The applicant had been denied the right to a fair trial.

It is clear from *Teixeira* that the ECtHR has not gone as far as the common law in sanctioning the use of improperly obtained evidence and it is more willing to find that the use of such evidence in an entrapment case deprives the applicant of a fair trial under Art 6 if the use of such evidence makes the trial as a whole unfair. The question is not whether the evidence was improperly obtained but the use to which it was put at the trial.

Other key cases

In *R v Smurthwaite* (1994) the Court of Appeal looked again at the question of entrapment and conceded that it could be excluded if it had the necessary adverse effect on the fairness of the proceedings. It is arguable that the guidelines set out in this case for the potential exclusion of such evidence demonstrate a pragmatic rather than a principled approach. The questions to ask were:

- was the officer acting as an ***agent provocateur*** in that he was enticing the defendant to commit an offence he would not otherwise have committed?
- what was the nature of the entrapment – was it evidence of admission to a completed offence, or does it consist of the actual commission of an offence?
- how active or passive was the officer's role? and
- is there an unassailable record of what occurred or is it strongly corroborated?

Another notable English case on entrapment is *R v Shannon* [2001] where the court added the potential violation of a Convention right to the list of criteria to be considered. There the defendant was convicted of supplying drugs to a journalist posing as an Arab sheikh, part of a stratagem to obtain evidence of drug offences against him. The judge refused an application to exclude the evidence as unfairly obtained. The Court of Appeal held that the appeal against conviction be dismissed. There was no general rule requiring a court on grounds of fundamental fairness not to entertain a prosecution in all cases of incitement or instigation by an ***agent provocateur*** regardless of whether the trial as a whole could be fair in the procedural sense. The judge found correctly in that the evidence fell short of establishing actual incitement or instigation of the offences and in any event the admission of the evidence would not have an adverse effect on the procedural fairness of the trial. The Court of Appeal were referred to *Teixeira de Castro v Portugal* and considered that the end result of that case, couched as it was in terms of incitement and causation, was not necessarily at odds with English law. It considered that the approach of the Strasbourg court was not inconsistent with the approach in *R v Smurthwaite* namely that the evidence would be open to exclusion only if the incitement had caused the offence.

✅ Looking for extra marks?

This is an area which is predominantly based on the case law and you should familiarise yourself with the facts of the cases which may form the basis of a problem question scenario. A controversial decision is that in *Williams and O'Hare v DPP* (1993). There police had set a trap in an area plagued by car theft. They parked a van filled with cigarette cartons with its door open. Two young men helped themselves and were arrested, charged, and convicted. The convictions were upheld since the police had acted lawfully and there was no incitement. The ethical dilemmas presented by such a case when arguably the two thieves did not start out with crime in mind, makes a good basis for an essay question on discussion of policy on police undercover tactics.

PACE and illegally obtained evidence

A pertinent question to ask is whether the courts take a different stance when the police are breaking the law as opposed to acting unfairly or improperly in a way which fell short of unlawfulness. The ECtHR has held that evidence so obtained is not necessarily to be excluded. The leading case is *Khan v UK* (2000). The applicant had been convicted of involvement in importing heroin. The evidence against him came from an electronic listening device installed by police in a private house he visited. The police had allegedly committed criminal damage in planting the device. K claimed violations of Arts 6 and 8. The Court held that the evidence had been obtained in violation of Art 8 but it had not been unlawful in the sense of being contrary to domestic criminal law. The authenticity of the recordings was not in question; only their admissibility. Since the domestic courts could exercise discretion whether or not to admit such evidence and had concluded its admission would not affect the fairness of the trial, there was no breach of Art 6. The Court found a breach of Arts 8 and 12 since there was no legal basis and thus no redress for the invasion of privacy.

Overwhelming cogency of evidence

On occasion, police evidence obtained unlawfully is so cogent that to refuse to admit it affronts justice. An example is the admissibility of unlawfully retained DNA specimens. In *A-G's Ref (No 3 of 1999)* (2001) the House of Lords reached what many regard as a sensible decision. Under s64(1) PACE a sample taken from a suspect during the investigation of an offence must be destroyed if that person is 'cleared' of the offence and according to s64(3B) such sample 'shall not be used in evidence against that person ... or for the purposes of any investigation of an offence'. In two cases, one involving murder and one rape, the Crown had put forward as part of its case **DNA** evidence collected during other investigations which had both led to the defendants being acquitted. The Court of Appeal had declared that s64 was mandatory and such evidence was inadmissible. The Court of Appeal at the request of the Attorney General referred a question for the opinion of the House of Lords as to whether in such circumstances a judge had a discretion to the relevant evidence notwithstanding the terms of s64(3B). The House of Lords reversed the Court of Appeal decision. Whereas s64 (3B) made express prohibition against the use of a DNA sample which should have been destroyed, s64(3B)(b), in prohibiting the use of an unlawfully retained sample for the purposes of any investigation, did not amount to a mandatory exclusion of evidence obtained as a result of a failure to comply with the prohibition. It should be read along with s78 which left the question of its admissibility to the discretion of the trial judge. A decision by a judge in the exercise of his discretion to admit such evidence would not be in breach of Arts 8 or 6 ECHR. The information obtained as a result of the failure to destroy the DNA sample ought not to have been rendered inadmissible.

Subsequently the law has been changed so that it is lawful for the police to keep such DNA specimens.

Revision tip

Bear in mind that it is always open to Parliament to give the police extensive additional powers so their scope for acting illegally is narrowed. Parliament, for example, had made substantial amendments to the law on the retention of DNA evidence of those who are arrested but not charged. Thus, the undercover operation undertaken by the police in *R v Khan* (1996) would now be authorised under PtIII of the **Police Act 1997** or PtII of the **Regulation of Investigatory Powers Act 1996**.

Police surveillance and legal professional privilege

The courts appear to take a trenchant stance on protecting this confidential relationship. In *R v Grant* (2005) police had secretly and without authorisation recorded the conversation of a suspect and his solicitor. This amounted to a breach of legal professional privilege and the trial was stayed. This contrasts with *R v Button* (2005) involving a secret recording of a suspect in his cell. There was breach of Art 8 but it was not unfair to admit the evidence. Note also that the House of Lords has now held that the police, in cases involving national security, may bug a solicitor client interview if authorised under the stringent provisions of the **Regulation of Investigatory Powers Act (RIPA) 2000**; see *In re McE; In re M; In re C and Another* (2009). **RIPA 2000** thus overrode legal professional privilege (see Chapter 11). In a powerful dissenting judgment Lord Phillips identified a distinction between legal professional privilege and the statutory right of a detained person to consult privately with a solicitor. He stated (at para 26), 'I would interpret the statutory right to consult a lawyer privately as one that confers on the detainee an absolute right to privacy that precludes covert surveillance in any circumstances.'

Of course, the decision does not mean that evidence obtained in such circumstances will be admissible at trial but it marks a significant step in legitimising what had been previously perceived as unauthorised police activity.

Stay of prosecution or exclusion of evidence?

The court has the option of staying a prosecution rather than just excluding evidence at trial and has adopted the former in relation to entrapment cases.

The leading House of Lords case is *R v Looseley (A-G's Ref No 3 of 2000)* (2001). An undercover police officer who had been given the defendant's name as a potential source of drugs, arranged with him to exchange heroin for money. The defendant was charged with supplying or being concerned in supplying to another a class A controlled drug, contrary to s4 Misuse of Drugs Act 1971. The trial judge refused a preliminary request to exclude evidence or stay proceedings. The defendant pleaded guilty.

In a separate case, two undercover police officers who offered contraband cigarettes for sale at a housing estate were introduced to the accused as a potential buyer. They sold him cigarettes and asked if he could get them heroin, a request to which he agreed and complied after initial hesitation. He was charged with supplying heroin. The trial judge stayed the proceedings on the ground that the police had incited the commission of the offence and that otherwise the accused would be denied his right to a fair hearing under Art 6(1) ECHR. The stay was lifted, the prosecution offered no evidence, and the accused was acquitted. The Attorney General referred, for the opinion of the Court of Appeal, the question whether in cases of **entrapment** the judicial discretion conferred by s78 PACE, and the power to stay proceedings as an abuse of process, had been modified by Art 6(1) ECHR. The Court of Appeal held it had not and that the trial judge had been wrong to stay the proceedings. The defendant in the first case appealed and the reference was made from the Court of Appeal in the second.

The judgment

The House of Lords held that the court must in such cases balance the need to uphold the rule of law by convicting and punishing those who committed crimes with the need to prevent law enforcement agencies acting in a way which offended ordinary notions of fairness. The House distinguished between entrapment which might lead to exclusion of evidence and entrapment which will lead to a stay of prosecution. There is not one simple test. The court must ask the central question which is whether the actions of the police were so seriously improper as to bring the administration of justice into disrepute. If there has been an abuse of state power, then the appropriate remedy is a stay of the indictment, rather than exclusion of the evidence under s78 PACE. The appeal of the defendant in the first case was dismissed since the undercover officer did no more than present himself as an ordinary customer to an active drug dealer and there was nothing in the officer's conduct which constituted incitement. In the second case, on the facts, the trial judge had been entitled to stay the proceedings on the ground that the officers had instigated the offence by offering inducements which would not ordinarily be associated with the commission of that offence. The decision of the Court of Appeal was reversed in part.

The House stated that the principle to be applied was that it would be unfair and an abuse of process if a person had been lured, incited, or pressurised into committing a crime which he would not otherwise have committed but that it would not be objectionable if the law enforcement officer, behaving as an ordinary member of the public, gave the person an exceptional opportunity to commit a crime and that person freely took advantage of the opportunity. The judgment demonstrated strong judicial recognition of the dangers of excessive police behaviour in cases of **entrapment** and the need for the courts to protect citizens.

Police misconduct and the integrity of the criminal justice system

Following this judgment the focus of the court's approach must be on an objective assessment of the conduct of the police rather than the predisposition of the defendant. Thus, for example, the defendant's criminal record is unlikely to be relevant. Lord Nicholls specifically recognised at para 16, p2067, that *R v Sang* (1980) had been 'overtaken' by statute and case law. Lord Hoffman, at para 36, p2071, stressed the importance of the 'protection of the integrity of the criminal justice system'. Their Lordships considered that their judgment was compatible with *Teixeira de Castro v Portugal* (1999). It did not follow from *Teixeira* that taking any active steps, such as offering to buy drugs, necessarily amounts to 'incitement'. The law was and is that entrapment is not a defence per se. Lord Nicholls stated that if there has been entrapment, then even where there is other evidence, the abuse of state power is such that the case should be stopped entirely by means of a stay. Among the factors to be considered will be the following:

- the nature of the offence;
- the factual basis for the police carrying out the operation; and
- the degree and extent of the police inducement.

The former test of whether the offender was predisposed to commit such an offence was not appropriate.

The test: an unexceptional opportunity?

Lord Nicholls of Birkenhead stated in *Looseley* (2001) (para 23):

> . . . a useful guide is to consider whether the police did no more than present the defendant with an unexceptional opportunity to commit a crime. I emphasise the word unexceptional. The yardstick for the purpose of this test is, in general, whether the police conduct preceding the commission of the offence was no more than might have been expected from others in the circumstances. Police conduct of this nature is not to be regarded as inciting or instigating a crime, or luring a person into committing a crime. The police did no more than others could be expected to do. The police did not create crime artificially.

✅ *Looking for extra marks?*

Your examiner will be impressed if you demonstrate that you understand the difference between impropriety carried out by non-state actors as opposed to those who represent state power. Thus, in *R v Shannon* (2001) an undercover reporter attempted a 'sting' by posing as an Arab sheikh wanting to buy drugs. The Court of Appeal refused to apply the 'abuse of process doctrine'. However, this area of law is under constant change.

(!) Conclusion

Roberts and Zuckerman (2004) review the rationales for exclusion of improperly obtained evidence and observe that it is short-sighted not to take account of the fact that the evidence exists and then 'our knowledge of the world has changed forever and moral evaluation must take account of the realities of the situation' (p153). They call (p158) for a development of 'principles of attribution specifying the circumstances in which the state is properly answerable for the activities of its servants and agents'. They see that a 'blanket rule of exclusion' (p159) or an 'all-purpose rule' would not be appropriate. Recent case law does suggest that English courts are now engaging with this moral dimension and have moved beyond the view that reliability is the only criterion for admissibility in relation to improperly obtained evidence. The approach evidenced in *Chalkley* (1998) that factual guilt was sufficient may be short-lived. In particular, it does seem that the law on entrapment has thus moved away from *Sang* (1980). It is still not a defence but a more robust approach to exclusion or stay of prosecution is now taken, recognising that fair trial rights extend to pre-trial proceedings including police investigations. The issues are complex policy ones. The investigative authorities, particularly the police will argue that their hands should not be tied by technicalities, especially given the threat from organised crime and hardened offenders. Civil libertarians will argue that it is vital that the integrity of the criminal justice process is upheld by high standards.

It is clear that on occasion, albeit unusually, the courts will exclude such evidence or stay a prosecution because however compelling it might be, the integrity of the criminal process might otherwise be at risk. This is particularly so in cases of **entrapment** and far less so, torture cases aside, in other situations where the evidence is reliable. It is expected that the jurisprudence from Strasbourg applied under the **Human Rights Act** will lead to more careful delineation of the principles on which the courts should approach such cases. The tension is between concentrating too much on the reliability of the evidence to the detriment of considerations of fairness. It is notable of course that s78 refers to 'fairness to the proceedings' and not just to the defendant. Finally, of course, it is always open to Parliament to authorise extended police operations by statute and pass a law for example allowing bugging of police stations.

Other jurisdictions

It is generally agreed that the judicial exclusionary discretion is based on a pragmatic rather than a principled approach. Commentators have remarked on the position of other jurisdictions where in particular there is a more active stance on exclusion, particularly if there is a violation of a constitutional right. Examples are the United States' case *Mapp v Ohio* (1961) and **Section 24(2)** of the *Canadian Charter of Rights and Freedoms*,

> Where ... a court concludes that evidence was obtained in a manner that infringed or denied any rights or freedoms guaranteed by this Charter, the evidence shall be excluded if it is established that, having regard to all the circumstances, the admission of it in the proceedings would bring the administration of justice into disrepute.

(✱) Key cases

Case	Facts	Principle
R v Sang [1980] AC 402	The defendants were convicted of conspiracy to issue forged banknotes. It was argued that evidence had been obtained by the activities of an **agent provocateur**.	**Entrapment** was not a defence. There was no common law discretion to exclude relevant evidence, other than confession evidence or evidence obtained after the commission of the offence, because it was improperly obtained.
R v Smurthwaite (1994) 98 Cr App R 437	An undercover police officer posed as contract killer and secretly recorded conversations with the defendant. The defendant had said he wanted to hire a killer for his wife. Trial judge refused to exclude evidence in trial for solicitation to murder.	The Court of Appeal reviewed the factors to be considered in exercising judicial discretion to exclude evidence obtained by entrapment. There was no defence of entrapment but s78 could in principle be applied to exclude such evidence on grounds of unfairness to the proceedings.
R v Chalkley and Jeffries (1998) 2 Cr App R 79	A covert listening device had been planted and police had unlawfully entered the appellant's home to replace batteries.	The evidence should not be excluded. The evidence was authentic, probative, and relevant. The quality of the evidence had not been affected by the police action.
Khan v UK (2000) 31 EHRR 1016	Police planted a covert listening device to a property frequented by a suspected drug dealer. There was no statutory authority for their action. The evidence from the recordings founded the conviction. The House of Lords rejected the argument that there was a violation of Art 8.	There had been a violation of Art 8 but not Art 6. The admissibility of evidence was primarily a matter for the domestic court and this had properly applied the law. The question was whether the proceedings as a whole were fair.
Nottingham City Council v Amin [2001] 1 WLR 1071	Plain clothes officers hired a taxi without a licence. The magistrate had excluded the evidence on the grounds of entrapment and violation of Art 6.	Evidence should be admitted. D would have behaved in the same way if others had offered the opportunity.
R v Looseley; Re Attorney-General's Reference (No 3 of 2000) [2001] UKHL 53	Two joined cases where the appellants claimed they had been incited into supplying heroin to the police.	The proper approach is to ask did the police do more than present the defendant with an unexceptional opportunity to commit a crime. It would be

Case	Facts	Principle
continued		unfair to offer inducements and entice a person into actions he would not normally have taken. The proper approach is **stay of** proceedings but evidence may be excluded if trial has commenced. In one case, that of a known drug dealer, the conviction was upheld but in the other it had been properly stayed as an abuse of process in that there had been the encouragement of an uncharacteristic offence.
Allan v UK (2002) 36 EHRR	Police had trespassed and committed criminal damage in attaching a covert listening device to a property visited by a suspected drug smuggler. At the time there was no statutory system to deal with such devices. The House of Lords had held that evidence from the tapes was properly admitted at trial.	This amounted to a breach of Art 6 and a violation of the suspect's privilege against self-incrimination. The evidence should be excluded.
A and others v Secretary of State for the Home Department (No 2) (2006) 2 AC 221	The Special Immigration Appeals Commission and the Court of Appeal had held that evidence obtained by torture abroad was admissible for the purpose of deciding whether a person was a terrorist and a threat to national security.	The exclusion of evidence obtained by torture, including outside the jurisdiction, is a principle of the common law.

⑨ Key debates

Topic	**Should the discretion under s78 be structured and should there be a presumption of exclusion?**
Authors	D Ormerod and D Birch
Viewpoint	The authors set out the arguments for and against a statutory adoption of a more structured approach to exclusion of evidence. One risk of a structured approach is that it might be resisted by the judiciary and signal a return to the common law discretion.
Source	'Evolution of the Discretionary Exclusion of Evidence' [2004] Crim LR 138

Exam questions

✲✲✲✲✲✲✲✲✲✲

Topic	Legal values and discretionary exclusion of evidence
Author	A Ashworth
Viewpoint	Puts the theoretical argument for the principle that those who enforce the law should obey it and if government officials have played a part in creating an offence the trail should be stopped.
Source	'Testing Fidelity to Legal Values: Official Involvement and Criminal Justice'(2000) 63 *Modern Law Review* 633

⑦ Exam questions

Essay question

'Section 78 of the Police and Criminal Evidence Act 1984 empowers the court to exclude prosecution evidence if its admission "would have such an adverse effect on the fairness of the proceedings that the court ought not to admit it". However so far there has been little inclination to elucidate the principles which should govern the exercise of this discretion.' (Zuckerman (1989, 352))

Explain, with reasons, whether Zuckerman's comment is still valid in 2008 in relation to the discretionary exclusion of improperly obtained evidence other than confessions.

An outline answer is available at the end of the book.

Problem question

The police are concerned about a spate of thefts from houses and shops on the Stafford Cripps Estate. The offenders have not been caught. Inspector Tamara, acting undercover, engages a group of women in conversation at the school gates when they are collecting their children. She admires the earrings they are wearing. Janet, one of the mothers, agrees to get them for Tamara. They arrange to meet the next day and the earrings are exchanged for money. They turn out to have been stolen from a jewellery shop on the estate. Janet is arrested for dealing in stolen goods. Advise on evidence.

An outline answer is available online at http://www.oxfordtextbooks.co.uk/orc/concentrate/

#5
Character evidence

- Two processes are at stake in discussing character evidence, whether it is admissible or not, and if it is admissible, what is its use as evidence or what is its evidential worth.
- Character evidence if admitted may be evidence of either propensity, or **credibility**, or both.
- Character has two aspects, good character and bad character.
- The admissibility and evidential worth of good character is governed by the common law.
- Good character is defined as general reputation, or lack of criminal record.
- Good character may be evidence of lack of guilt (**propensity**) and of trustworthiness as a witness (credit).
- Under the common law there was a presumption that bad character evidence of defendants was not admissible, the exceptions to this were i) the '**similar fact**' common law principle and ii) the statutory provisions relating to cross examination of the witness who chose to testify under **s1(3) Criminal Evidence Act (CEA) 1898**.
- Bad character evidence of both defendants and non-defendant witnesses is now defined by statute, **s98 Criminal Justice Act (CJA) 2003**.
- The admissibility of bad character as evidence of non-defendants is determined by **s100 CJA 2003**.
- The admissibility of bad character evidence of defendants is governed by **s101(1) CJA 2003**.
- Bad character of the defendant may be admissible whether he testifies or not, in contrast to the position under **CEA 1898**.

Related areas

Character evidence may be considered alongside that on confessions since the defendant may choose to challenge the admissibility of his confession by attacking the behaviour of the police. This may lay him open to having his criminal record revealed. Since previous bad behaviour may involve testimony from witnesses making out of court statements the law on hearsay may also play a part. Finally, Chapter 8 in relation to sexual history evidence of complainants in rape trials needs to be read in conjunction with this chapter.

The assessment: key points

This area falls into three distinct parts and although a question may contain elements of all three, the law relating to each is quite different:

- good character of the defendant;
- bad character of the defendant; and
- bad character of a non-defendant witness.

The first part is relatively straightforward and you need to familiarise yourself with the leading cases under the common law. The second and third are more difficult in that they are covered by a very complex statute, CJA 2003, and a growing body of case law. You should be very careful you understand the statutory provisions and treat the cases as examples of its operation. The cases should not be seen as exact precedents since each situation turns on its own facts. In many instances the cases are conjoined appeals covering many first instance trials. They will be referred to here for the most part by the first named case.

Character evidence comprises a controversial series of provisions where the old common exclusionary rule that the defendant's previous convictions should not be disclosed to the court has in many ways been turned on its head. There is now, in effect, a presumption that a criminal record should be admitted but in order to achieve admissibility the provisions of the statute should be scrupulously followed. This again is an area where it does help to have at least outline knowledge of the history of the law. Some of the cases on bad character that are cited in the judgments under CJA 2003 are determined under the common law or the CEA 1898 and these will be incomprehensible unless you familiarise yourself to some extent with the old law which is set out below.

Propensity and credit

You need to clarify in your mind the sometimes obscure distinction between relevance to **propensity** (lack of guilt) and relevance to credit (trustworthiness). The criminal justice system and the legal profession, with little if any support from psychological research, have long maintained that both good and bad character may be predictors of behaviour in two regards:

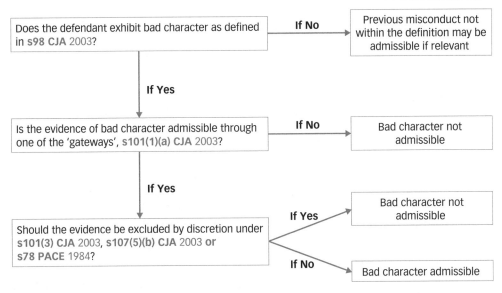

Figure 5.1 Overview of law on admissibility of defendant's bad character evidence

- they may indicate that the defendant is, respectively, either less or more likely to have committed the offence; and
- that he or she is, respectively, more or less likely to be telling the truth as a witness.

The distinction between evidence for guilt or lack of it and evidence for **credibility**, or lack of it, although formally disapproved, still complicates this area of law. Thus assessments may require you to consider two distinct issues; firstly, is the evidence admissible or not, and secondly, if it admissible what is it evidence of?

The above chart (Fig 5.1) provides a guide to the admissibility of bad character evidence of the defendant.

Revision tip

It is sound practice, particularly in preparation of essay questions, to read the consultation papers and reports produced by the Law Commission which provide helpful guides to the principles and public policy considerations underlying this area of law. Thus, in its Consultation Paper, No 141, produced in 1996 (available at http://www.lawcom.gov.uk/docs/cp141.pdf) it referred to the light that psychological research had thrown on this area. It pointed out (paras 6.16-6.17) that there was no sound psychological research confirming a link between criminal record and lack of truthfulness as a witness. In its 2001 Report (Cm 5257) it explained the reasons for the proposed change in the law. It is a good exercise to contrast its proposals with the shape of the final statute which arguably has taken a more prosecutorial approach.

Key features and principles
Rationale and evolution of the law on character

This area is one of the most controversial in the law of evidence. To what extent should a defendant have a 'clean slate' when facing trial? It helps to have some overview of the history, particularly of the provisions on bad character. There are two strands to this, one under the common law and one under statute.

To deal with statute first, until 1898 the defendant was not allowed to testify, so was protected from being questioned about any previous convictions, unlike other witnesses who were not so protected. However, if evidence was given on his behalf of his good character the prosecution was allowed under the common law to admit any bad character. In 1898 the defendant was permitted to testify in his own behalf. The **Criminal Evidence Act 1898** brought about a compromise whereby if the defendant chose to testify, he was shielded from questions in cross examination about any bad character unless he:

- claimed to be of good character;
- impugned a prosecution witness or a dead victim (a 1994 amendment to the 1898 Act); or
- made an attack on a co-defendant.

If he did any of these he lost his 'shield'. Note that this only applied to the testifying defendant. The evidence, if admitted, was only evidence for lack of **credibility**.

The common law strand of cases on bad character related to what was known as '**similar fact**'. The starting point was the exclusionary rule that previous bad character was not admissible to show guilt. The exception was that if the previous behaviour was so relevant that it shed more probative light than prejudice on the instant charge it was admitted. A leading case under the common law was *R v Smith* (1915).

· ·

R v Smith (1915) 11 Cr App R 229

S was on trial for the murder of his wife whom he had just married. He claimed her death in the bath was an accident. Evidence was admitted of two of his earlier 'brides' who had died in unlocked bathrooms and on whose death Smith collected insurance. The extent of the coincidences was such that it defied belief that the deaths were accidental.

· ·

Gradually, the case law demonstrated a lowering of the threshold of admissibility in such cases. The rule on admissibility applied whether the defendant testified or not and the evidence, if admitted, was evidence of guilt.

The complexities of the law in this area and the pressure to secure more convictions led to a review of the law. The Law Commission published two reports in which they identified the dangers of too readily admitting the defendant's bad character. The jury might give it too much weight and thus fall into a 'reasoning prejudice' or they might fall into 'moral prejudice' by not looking at the evidence carefully since they had formed a prejudicial view of the defendant on the basis of his record. The highly prejudicial effect of admitting defendants' previous convictions before both juries and magistrates has been identified in research by Lloyd Bostock (1973, 2006) and the risk, therefore, is that too ready an admissibility of bad character evidence may lead to miscarriages of justice.

In the event, the Government legislated in the **Criminal Justice Act 2003** to admit character evidence more readily than the Law Commission had recommended. The concept of a 'shield' for the defendant, which lay behind the **CEA 1898**, was replaced by that of 'gateways' (see Fig 5.2) of admissibility indicating that there is a presumption the bad character evidence will be admitted.

Section 99 CJA 2003 abolishes the common law rules on admissibility (but not on other aspects of character eg definition of good character or judicial directions to the jury on the evidential worth of character). It also repeals **s1(3) CEA 1898**.

Definition, admissibility and evidential worth of good character

Good character is defined by the leading common law cases: see *R v Rowton* (1865) and *R v Redgrave* (1982) in the Key Cases below. The strict rule is that only evidence of general reputation is admitted but in practice the rule is often not observed and good character is held to be synonymous with no criminal record. Good character is relevant to both credit and **propensity**. See *R v Vye* (1993).

In *R v Aziz* (1996) the House of Lords gave further guidance on the importance of a good character direction. Three defendants were charged with conspiracy to evade VAT payments. Two had no previous convictions but admitted separate acts of dishonesty at trial and were not given the propensity limb of the good character direction. The House stated that failure to give a good character direction could mean the conviction being overturned on appeal but that the judge had a residual discretion to refuse to give one if it was 'an insult to common sense'. In this case the convictions were overturned.

Definition of bad character

Section 98 CJA 2003 defines bad character for both defendants and witnesses as:

evidence of, or a disposition towards, misconduct on his part, other than evidence which –

(a) has to do with the alleged facts of the offence with which the defendant is charged, or

(b) is evidence of misconduct in connection with the investigation or prosecution of that offence.

The interpretive section, s112, misconduct is defined as 'the commission of an offence or other reprehensible behaviour'.

Definition of bad character

✳✳✳✳✳✳✳✳✳✳✳

The term 'reprehensible behaviour' has not featured in other statutes and its vagueness in meaning has been the subject of academic and judicial debate.

Evidence which falls within this definition is admissible only if one of the 'gateways' set out in s101(1) applies (see Fig 5.2).

Previous convictions

Bad character certainly includes previous convictions. The Explanatory Notes which accompanied the Act gave a broad definition of 'bad character' as including 'evidence such as previous convictions as well as evidence on charges being tried concurrently and evidence relating to offences for which [the accused] has been charged, where the charge is not prosecuted, or for which [the accused] was subsequently acquitted'. In *R v Edwards (Stewart)* (2006) evidence of allegations that did not go to trial because of abuse of process were considered bad character and therefore subject to admissibility under s101(1)(d). Thus, unproven behaviour may be held to be bad character. Note, however, that s108(2) provides that convictions committed while the defendant was under 14 years old are not admitted in trials where the defendant is over 21 years. The exception is if offences allegedly committed at the current trial and when the defendant was under 14 years are only triable on indictment and the court considers that 'the interest of justice require the evidence to be admissible'.

Revision tip

You have to be careful in citing earlier cases when applying the CJA 2003 but it is appropriate to cite the case of *R v Z* (2003) in explaining how acquittals may be considered bad character and also how the common law cases influence the shape of a statute. In the trial of a rapist the House of Lords allowed evidence of previous acquittals for rape where the defendant had exhibited similar behaviour to that in the current charge and put forward the same defence. He was subsequently convicted. Earlier authorities had held that previous acquittals were irrelevant to the question of guilt see *Maxwell v DPP* (1935).

You must be careful to examine the facts of any problem you are set since acquittals will by no means be routinely admitted. See *R v Edwards* (2006) where it was held that behaviour which was the subject of a prosecution which resulted in an acquittal was 'reprehensible behaviour' under s98 CJA 2003.

The test for 'reprehensible behaviour' has been addressed in a number of cases. Emson (2008, p58) writes that it 'would seem to require the trial judge to determine whether or not most reasonable people would strongly disapprove of the conduct on moral grounds'. In *R v Somanathan* (2006), case conjoined with *R v Weir* (2006), it was held that evidence from women that they had been propositioned sexually by a Hindu priest were admissible in the trial of the priest for a rape of another member of his congregation. In *R v Tine* (2006) by contrast, psychiatric illness was not reprehensible behaviour.

✅ *Looking for extra marks?*

You will impress the examiner if you connect the material in each of the specific areas with the general principles you have learnt and which are outlined in Chapter 1. Thus, for example, you will be aware that the question of the nature of prior bad character could be seen as a 'collateral fact' and the courts will not want to spend too much time on arguments about what amounts to 'reprehensible behaviour'. This point was made in *R v McKenzie* (2008). You could note, however, that on the facts of that case the definition did allow the Crown to **adduce** evidence of prior bad driving where there was no conviction to prove aggressive and impatient driving.

Relevant behaviour

If the behaviour does not fall within the definition of 'bad character' in s98 it may still be admissible if it is relevant. There are three sorts of behaviour for which the only test is relevance. The first is that which 'has to do with the alleged facts of the offence with which the defendant is charged' (s98(a)), the second is that which 'is evidence of misconduct in connection with the investigation or prosecution of that offence' (s98(b)), and the third is other behaviour which is not bad character and also falls outside of those categories. Taking each in turn:

The alleged facts of the case

In *R v Edwards and Rowlands* (2006) the discovery of a cartridge buried in the defendant's garden was admissible under this head and not as evidence of bad character. The cases suggest that the courts give this section a wide interpretation. It clearly overlaps with s101(1)(d) the test being whether it is evidence of **propensity** or not. See also *R v Benguit* (2005) where the defendant contested evidence that he had ever carried a knife. This should have been considered under s101 since it did not have to do with the alleged facts of the instant case.

Evidence of misconduct in connection with the investigation or prosecution of that offence

This might include, for example, evidence of witness intimidation after the alleged commission of the offence.

Other behaviour

This is subject only to the test of relevance. Here the earlier common law tests in the **'similar fact'** cases may be helpful. It will need to be more probative than prejudicial. Behaviour here may be neither criminal nor morally reprehensible.

In *R v Manister* (2006), M was on trial for sexual offences against an underage girl. Evidence that he had had lawful sexual involvement with a 16-year-old when he was 34 was admissible under the common law test to show his sexual preferences given that he contested he had no sexual interest in the alleged victim.

Cases involving incriminating but not necessarily reprehensible possession of articles may be admitted under this head. This might include, for example, legal pornography.

Admissibility and evidential worth bad character of defendant

Evidence of the defendant's bad character (as defined above) is only admissible if one of the gateways in **s101(1)** applies. **Subsections (c)–(g)** have an accompanying explanatory section (**ss102–106**) which is also given in the Fig 5.2 table:

Figure 5.2 The gateways and explanatory sections

Gateway	Provision
s101(1)(a)	All the parties agree
s101(1)(b)	Evidence is **adduced by** defendant, or given in examination or cross examination
s101(1)(c)	It is important explanatory evidence. See also ss102
s101(1)(d)	It is relevant to an important matter in issue between the defendant and the prosecution. See also s103
s101(1)(e)	It has substantial probative value in relation to an important matter in issue between the defendant and a co-defendant. See also s104
s101(1)(f)	It is evidence to correct a false impression given by the defendant. See also s105
s101(1)(g)	The defendant makes an attack on another person's character. See also s106

Note the differing descriptors of the test for admissibility between the sections. Under **s112** ' "an important matter" means a matter of substantial importance in the context of the case as a whole'. This appears to blur the distinction between 'relevant to an important matter' and 'substantial probative value in relation to an important matter in issue'.

Note also that 'probative value' and 'relevant' are to be read in accordance with **s109**:

(1) ... the relevance or probative value of evidence is a reference to its relevance or probative value on the assumption that it is true

(2) In assessing the relevance or probative value of an item of evidence ... a court need not assume that the evidence is true if it appears, on the basis of any material before the court (including any evidence it decides to hear on the matter) that no court or jury could reasonably find it to be true.

The gateways heading

Taking each gateway in turn their scope and important case law will be reviewed:

Section 101(1)(a)

All the parties agree:

This is not a controversial provision and it may occur if the defendant thinks tactically it is best to pre-empt the prosecution admitting the bad character evidence or it might be necessary in establishing an alibi. Note that under this head any co-defendants would have to also agree.

Section 101(1)(b)

Elicited in examination or cross examination:

Again this might be a tactical decision by the defendant. The risk for the defendant in both these instances is that the evidence may then be used by the prosecution to demonstrate lack of **credibility** and **propensity**. In other words he may control its admissibility but not its use.

Section 101(1)(c) and s102

Important explanatory evidence:

Under **s102b**, evidence under this gateway will be admitted if, without it, the court would find it 'impossible or difficult properly to understand other evidence in the case, and its value for understanding the case as whole is substantial'.

The provision overlaps to some extent with evidence which is part of the offence as provided for in **s98**. There was provision under the common law for what was known as background evidence and here the overlap is with **s101(d)**. Thus Roberts and Zuckerman (2004, p529) cite the case of *R v Straffen* (1952). The defendant had absconded from Broadmoor (and thus obviously had a criminal past) and this information was given to the trial to explain his presence at the scene of the crime. These authors suggest that the new statutory test has increased the threshold of admissibility of this evidence compared with the laxer common law approach.

Section 101(d) and s103

It is relevant to an important matter in issue between the defendant and the prosecution:

Here the large amount of new case law indicates the complexity of the provision which is the successor the old '**similar fact**' rule. **Section 103** provides that:

matters in issue between the defendant and the prosecution include –

(a) the question whether the defendant has a **propensity to** commit offences of the kind with which he is charged, except where his having such a propensity makes it no more likely that he is guilty of the offence;

(b) the question whether the defendant has a propensity to be untruthful, except where it is not suggested that the defendant's case is untruthful in any respect.

Section 112(1) defines an 'important matter' as 'a matter of substantial importance in the context of the case as a whole'. **Section 103** contains a number of conditions concerning this evidence. They are:

- offence of the same kind includes offences of same description as if the indictment would be in the same terms and also offences of the same category. (The Home Office by Statutory Instrument has produced official lists of these concerned with theft and sexual offences against persons under 16);

Definition of bad character

****

- offences may be excluded 'by reason of the length of time since conviction or for any other reason, that it would be unjust for it to apply in this case'. (Note also the overlapping discretion under s101(3) and (4)); and

- only the prosecution may **adduce** evidence under this gateway.

Propensity to commit offences of the same kind

Under the common law, propensity or disposition evidence was circumstantial evidence of guilt. There are three main differences between the common law and statute:

- the common law position of a rule of exclusion subject to an inclusionary discretion is reversed. The Court of Appeal in *R v Weir and Others* (2006) stated that s101(1)(d) 'completely reverses the pre-existing general rule . . . if the evidence of a defendant's bad character is relevant to an important issue between the prosecution and the defence . . . then, unless there is an application to exclude the evidence, it is admissible . . . The pre-existing one-stage test which balanced probative value against prejudicial effect is obsolete.' The balancing act is performed when an application is made under s101(3) and the judge must consider whether 'the admission of the evidence would have such an adverse effect on the fairness of the proceedings that the court ought not to admit';

- the Court of Appeal will not readily reverse the exercise of judicial discretion to admit evidence; and

- the courts are aware of Parliament's intention to increase the instances of admissibility of bad character. In *R v Edwards (Stewart)* (2006) it stated that it 'was apparent that Parliament intended that evidence of bad character would be put before juries more frequently than had previously been the case'.

You cannot treat the cases necessarily as binding precedents since they turn on their specific fact situations. However, the following case does set out general guidelines. The account below is an attempt to derive some principles on admissibility in relation to propensity to commit the offence from a selection of the leading cases.

In *R v Hanson* (2005) (one of three conjoined appeals) the appellant had allegedly stolen money from a bedroom above a public house. He had been drinking in the pub and according to the prosecution was the only person who had had the opportunity to enter the bedroom. His previous convictions for dishonesty offences were admitted to suggest **propensity**. Some offences such as handling stolen goods were not evidence of propensity but the burglary offences were. The court held that:

- three questions are to be considered where propensity to commit the offence is relied upon: (1) Does the history of convictions establish a propensity to commit offences of the kind charged? (2) Does that propensity make it more likely that the defendant committed the offence charged? (3) Is it unjust to rely on the convictions of the same category; and in any event will the proceedings be unfair if they are admitted?

- decisions on the exercise of discretion should take into account the degree of similarity between the previous convictions and the offence charged, the respective gravity, and the strength of the prosecution case. If there is little other evidence against the defendant it may be unfair to admit the evidence;

- old convictions with no special features shared with the offence charged are likely seriously to affect the fairness of proceedings adversely unless they show a continuing propensity;

- when the Crown begins the process of applying **to adduce** evidence of bad character it must specify the relevant gateway. This may include the facts of the conviction or, additionally, the surrounding circumstances; and

- although there is no minimum number of convictions necessary to show **propensity** the smaller the number the less likely it is that propensity will be demonstrated.

In *R v Somanathan* (2006) (see above) the Court of Appeal held that the evidence from the women members of the congregation was admissible even though it would have not been admissible under the old '**similar fact**' rule; 'enhanced probative value' was not required.

R v Tully (2006) is one of the small number of cases where the Court of Appeal has held that character evidence was wrongly admitted at trial. A general propensity to obtain property belonging to another should not have been admitted to prove the **propensity** in a case where the defendant was charged with the robbery of a taxi driver. Factually, the cases were quite different.

A number of cases have held that the use to which the evidence is put once it is admitted does not depend on the gateway. Thus, in *R v Highton* (2005) the defendant's previous convictions had been admitted under s101(1)(g), see below. However, the judge was correct to also give a direction on **propensity**. His previous convictions for violence and dishonesty where relevant to his current charge of kidnapping, robbery and theft. Moreover, during the course of the trial the ground may have shifted since the bad character evidence was admitted and the judge may need to direct that the character evidence has little weight. The specimen directions should be carefully followed but failure to do so should not automatically be grounds of appeal.

Revision tip

Many of the Court of Appeal decisions in this area could arguably be seen to be of prosecutorial benefit, which was of course the objective of the statute. Note, by contrast, *R v Davies* [2008] where the Court held that it may be unfair to admit relevant evidence under s101(1)(c), explanatory material, or false information (f), or imputation (g) if it has been held to be inadmissible under (d) as evidence of propensity. The court or jury might under those circumstances misunderstand its purpose and s78 PACE should be used to exclude the evidence.

Propensity for untruthfulness

The Explanatory Note which accompanied the Act explained:

Section 103(1)(b) makes it clear that evidence relating to whether the defendant has a propensity to be untruthful (in other words, is not to be regarded as a credible witness) can be admitted. This is intended to enable the admission of a limited range of evidence such as convictions for perjury or other offences involving deception … as opposed to the wider range of evidence that will be admissible where the defendant puts his character in issue by, for example, attacking the character of another person.

The definition of untruthfulness has caused some problems. In *R v Hanson* (2005) (at p3174) the Court of Appeal stated that a **propensity to be** untruthful is not the same as a propensity to be dishonest. Perjury aside, the question is not so much the nature of the previous offences but whether the facts surrounding them demonstrate a propensity to be untruthful such as a not guilty plea when the defendant is convicted. The effect of the open approach taken in *Hanson* is that judicial directions on **credibility** are not confined to those situations where **s103(1)(b)** is the gateway as long as the evidence is relevant to the defendant's truthfulness.

Further light on the position is given in *R v Campbell* (2008). The defendant was charged with false imprisonment and assault against a woman with whom he had a sexual relationship. The prosecution was permitted to **adduce** evidence of recent crimes of violence against girl friends since they showed propensity under **s101(1)(d)**. He had pleaded guilty to those offences. On appeal the defendant argued that the judge should not have directed the jury that the previous convictions were relevant to credibility as well as propensity. The following observations are derived from the case:

- the courts had in the past drawn a distinction between propensity to offend and credibility. The distinction was usually unrealistic;

- it would be comparatively rare for the case of a defendant who had pleaded not guilty not to involve some element that the prosecution suggested was untruthful. However, the question of whether a defendant had a propensity for being untruthful would not normally be capable of being described as an *important* matter in issue between the defendant and the prosecution; and

- whether or not a defendant was telling the truth was likely to depend simply on whether or not he committed the offence. The jury should focus on that question.

Section 101(1)(e) and s104

It has substantial probative value in relation to an important matter in issue between the defendant and a co-defendant:

The dilemma for legislators and courts here is balancing the rights of co-defendants who might be running what is known as 'cut-throat' defences, each blaming the other. The current provision is a broader version of one contained in the CEA 1898 and some of the earlier case law is cited in recent judgments. The main differences is that the new statute explicitly states it is only to be used by co-defendants, thus the prosecution cannot apply to have evidence **adduced**.

The Act also requires that the evidence has 'substantial probative value' whereas **s101(d)** refers to 'relevant to an important matter', which means **s112** is a matter of substantial importance in the context of the case as a whole. A distinct feature of s101(1)(e) is that the discretion to exclude does not cover this section.

According to s104(1), 'Evidence which is relevant to the question whether the defendant has a propensity to be untruthful is admissible under s101(1)(e) only if the nature or conduct of his defence is such as to undermine the co-defendant's defence.' Note also that s78 is confined to prosecution evidence. The court may of course decide to hold separate trials, in which case the defendants will not be co-defendants.

The leading case on the 1898 provision of the meaning giving evidence 'against' a co-defendant was *Murdoch v Taylor* [1965] and this may still be cited. Such evidence was defined as evidence 'which supports the prosecution's evidence in a material respect or which undermines the defence of the co-accused'.

The differing approaches the courts may take to s101(1)(d) and (e) in relation to admissibility of evidence on '**propensity to be** untruthful' is illustrated by the case of *R v Lawson* (2007). In that case D1 was allowed to **adduce** evidence of D2's behaviour even though it did not involve offences of dishonesty. The court stated that 'it was wholly rational that the degree of caution which is applied to a Crown application against a defendant who is on trial when considering relevance or discretion should not be applied when what is at stake is a defendant's right to deploy material to defend himself against a criminal charge'. It was for the judge to decide whether D2's bad character had substantial probative value in relation to his **credibility** and the appeal courts would only interfere with this on grounds of *Wednesbury* unreasonableness. The courts will also have to consider the House of Lords' decision in *R v Randall* (2004). In that case, two defendants on trial jointly for murder blamed one another. Their previous convictions were admitted under s1(3)(iii) CEA 1898. D1's convictions were less serious than D2's which were for burglary and robbery. The House of Lords upheld the trial judge's ruling that D2's convictions were relevant to propensity for violence and lack of credibility. Lord Steyn stated that in such a situation, 'To rule that the jury may use the convictions in regard to his credibility but that convictions revealing his propensity to violence must otherwise be ignored is to ask the jury to put on one side their common sense and experience'.

✔ Looking for extra marks?

Good students will not only revise the leading authorities such as *Randall* but also be aware of how the courts have subsequently tried to apply them. See *R v Robinson* (2005) and *R v Merkens* (2005), suggesting that the prosecution could not make use of convictions admitted under s101(1)(e).

Section 101(1)(f), s105

Evidence to correct a false impression given by the defendant:

Section 105(1)(a) refers to the defendant 'making an express or implied assertion which is apt to give the court or jury a false or misleading impression about the defendant'. The impression may be given by conduct such as appearance or dress (s105(4) and (5)) and can be given by the defendant in pre-trial interviews or at the time of being charged or at trial. It can also be given by his witness. However, under s105(3) the defendant will not be responsible for making the assertion if he withdraws it or otherwise actively dissociates himself from it (see *R v Renda* (2006)).

In this area the cases cannot be seen as providing clear definitions of what is meant by a 'false impression' since as the Court of Appeal noted in *R v Weir* [2005] at para 43 it is 'fact specific'. Evidence in rebuttal must go 'no further than is necessary to correct the false impression' (s105(6)).

Exam tip

If you are having to make as assessment of the ways the new Act helped the defence or prosecution, an example from s105(6) could suggest that it is not entirely pro-prosecution. You could refer here to the abolition of the common law rule on the indivisibility of character (s105(6)). In **R v Winfield** (1939) a defendant who claimed to be of high moral standing sexually, lost his shield and faced having his offences for dishonesty adduced. This pro-prosecutorial advantage is not available under **CJA 2003**.

Section 101(1)(g) and s106

The defendant has made an attack on another person's character:
The differences with the former law are:

- it is not confined to prosecution witness or dead victim;
- it may be made by non-testifying witness; and
- it may be made pre-trial, see s106(1)(c).

Note that 'attacking another person's character' is broadly defined. It includes evidence of committing an offence as well as evidence that the person 'has behaved, or is disposed to behave, in a reprehensible way' (s106(2)). The section only applies to the prosecution.

An example of what is meant by an 'attack' short of a criminal conviction is *R v Renda and others* (2006) where the allegation was one of loose sexual morals on the part of the victim.

R v Singh (James Paul) [2007] gives guidance on the application of this section:

- the purpose of gateway 'is to enable the jury to know from what sort of source allegations against a witness (especially a complainant but not only a complainant) have come';
- gateway does not depend upon evidence demonstrating **propensity to** offend as charged or propensity to be untruthful;
- however, evidence once admitted may be used to demonstrate both such propensities following *R v Highton* (2005) (but this was not the situation in this case);
- evidence may be relevant to **credibility** while not showing a 'track record for untruthfulness';

- once admitted under (g) bad character evidence goes to **credibility**; and
- the court will only interfere with the judge's discretion to exclude under s101(3) or s78 on grounds of *Wednesbury* unreasonableness.

Exam tip

In assessing the impact of the statute this section provides a good example of how the final legislation departed from the more liberal approach of the Law Commission proposals. This relates to what is known as the 'no stymie rule' evidenced by the case of *Selvey v DPP* [1970] whereby the defendant lost his shield even where the imputation was a necessary part of his defence; here that the alleged victim was a male prostitute. The Law Commission had proposed that imputations should not include evidence to do with the alleged facts of the defence. This was not accepted in the legislation.

Exclusionary discretion

Section 101(3) and (4) also include an exclusionary discretion which only applies to ss101(1)(d) or (g) namely that 'The court must not admit evidence under these section if, on application by the defendant to exclude it, it appears to the court that the admission of the evidence would have such an adverse effect on the fairness of the proceedings that the court ought not to admit it. On application to exclude evidence the court must have regard to the length of time between the matters to which that evidence relates and the matters which form the subject of the offence charged.'

Bad character of non-defendant

Section 100 provides for the admissibility of bad character evidence of the non-defendant. This can include those who are not witnesses. The definition of bad character is that in s98 (see above). There are a number of safeguards against the too ready admissibility of such evidence:

- its admissibility needs the leave of the court, s101(1)(c), unless all the parties agree and the criteria for giving leave are set out; and
- it must be either important explanatory evidence or have substantial probative value in relation to a matter which (i) is a matter in issue in the proceedings and (ii) is of substantial importance in the context of the case as a whole.

The purpose here is to encourage victims and witnesses to testify and to avoid witnesses routinely having their bad character admitted as was the case under the common law. Issues relating to the **credibility** of the witness are likely to have such substantial probative value.

Conclusion

✱✱✱✱✱✱✱✱✱✱

① Conclusion

It is quite a good exercise to review the ways the statute sets out protective measures and compare how they apply to defendants and non-defendants. See Fig 5.3.

Figure 5.3 Safeguards and admissibility of bad character evidence

Safeguard	Explanation
Leave of court	Leave of court required for admissibility of bad character of non-defendant but not for defendant.
Discretion to exclude under s 101(3) & (4) CJA 2003.	Applies to ss101(1)(d) and (g) CJA 2003.
s78 PACE discretion.	May apply to s101(f) CJA 2003 (see *Highton*). Cannot apply to s101(1)(e) CJA 2003.
Stopping the case where evidence is 'contaminated' under s107 CJA 2003. The term is defined in s107(5) CJA 2003 as 'false or misleading' evidence including that resulting from collusion between the witness and others.	Applies to ss101(1)(c) to (g) CJA 2003.

In a critical concluding comment on the complex provisions of the **CJA 2003**, Choo (2009, p 275) sees a worrying tendency on the part of the Court of Appeal to leave too much freedom to trial judges in admitting character evidence. He writes,

> The rapidly growing body of case law from the Court of Appeal on the new statutory provisions demonstrates the Court's desire to take an approach supposedly based on 'common sense' and on the idea that the trial judge should have considerable leeway in determining admissibility. It is arguable that such an approach may not protect defendants sufficiently and that gateway (d), at least, should be the subject of a thorough and authoritative consideration by the House of Lords.

✅ Looking for extra marks?

It is generally acknowledged that the Court of Appeal rarely overturns the trial judge's decision on admissibility of bad character. In writing an evaluation of the Act, however, it is a good idea to give an example where the Court did rule the judge had been wrong. One such case is *R v M* (2006) where it was held that a single conviction for possessing a sawn-off shotgun 20 years earlier did not demonstrate the defendant's propensity to commit firearms offences.

(✱) Key cases

Case	Facts	Principle and comment
R v Rowton (1865) Le and Ca 520	A teacher charged with indecently assaulting a pupil called a number of character witnesses to attest that he had a good general reputation in the community. The prosecution's evidence of a contrary individual opinion was not admissible since evidence of character should be that of general reputation, not isolated acts.	This case is still authority for the definition of good character which is governed by the common law. The principle in many ways reflects nineteenth century society with its more static population. It was, however, confirmed in the case of *R v Redgrave* (1982), where a defendant charged with importuning for immoral purposes was not permitted to produce good character evidence that he had a loving heterosexual relationship.
R v Vye [1993] 3 All ER 241	A man with no criminal record was convicted of rape. His defence was consent. The Court of Appeal held that the judge had been wrong not to direct that his good character was relevant to both his lack of guilt or propensity and his credibility.	It set out general guidelines on the correct judicial directions. If the defendant does not testify but makes an exculpatory statement to the police then a direction on **credibility** should still be given. If he neither testifies nor makes an out of court exculpatory statement then only the direction on propensity should be given. A defendant with good character is entitled to a good character direction even if tried with a defendant with a record. Failure to give such a direction could lead to the conviction being overturned.
R v Hanson [2005] 1 WLR 3169	The appellant had been convicted on circumstantial evidence of the theft of cash from a public house where he had been drinking. His previous convictions for dishonesty included offences for handling stolen goods and aggravated taking and driving away a vehicle. They were admitted as evidence of propensity to commit offences of the kind charged. His appeal failed.	The court set out guidelines for the admissibility of propensity evidence. Merely establishing the offences were of the same description or the same category (according to Home Office prescriptions) was not sufficient. The court should ask if the history of convictions established propensity to commit offences of the kind charged and if yes, whether such propensity made it more likely that the defendant had committed the offence. Finally, it should consider if it would be unjust to rely on the convictions and if admitting the evidence would have such an adverse effect on the fairness of the proceedings that it ought not to be admitted.

Key cases

✶✶✶✶✶✶✶✶✶✶✶

Case	Facts	Principle and comment
R v Edwards (Stewart) [2006] 1 WLR 1524	The appellant had been convicted of gross indecency with a child. Evidence had been admitted of stay of prosecutions for other sexual offences. The Court of Appeal held that these allegations had been rightly admitted. The court distinguished *R v Bovell* (2005) 2 Cr App R 401 where Rose LJ had expressed doubt whether making an allegation was admissible under s100(1). There the allegation had been withdrawn.	Whether criminal allegations may be admissible when they do not lead to convictions depends on the facts of the case. Scott Baker LJ stated that the courts should consider whether the evidence may be admitted under s98 since the definition of bad character does not embrace evidence that 'has to do with the facts of the offence charged' and also evidence of 'misconduct in connection with the investigation or prosecution of that offence'.
R v Weir [2006] 1 WLR 1885	The appellant had been convicted of sexual assault on a girl under the age of 13. The victim alleged previous indecent behaviour by W which he denied. A **caution** for taking an indecent photograph of a child was admitted. W claimed this should not have been admitted since it did not fall into the same category of sexual assault listed in the Categories of Offences Order 2004 under the CJA 2003. The appeal was dismissed. The word 'may' in s103(2) and the reference to 'without prejudice to any other way of doing so' indicated that the listing in the Order was not the only way of admitting offences.	'Reprehensible behaviour' short of conviction may be admissible. The Court stated that s101(1)(d) 'completely reverses the pre-existing general rule'. The rule of exclusion, subject to an inclusionary discretion, is replaced by a presumption of inclusion with a discretion to exclude.
R v Renda [2006] 1 WLR 2948	R was convicted of attempted robbery. He had claimed that he had been injured while serving in the British Army and that he worked regularly as a security guard. Both were false claims. The Court of Appeal held he was rightly cross examined under s101(1)(f) on his 'reprehensible behaviour', which included a violent attack not leading to a conviction.	The decision may be contrasted with that in *R v Weir and Others* where the court referred to s105(6) in that the accused should only be cross examined on previous bad character necessary to correct the false impression he had given. In general, the Court of Appeal will defer to what it referred to (at p2950) as the trial judge's 'feel for the case'.
R v Singh (James Paul) [2007] EWCA Crim 2140	S was convicted of robbery. He had made an attack on a prosecution witness claiming he took drugs and had lied in his evidence. S's previous convictions were admitted under s101(1)(g). The appeal was dismissed.	In reviewing the exercise of the discretion to exclude under this section, the court referred to the continuation of the practice which had been evidenced under the old law. This was that the fact that an attack on a witness was necessarily

Case	Facts	Principle and comment
continued		involved in the case the accused chose to make, was no reason to allow the jury to assess the reliability of the defendant by seeing 'the full nature of the source from which the allegation comes'.

🔢 Key debates

Topic	**Bad character and co-defendants**
Author	R Munday
Viewpoint	The CJA 2003 gives the trial judge too much discretion in deciding to admit evidence.
Source	'Cut Throat Defences and "The Propensity to be Untruthful"' [2005] Crim LR 624

Topic	**Jury's treatment of bad character**
Author	M Redmayne
Viewpoint	Challenges the traditionally held view that juries put too much weight on bad character evidence.
Source	'The Relevance of Bad Character' [2002] CLJ 684

❓ Exam questions

Essay question

Has the concept of the indivisibility of character evidence survived the **Criminal Justice Act 2003**?

An outline answer is available at the end of the book.

Problem question

John and Lewis are both charged with assaulting Peter. Each mounts a cut-throat defence and blames the other. Jones was a witness to the assault and gives evidence for the prosecution. John was sacked from his post as a security guard after an internal works disciplinary hearing found he had stolen petty cash. Lewis has previous convictions for criminal damage and shoplifting. Jones has a conviction for benefit fraud and is a known drug user. Advise on evidence. John claims that Peter had sexually propositioned him. Peter is too ill to be called as a witness.

An outline answer is available online at http://www.oxfordtextbooks.co.uk/orc/concentrate/

#6
Hearsay evidence

Key Facts

- The rule against hearsay originated as a common law rule which provides that a statement made out of court may not be tendered in evidence as proof of its contents.
- The rule applies to out of court statements of witnesses who are testifying as well as of those who are not called as witnesses.
- Statements include oral and written statements and gestures; documents are anything in which information of any description is recorded.
- The rule applies equally to defence and prosecution.
- Different rules apply in civil and criminal cases.
- In criminal proceedings the rule still exists but with a large number of statutory and common law exceptions.
- In criminal proceedings hearsay is admissible i) if any of the statutory provisions in the **Criminal Justice Act (CJA) 2003** allow it, or ii) under the common law provisions preserved under **CJA 2003**, or iii) if all the parties agree or iv) under the statutory discretion conferred on the court, namely that it is satisfied it is in the interests of justice for it to be admissible.
- In criminal law no new exceptions can be made under the common law.
- In civil proceedings the rule has been abolished by statute, **Civil Evidence Act (CEA) 1995**.
- The law distinguishes between first hand (what X told Y) and multiple hearsay (what X told Y who told Z).

Related areas

The whole question of hearsay evidence is closely related to additional protections for victims dealt with in Chapters 7 and 8. Hearsay evidence may be tendered by a witness who is reluctant, unwilling, or too frightened to testify so there is considerable overlap between this section and Chapter 7. You will find in Chapter 8 discussion on the closely related issue of the evidential status of some out of court statements which were previously only admissible as evidence of consistency such as those by rape victims.

Arguably, the biggest exception to the rule against hearsay, and one which aids the prosecution, is confession evidence. There is, therefore, considerable overlap between this chapter and Chapter 3. Note that **s76A(1) Police and Criminal Evidence Act (PACE) 1984** creates a hearsay exception for the admissibility of confessions by co-accused and it is on the question of such out of court third party confessions that the relationship between confessions and hearsay is shown most powerfully, as the table in Fig 6.1 indicates.

Figure 6.1 Third party confessions and hearsay

Case/statutory section	Principle and comment
R v Blastland (1985)	B was convicted of murder and appealed on the grounds that evidence should have been allowed that a third party, M, had spoken to others that a boy had been murdered before it was public knowledge. M was not called as a witness. The House of Lords held that the evidence was irrelevant and hearsay and therefore inadmissible.
s76A(1) PACE	Confessions may be given in evidence for the co-accused.
s116(2) CJA 2003	Oral or written third party confessions may be admissible if the conditions are satisfied.
R v Finch (2007) and s114(1)(d) CJA 2003	F wanted the statement of his former co-accused, R, exonerating him, admitted under the CJA. The Court of Appeal held this was inadmissible since R could have been compelled to give oral evidence. The evidence was thus not available for the defence. The Court here drew a distinction between a witness who was unavailable and one who was unwilling. It stated (at para 24), 'It is not, in short, the law that every reluctant witness's evidence automatically can be put before the jury under s114 of the 2003 Act.'
R v Y and s114(1)(d) CJA 2003	Y was tried for murder. X had previously pleaded guilty to the same offence. The trial judge refused to allow a statement of X implicating Y under s114(1)(d) on the basis that this did not apply to third party confessions.

Case/statutory section	Principle and comment
continued	The Crown made an interlocutory appeal which was allowed. The court held that s114(1)(d) was available in law for all types of hearsay, and on application by any party to a criminal trial. The evidence was available for the prosecution.

The CJA 2003, in creating a number of new statutory exceptions to the rule against hearsay, has connected this area with that of examination and cross examination more closely, particularly on the question of the new status of previous consistent and inconsistent statements and identification evidence, see Chapter 8. Hearsay also overlaps with the question of the compellability of witnesses, witness anonymity, and the right to confrontation, see Chapter 7.

The assessment: key points

This is another area where it does help to have at least an outline knowledge of the history of this notoriously complex rule. The CJA 2003 has in part codified the law but you will see that the common law exceptions can still apply. It is important that you go through a logical sequence of questions. First, see if the statement is hearsay or not, then if it is, whether any of the exceptions to the rule of exclusion apply and, if they do not, finally if it may be admitted by the new inclusionary discretion. The chart in Fig 6.2 explains the overall process.

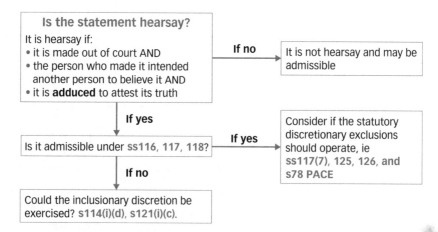

Figure 6.2 Admission of contested statements

Revision tip

Do not forget the central point that evidence in order to be admitted must first of all be relevant. You must make it clear to the examiners that you understand this as the starting point for all evidence. In *R v T* (2006) a woman alleged she had been indecently assaulted by her father and her uncle. Her father had subsequently died and a confession by the father had been improperly **adduced** under s116 CJA 2003 at the uncle's trial. It had no relevance.

Key features and principles

Rationale and evolution of the exclusionary rule

Hearsay evidence is one of the great exclusionary rules of evidence. The reasons for the rule are derived both from efficiency and from principle. From the point of view of the most effective evidence, out of court statements which cannot be tested on cross examination risk introducing mistake, false recollections, ambiguity, and insincerity (see Tribe (1974)). On the question of principle there are two aspects to the exclusion. Firstly, such statements have not been made on oath in open court. Secondly, and more controversially, it has been argued that the rule against hearsay protects what in the US constitution is known as the 'right to confrontation', the right to confront one's accuser. The latter's existence, however, has never been fully acknowledged in English common law and it should be noted that Art 6 refers to the right of defendants to examine or *have examined* witnesses called against them (see below for a fuller discussion on this).

Abolition of the rule against hearsay in civil proceedings

The relatively uncomplicated law relating to hearsay in civil proceedings will not be covered in great depth in this chapter. Below, in Fig 6.3, are the key provisions taken from the CEA 1995.

Figure 6.3 Overview of the Civil Evidence Act 1995 provisions

Section	Provision
s1(1)	Evidence in civil proceedings shall not be excluded on the ground that it is hearsay. This applies to first hand as well as multiple hearsay.
s2	Sets out Notice provision for admission of hearsay but failure to comply does not in itself mean statement is inadmissible.
s3	Power to call witnesses for cross examination on hearsay provisions.

Section	Provision
s4	Sets out factors to consider in weighing hearsay statements
ss5–6	Sets out rules on assessing the competence and **credibility** of the person who made the statement and whether there had been previous inconsistent statements.
s70	Provisions relating to common law rules.
s8–9	Status of copies of documents and proof of records of a business or public authority.

Key stages in history of hearsay in criminal proceedings

Common law: In the case of **Myers v DPP** (1965) the House of Lords held that it was not open to the courts to create new exceptions to the rule against hearsay. Some common law exceptions are preserved in **CJA 2003**.

Criminal Justice Act 1988: Admitted first-hand documentary hearsay where the maker was not available to give evidence and there was an acceptable reason for not calling him. Admitted multiple documentary hearsay if it was created in the course of trade, business, etc.

Law Commission: Law Commission Report No 245 (Cm 3670) 1997, 'Evidence in Criminal Proceedings, Hearsay and Related Topics' recommended the rule against hearsay should be retained but the number of exceptions increased and an inclusionary discretion introduced.

CJA 2003: This act introduced new exceptions for first-hand oral hearsay and an inclusionary discretion. Certain common law exceptions were preserved. Extended the acceptable reasons for non-appearance of a witness including fear of financial loss.

Definition of hearsay in criminal proceedings

The definition of hearsay is covered in several statutory sections:

- s114(1): 'A statement not made in oral evidence in the proceedings ...'
- s115(2) and (3): 'A statement is any representation of fact or opinion, made by a person by whatever means; and it includes a representation made in a sketch, photofit, or other pictorial format. (3) A matter stated is one to which this chapter applies if (and only if) the purpose, or one of the purposes, of the person making the statement appears to the court to have been – (a) to cause another person to believe the matter, or (b) to cause another person to act or a machine to operate on the basis that the matter is as stated.' (NB The effect of this definition is that implied assertions are not hearsay.)
- s121(2): In this section [covering multiple hearsay] 'hearsay statement means a statement, not made in oral evidence, that is relied on as evidence of a matter stated in it'.

Revision tip

Before the passing of the CJA 2003 evidence students would have spent much effort in assessments, trying to decide if a statement was hearsay or not. Although that logical chain of reasoning must still be followed you should let the examiner know that you are aware that this definitional exercise has now changed. A useful case is *R v Isichei* (2006). In that case the disputed evidence was that of identification, referring to an alleged assailant by name. The judge ruled that the evidence was admissible as non-hearsay under s115(3) since the name had not been said for the purpose of causing a person to believe the matter stated. Alternatively, it was admissible under s114(1)(d). The Court of Appeal held that even if the application of s115(3) was in doubt, the statement was admissible under s114(1)(d) as 'part of the story of a common sense series of events'.

Thus, s114(1)(d) may apply to non-hearsay statements.

Current rules on hearsay exceptions in criminal cases

Hearsay is only admissible as stated in s114(1) CJA 2003:

- if any provisions in statute make it admissible;
- if any preserved common law provisions in s118 CJA 2003 make it admissible;
- if all the parties agree; or
- if the court is satisfied that it is in the interests of justice for it to be admissible.

Under the statutory regime, the form of the statement has an effect on its admissibility.

Oral first-hand hearsay

This form of hearsay evidence is admissible under s116 if conditions apply *or* under s114(1)(d) *or* if parties agree. Conditions: must be one of the statutory reasons for not calling the witness who made the statement. The person to whom the oral statement was made may give the testimony in court. If the out of court statement was made by the witness who is testifying then it may be admissible under ss119 or 120 (see Chapter 8).

Oral multiple hearsay

Only admissible under s114(1)(d) *or* s121(1)(c) *or* if parties agree. Conditions: see *R v Taylor* (2006) where the court allowed multiple oral hearsay (conveyed by video tape interview) to be admissible under s114(1)(d) or s121(1)(c). The trial judge's approach could not be challenged even though he had not specifically considered the fact that the evidence was multiple hearsay.

Written first-hand hearsay

Admissible under s116 if conditions apply *or* under s114(1)(d) *or* if parties agree. Condition: must be one of the statutory reasons for not calling the witness.

Key features and principles

✱✱✱✱✱✱✱✱✱✱

Written multiple hearsay

Admissible under ss117, 119, 120, *or* s121(1)(c) *or* s114(1)(d) *or* if parties agree. Conditions: see *Maher v DPP* (2006) where multiple documentary hearsay evidence, inadmissible under s121(1)(a) was admitted. The court accepted that it was admissible under either s121(1)(c) or s114(1)(d).

Written business documents, first hand and multiple

Admissible under s117 if conditions apply *or* under s114(1)(d) *or* if parties agree. Conditions:

- person supplying the information was acting in the course of trade etc; *and*
- may reasonably be supposed to have had personal knowledge of the matters dealt with; *and*
- each person through whom information passes was acting in the course of trade etc.

Note that the court may refuse to admit document even if conditions apply, s117(6) and (7).

Documents prepared for criminal proceedings

Admissible under s117 if conditions apply *or* under s114(1)(d) *or* if parties agree. Conditions: in addition to the above there must be one of the statutory reasons for not calling the witness (see above p 94) or additional reason that 'the maker cannot reasonably be expected to have any recollection of the matters dealt with in the statement'.

Exam tip

In a problem question, reference could be made to documents generated as part of the police investigation into a crime. *Kamuhuza* (2008) shows the approach of the courts to the admissibility of documents generated by the police.

In that case the court considered the admissibility of an analysis of fingerprints left by the defendant at the scene of the crime some five years before the trial. The prosecution had not traced the police forensic expert. The court held that s116 was not the appropriate section since it could not be realistically assumed that a public servant in that post could not be traced. Section 117(5)(b) applied and since the document was prepared for the purpose of criminal proceedings, and the maker could not reasonably be expected to remember the contents of the document.

Common law exceptions

The CJA 2003 specifically preserves some but not all of the common law exceptions. Their admissibility is not subject to the rather complex statutory provisions and the common law does not make a distinction between oral or written statements.

Figure 6.4 Common law exceptions preserved in s118 CJA 2003

Exception	Comment
Records containing public information: s118(1) para 1	Much of the evidence under this head would be admissible also under s117.
Reputation as to character: s118(1) para 2	See *R v Rowton* (1865). See p 81.
Reputation or family tradition: s118 (1) para 3	This refers to evidence of pedigree, the existence of a marriage, the existence of a public or general right, or the identity of any person or thing.
Res gestae i) Excited utterances: s118(1) para 4(a)	The leading case on excited utterances prompted by an event is *R v Andrews* [1987]. This set out a test for admissibility of the statement replacing the earlier test which had concentrated on closeness in time between the utterance and the event. The new test rested on discounting the possibility of mistake or concoction. In *R v Callender* [1998] the Court of Appeal proposed that the same test applied to all aspects of the *res gestae* exception.
Res gestae ii) Statements accompanying an act: s118(1) para 4(b)	A good example of this exception is *R v McCay* (1990). The police officer at a trial arising from an assault in a public house was allowed to state which number the witness had given identifying the defendant at a pre-trial identification parade. See further p 121 on identification evidence.
Res gestae iii) Statements related to the maker's physical sensation or a mental state (such as intention or emotion): s118(1) para 4(c)	In *R v Gilfoyle* (1996) (now under review) the defence said that the victim had committed suicide and the prosecution that she had been murdered by her husband. She had left suicide notes. The Court of Appeal held that statements by the wife to her friends that G had asked her to write the notes to help with a course he was taking were admissible as evidence of her non-suicidal state of mind. They were not evidence as to the cause of her state of mind. They would also have been admissible under the *Andrews* test.
Confessions or mixed statements: s118(1) para 5	See Chapter 5.
Admissions by agents: s118(1) para 6	Such vicarious admissions are rarely admissible in criminal proceedings.
Statements made in furtherance of common purpose: s118(1) para 7	A statement made by one party to a conspiracy is admissible against any other party to the conspiracy as evidence of its truth if it demonstrates that the conspiracy is in operation. In *R v Hulme* (2005) the court properly admitted text messages sent between alleged IRA terrorists.
Expert evidence: s118(1) para 8	See Chapter 9.

Key features and principles

✳✳✳✳✳✳✳✳✳✳

Revision tip

Assessment questions are most likely to refer to *res gestae*.

Roberts and Zuckerman (2004, p643) describe this list as a 'rag-bag' and you must be careful you understand that not all the common law exceptions are preserved. Thus, for example, if you have a question that includes a dying declaration you will need to apply the *res gestae* exception, which is preserved, or the inclusionary discretion under **s114(1)(d)**. On this, see **R v Lawson** (1998).

There is at the time of writing, limited case law under **s118** but note **Walker (Levi Soloman)** (2007) where the Court of Appeal preferred to apply the statutory discretion to a statement where arguably the case was one of common enterprise. The case involved a statement by a third party as to what a co-defendant had said which the trial judge had admitted against both defendants.

Questions on the safeguards under CJA 2003

How is the inclusionary discretion to admit structured?

Section 114(2)(a)–(d) sets out considerations the court should bear in mind before exercising the inclusionary discretion, namely that it is in the interests of justice to admit an otherwise inadmissible statement:

- probative value;
- the extent of other evidence;
- how important it is in the context of the case as a whole;
- circumstances in which it was made;
- reliability of maker of the statement;
- reliability of the evidence in the statement;
- if oral evidence on this can be given and if not why;
- difficulty in challenging the statement; and
- the extent to which such difficulty would prejudice the party.

In *R v Taylor* (2006) the Court stated that although the court must take these factors into consideration, it is not required to specifically consider each one or to come to a conclusion on each one individually. However, contrast the apparently light touch with the greater emphasis on a more thorough assessment of the factors in *R v Y* (2008). Tapper (2009, p83) points out that 'although in *R v Y* the Court of Appeal reversed the trial judge who had held that s114(1)(d) was inapplicable, this was on a question of law, not on the merits, and was in effect against the non-exercise of discretion rather than against its exercise'.

Although the wording of the statute suggests that the inclusionary discretion should only be applied if the statement is not admissible, under the statute note that the courts in some cases take a two-stage approach. There is first a consideration of whether the statutory sections apply and then a screening of the statement against the factors in s114(2). Thus, in *Cole and Keet* (2007) earlier written evidence taken from a woman subsequently suffering from dementia was admissible under s116(2)(b) and the court then considered whether it was fair to admit it considering the factors in s114(2). The court referred to the factors set out in s114(1)(d) as being applicable in considering s78 PACE 1984 in hearsay cases. Thus, the inclusionary discretion criteria may also be relevant to exclusion.

Figure 6.5 Cases under s114(1)(d) CJA

Case	Principle
McEwan v DPP (2007)	Section may be relied upon even if another hearsay exception is available.
R v Xhabri (2005)	Section may be relied upon even if evidence is inadmissible by another section.
R v Finch (2007)	Trial judge's ruling will only be reversed on grounds of Wednesbury unreasonableness.
R v Y (2008)	The section was not limited to hearsay assisting the defence, The Court did, however, stress the general unreliability of hearsay, and the need to consider the factors set out in s114(2) extremely thoroughly. Since the trial judge had in consequence of his preliminary ruling not considered these at all, the case was sent back for the resumption of the trial.
R v L (2009)	A wife made a statement to police who had not advised her that she was not compellable to give evidence against her husband in his trial for alleged rape of their 19-year-old daughter. She declined to testify. The statement was admissible under s114(1)(d). PACE s 80 did not preclude a witness from giving evidence of a voluntary statement made in the past by the defendant's wife. Whether it was just in such instances to admit the statement depended on the specific facts.

Note that the application of the comprehensive inclusionary discretion in s114(2) is made more complex in that there is another inclusionary statutory provision:

S121 (1)(c): the court may admit multiple hearsay that is not otherwise admissible under the section (see further below) if it 'is satisfied that the value of the evidence in question, taking account how reliable the statements appear to be, is so high that the interests of justice require the later statement to be admissible for that purpose'.

How is the exclusionary discretion exercised?

There are two specific sections dealing with exclusion of evidence, namely s125(1) (see below) and s126(1). The latter is written in narrow terms, 'taking account of the danger that to admit the evidence would result in undue waste of time'.

In addition s116(4) gives the court a power to exclude evidence if the witness is not appearing through 'fear' (see further below)

and

s117(6) and (7) giving the court power to exclude otherwise admissible business and other documents.

Key features and principles

✳✳✳✳✳✳✳✳✳✳

In practice, the courts have considered s126(1) more widely than its terms suggest. In *Cole & Keet* (2006) the court was of the view that even if the conditions of admissibility were satisfied, here the relevant section being s116(2)(c), there would still be a need to consider the general discretion under s126(1) and on occasion s78 PACE. Contrast this with the case of *Cole and Keet* where s114(1)(d) was considered. See also *R v Gyima* (2007), where the judgment does not make it clear whether the evidence of a video recording made by a foreign witness before going back home was admitted under s114(1)(d) or s116(2)(c) or not excluded under the exclusionary discretions.

What is the application of the acceptable reasons for not calling the witness?

Under s116(2) the acceptable reasons for not calling the witness are that the witness is:

- dead;
- unfit to be a witness because of bodily or mental condition;
- outside the United Kingdom and it is not reasonably practicable to secure his attendance;
- not to be found although such steps as is reasonably practicable to take to find him have been taken; or
- is not giving or not continuing to give oral evidence in the proceedings through fear, either at all or in connection with the subject matter of the statement and the court gives leave for the statement to be given in evidence. NB fear is to be widely construed and (for example) includes fear of the death or injury of another person or of financial loss.

One question is whether the broad interpretation of 'fear' is open to abuse. There is a safeguard in that the court has to give leave to allow such a statement. In addition, there is somewhat of an acknowledgement of the 'equality of arms principle' in that the statement is not restricted to investigating officers, thus opening up the possibility of admitting defence evidence under this head.

In *R v Boulton* (2007) the Court of Appeal again considered the sort of evidence required to establish fear for the purposes of s116(2)(e). The facts of the offence, although not sufficient reasons, could constitute the conditions in which to evaluate the evidence. It was not relevant that fear was not the only reason for not testifying if fear was a significant ingredient.

Some of the earlier case law may be relevant. Thus, in *R v Acton Justices ex p McMullen* (1990) the court held that the fear need not be a reasonable one, nor, according to *Martin* (1996) need it be linked to actions by the defence.

What protection is afforded when the statements are prepared for criminal proceedings?

Section 117(4) covering the admissibility of statements prepared for criminal proceedings contains similar provisions to those in the 1988 Act. The reason for the additional safeguards is the need to avoid purely paper trials. Thus, relevant 'the person, who supplied the information' of the documents should be called to give oral testimony unless one of the acceptable reasons for not calling him applies. Note also that the case of *Kamuhuza* (2008) (see p 90) suggests that first-hand documentary statements made by the police, and presumably this would include an endorsed witness statement, could in principle be admissible under s116 (the successor to s23 CJA 2003) if there is a statutory reason for not calling the witness.

How are business etc documents treated?

The statutory business etc document exception has a long history. It is obviously the case that such documents, by definition in a permanent form, will not suffer in the same way as personal, oral, or written documents from false recollections, mistake, ambiguity, and insincerity. Their authenticity is more assured. The conditions for admitting such documents are set out in s117. The wording is complex. A good illustration of its operation is the case of *Maher v DPP* (2006).

The case involved a driver M, who had left the scene of an accident in a car park but who was traced in the following way. An onlooker (O) who saw the crash left a copy of M's number plate on the bonnet of the stationary car that M had damaged. The driver of the damaged car (V) passed it to the police (P) whose record was admitted at trial under s117. M was convicted and appealed. The Divisional Court considered whether the statement was admissible under s117 and held it was not.

Figure 6.6 *See Maher v DPP (2006)*

O passes the note to V who passes it to P
*O fulfils s117(2)(b) – supplied information and may reasonably be supposed to have had personal knowledge of the matters dealt with
* V does NOT fulfil s117(2)(a) since the document was not created or received by a person in the course of a trade etc. The chain therefore was broken (even though P is acting in the course of a trade etc, s117).

This was a case of multiple hearsay which is only admissible under s121(a) if ss117, 119, or 120 were fulfilled (see Chapter 8 for ss119 and 120 which are not at issue here). Section 121(b) did not apply since the parties did not agree. That left s121(c), 'the court is satisfied that the value of the evidence in question, taking into account how reliable the statement appears to be, is so high that the interests of justice require the later statement to be admissible for that purpose'. The court considered that the trial judge should have considered this section as well as s114(1)(d). However, since the trial judge did not express any concerns about the statement's reliability under s117, the statement could be considered to be properly admitted.

Note also that the police log was a document prepared for the purpose of criminal proceedings but the criteria here were not fulfilled since, although the person who gave the

Key features and principles

✱✱✱✱✱✱✱✱✱✱

information could not reasonably be expected to have a recollection of the number (see s117(5)(b)) the chain of business etc documents had been broken.

The case is a good illustration of the complexities of the statute and the relationship between the differing sections.

✅ Looking for extra marks?

You should make it clear to the examiners that you are aware that the courts are not willing to allow witnesses to give evidence by the hearsay provisions if the reason the witness cannot be brought to court is prosecution mistakes. In *R v Adams* (2007) the Court of Appeal rejected any suggestion of a distinction between being unable to find and being unable to contact a witness. It emphasised the unsatisfactory procedure adapted by the prosecution in this case to alert witnesses to the need to attend to testify at trial. Thus, s116(2)(d) did not apply.

How does the statute deal with multiple hearsay?

The *Maher* case is a good example of the complexities of multiple hearsay which of course is even more problematic in the case of oral hearsay where there is not an unassailable record. See also *R v Taylor* (p 92). Worthen (p 440) comments, '... following the precedent laid down by *Taylor*, a judge can now admit evidence under s114(1)(d) though knowing nothing about the reliability of the evidence or the circumstances in which it was obtained'.

How does the court treat the question of the witness's **credibility**?

Section 124 provides that evidence which would have been admissible as relevant were s/he to have testified is also admissible in his/her absence. The person against whom the hearsay statement is admitted may seek to use evidence to discredit the maker of the statement or to show he has contradicted himself.

How is the power to stop the case exercised?

Section 125(1) is an important safeguard in that the court has the power to stop the case under the following conditions:

- case is wholly or partly based on hearsay;
- such evidence is so unconvincing that a conviction would be unsafe;
- the case is a trial on indictment before a jury.

Section 125(1) was considered in *R v Joyce* (2005). The disputed evidence in the trial of appellants, who were convicted of possessing a firearm with intent to cause fear of violence, was identification evidence which was retracted by witnesses who then claimed they had been mistaken. Their testimony at trial was not consistent with their earlier statements (for further details on s119 which applied here see Chaper 8). The court compared the test under s125(1) to that in *Galbraith* (1981) (see p 122) which applies to identification evidence.

The court considered that it was not believable that all three witnesses were indeed mistaken and refused to apply s125(1).

What safeguard is there as to the capacity of the absent witness?

Under s116(1) it is required that the witness whose hearsay evidence is being used is competent and compellable to give evidence and that he is identified to the court's satisfaction. There has also to be an acceptable reason for the absence..

Are there rules of court setting out additional procedures?

These may be made under s132. It is noticeable that such rules are well established in the case of hearsay in civil proceedings.

Hearsay evidence and ECHR

Article 6(3)(d) provides that everyone charged with a criminal offence has the right to examine or have examined witnesses against him. Thus, the right to confront a witness personally is not absolute since 'have examined' may include a pre-trial examination by an advocate. In some cases the court has upheld that this section has been violated by the non-appearance of a witness as for example *Kostovski v Netherlands* (1990), where the out of court statements were either the only evidence or an important part of the evidence. On the other hand there was no violation in *Doorson v Netherlands* (1996). In this case, frightened witnesses in a trial involving large scale drug dealing were cross examined in a pre-trial hearing without the presence of the defendant.

The hearsay provisions in the CJA 1988 have been held by the English and Strasbourg courts to be compliant with the ECHR in that there were in place safeguards such as the exclusionary discretion. In *R v Sellick* (2005) the Court of Appeal went further however than the Strasbourg jurisprudence in holding that where a court had allowed a witness's statement to be read out in court there was no absolute rule that even where the evidence was the decisive element, its admission would automatically lead to an infringement of the defendant's rights under the European Convention on Human Rights (ECHR) The court stressed the safeguards of allowing the admission of evidence relating to the **credibility** or inconsistency of the witness as important in considering whether a defendant's rights had been infringed.

Doubt will now be cast, however, on this argument by the Strasbourg Court's subsequent decision in *Al-Khawaja and Tahery v UK* (2009). In Al-Khwaja's case a witness statement had ben admitted under the now repealed s23 CJA 1988 which allowed a written statement to be admitted if the witness is dead and the court considered it was in the interests of justice to admit it. In Tahery's case the witness statement was admitted under s116(2)(e) which allows a statement to be admitted where the witness does not attend to give oral evidence through fear. The Court held that allowing a witness statement to be admitted as evidence where the witness is not available for cross examination, and that evidence is the sole or decisive basis for convicting the accused, is a violation of the right to a fair trial under Art 6(1) and 6(3)(d).

Conclusion

✱✱✱✱✱✱✱✱✱✱

✅ Looking for extra marks?

One difficult question is under what conditions evidence of motive is admissible as an exception to the rule against hearsay. The common law exception for statement of intention is preserved (s118(1)4(c)). Your answer to a question on this area must make it clear that the case law is unclear as to whether the court is able to infer from the statement that the intention was carried out. This is an instance where a detailed knowledge of the judgments will increase your marks.

In *Mohgal* (1977) the Court of Appeal (*obiter*) was of the view that a tape-recording by the accused's mistress six months earlier was admissible to suggest she had carried out the murder. On the other hand, some doubt was thrown on this in *Blastland* (1986) and see also *R v Thompson* (1912) where a statement by the victim that she had intended to carry out an abortion on herself was not admissible in a trial of her alleged murderer. Support for statements of intention as evidence of subsequent action is found in the more recent case of *R v Valentine* (1996) where the earlier statement of intention by an alleged rapist was admissible as relevant to his *mens rea*.

① Conclusion

Commentators differ as to whether the changes detailed in this chapter have been an improvement. They certainly appear to have generated a flexible approach but one which arguably makes the law more complex and uncertain. The mixture of detailed rule-based provisions with open textured discretion has overall created a certain amount of tension in its operation.

✱ Key cases

Case	Facts	Principle and comment
Subramanian v DPP [1956] 1 WLR 965	S was convicted in British-held Malaya with having ammunition without lawful authority. He argued duress in his defence in that he had been threatened by terrorists. The appeal to the Privy Council turned on whether the alleged statements made by the terrorists to him should have been admitted or whether they were, as the trial court held, inadmissible hearsay. The PC held that they were not hearsay since the purpose of tendering them was not to suggest they were true or not but whether they were made. Appeal allowed.	This case illustrates the importance of the second aspect of the definition of hearsay. Even if made out of court a statement is only hearsay if it is tendered to suggest it is true or, as s114 CJA now puts it, is 'admissible as evidence of any matter stated'. Here the purpose of putting evidence of the threats was simply to suggest that they had been made. The truth of their content was not in issue.
Sparks v R [1964] AC 964	At S's trial for assaulting a young girl the victim was too young to testify. The defence was not allowed to tender a	The rule against hearsay applies equally to defence and prosecution and under the common law it was

Case	Facts	Principle and comment
continued	statement she had made to her mother shortly after the offence. She had said, 'It was a coloured boy.' S was white. The PC upheld the judge's ruling that the statement was inadmissible hearsay.	applied strictly. There was no judicial discretion to admit even arguably good quality evidence. The rule, if it applied, was inflexible.
R v Andrews [1987] AC 281	The victim of a robbery and stabbing was able to tell police at the scene who his assailants had been. He died before the trial. The statement to the police was held by the House of Lords to be hearsay but admissible under the *res gestae* exception, the test for which was redefined.	The House here was marginalising the element of contemporaneity which had previously been the feature of the *res gestae* test. The statement to the police had of course been made some time after the stabbing.
Trivedi v United Kingdom [1997] EHRLR 520	The prosecution at the trial of T for false accounting had been allowed to **adduce** hearsay statements made by C under ss23 and 26 CJA 1988. C was in a poor mental state. The EctHR rejected the claim that this breached Art 6.	The Court identified the following safeguards which would apply also under the new Act. i) The trial judge had heard evidence about the quality of the evidence and the reason for the non-appearance of the witness before admitting the statements. ii) there was other evidence of T's guilt. iii) T had been able to give evidence which C could not challenge iv) T's counsel had the opportunity to impugn C and v) the judge had directed that the jury should give less weight to C's evidence.
R v Sellick [2005] 1 WLR 3257	Hearsay statements had been admitted under CJA 1988. In two cases the witnesses did not give evidence through fear. The appellants alleged this infringed Art 6(3)(d). The Court held that the evidence was properly admitted since the defendant had put the witness in fear. There had to be clear directions to the jury but in such a situation the defendant cannot claim that his rights have been infringed even if the hearsay evidence is the sole or decisive evidence against him.	The court took a robust approach to the admissibility of hearsay, particularly bearing in mind that the defendant was alleged to have caused the witnesses to be in fear. Controversially, it accepted that the conviction could stand even where the hearsay evidence was the main evidence.
R v C [2006] EWCA Crim 637	At the defendants' trial for fraud, the prosecution was proposing to **adduce** a witness statement made by a resident of South Africa, who was related to one of the defendants. The witness was not willing to attend trial. The judge admitted the witness	The court here indicated the scope of the exclusionary discretion even where the evidence was admissible under the statutory provisions. It also indicated the use of s78 for prosecution hearsay evidence.

Key cases

✳✳✳✳✳✳✳✳✳✳✳

Case	Facts	Principle and comment
continued	statement under s116(2)(c) CJA 2003 and refused to exercise his discretion to exclude it under s78 PACE 1984. The court held that the expression 'reasonably practicable' in s116(2)(c) had to be judged on the basis of the steps taken or not taken, by the party seeking **to adduce** the witness's evidence. There had been insufficient explanation of the reasons for the witness's refusal to attend, or to give evidence by video-link. The defendant's appeal at the interlocutory stage was allowed.	
R v Singh [2006] 1 WLR 1564	S's appeal turned on whether the prosecution should have been allowed **to adduce** evidence of entries in the memories of mobile phones. The inference from these was that S had taken part in a conspiracy. The Court held that this evidence was an implied assertion and not hearsay as defined in the CJA 2003. In any case there were two other routes to admissibility, namely s118(7) as common enterprise or by the inclusionary discretion s114(1)(d).	This case makes it clear that the common law definition of hearsay (which included implied assertions) no longer prevails. *R v Kearley* [1992] is thus overruled.
R v Xhabri [2006] 1 All ER 776	A woman who claimed she had been imprisoned, raped, and forced to work as a prostitute had made statements to others about her plight. The prosecution statements were held to have been properly admitted, either under s120(7) or s114(d), in a trial of her abductor. Appeal dismissed.	i) Evidence may be admitted under s114(1)(d) even where the conditions for admissibility under s120 are not met. ii) Section 114 was compatible with Art 6 since the court had the power to exclude hearsay evidence under s126 and was under a duty to do so under HRA 1998 where its admissibility would infringe Art 6. iii) Since the hearsay provisions CJA 2004 applied to prosecution and defence, there was **equality of arms**.
McEwan v DPP [2007] EWHC 740 (Admin)	The defendant was charged with criminal damage, namely scratching a car. The defendant was identified from photographs by a minor who said he had seen him scratch the car. The witness claimed to be unable to give evidence at trial because of a severe bowel condition. The magistrate	The Divisional Court commented on the prosecution delays and mistakes. It stated in relation to s114(1)(d) '... the safety valve is there to prevent injustice. It would have to be an exceptional case for it to be relied upon, as it is sought to do here, to rescue the prosecution from the consequences of its own failures.'

Case	Facts	Principle and comment
continued	admitted the witness's statement and the defendant was convicted. The court held that the bench had acted unreasonably in allowing the admission of the witness statement. Without the witness there was no case and the defendant would be acquitted.	
R v Cole and Keet [2007] EWCA Crim 1924	Keet was accused of having grossly overcharged an old woman for house repairs. By the time the case came to trial the householder had become demented and could not give evidence in person. The admission of her witness statement was contested. In Cole's case, the body of a woman who had committed suicide showed other injuries which were said to have been caused by the defendant. Before her death, the victim had told other people that the defendant had attacked her. The issue on appeal was whether their hearsay evidence could be used. The court held that there was no absolute rule that evidence of a statement could not be **adduced** unless a defendant had an opportunity to examine a witness.	In considering whether hearsay evidence should be admitted in a criminal trial, the only role of Art 6 ECHR was to determine whether the admission of the evidence was compatible with a fair trial. Hearsay evidence was not precluded by Art 6 even where it was the sole or decisive evidence against a defendant.

⑨ *Key debates*

Topic	**Abolition of the rule against hearsay**
Author	JD Jackson
Viewpoint	The rule against hearsay should be abolished. Emphasis should be placed on giving the defence greater opportunity to cross examine witnesses in pre-trial procedures and a more detailed code governing police investigations.
Source	'Hearsay: the Sacred Cow that Won't be Slaughtered' (1998) 2 E&P 166

Topic	**Review the operation of the hearsay provisions of CJA 2003**
Author	Tom Worthen
Viewpoint	The Act has brought some improvement in the law but overall has made the position worse. It is both unpredictable and not sufficiently flexible.
Source	'The Hearsay Provisions of the Criminal Justice Act 2003: So Far, Not So Good? [2008] Crim LR 431

Exam questions

✱✱✱✱✱✱✱✱✱

⑦ Exam questions

Essay question

'... if they are to act merely as the first stage of a process governed by broad discretions, one has to wonder whether it was really worth weighing the courts down with the complexities of the provisions in s116 and in particular, s117?. If a court can easily override these rules using general considerations of fairness, then might it not have been simpler to give the court a carefully defined discretionary power in the first place?' (Worthen (2008, p 442))

Critically evaluate the above comment on the operation of the hearsay provisions of the CJA 2003.

An outline answer is available online at http://www.oxfordtextbooks.co.uk/orc/concentrate/

Problem question

Anna and Fred are charged with stabbing their neighbour John. He had been found with a metal spike through his leg bleeding heavily. He died a few hours later. The prosecution case is that Anna, Fred, and John had a row over some broken garden gnomes and that Anna and Fred stabbed John with a metal tent spike. Anna argues in her defence that she and John had a discussion about the gnomes and that when Anna left to go to the Garden Centre, John was still gardening and chatting to Fred.

Discuss the admissibility of the following pieces of evidence.

i) Evidence from Tom, a milkman, who called the ambulance when he saw John injured in the garden. John said to Tom, 'It was that monster Anna who did it'.

ii) Evidence from Sally, Anna's daughter, that Anna had said to her a few hours after the incident that 'Fred had nothing to do with it'. Sally had sent an email detailing this to Harriet her friend. Sally was killed in a car accident before the trial.

An outline answer is available at the end of the book.

#7

Competence and compellability, special measures

Key Facts

- The presumption in both criminal and civil trials is that all witnesses are competent and compellable so a reason in statute or case precedent has to be found to apply an exception.
- The main criminal law exceptions in relation to competence are defendants testifying for the prosecution, or witnesses who are unable to give intelligible testimony.
- The main criminal law exceptions in relation to universal compellability are defendants themselves and spouses (or civil partners) and co-defendants testifying for the prosecution.
- The general expectation is that witnesses will give evidence on oath (**sworn evidence**).
- In criminal cases witnesses under the age of 14 years cannot give **sworn evidence**.
- In civil cases a child (a person under age 18 years) who understand the nature of the oath must give sworn testimony while others may give unsworn evidence under certain conditions.
- Special measures for vulnerable witnesses in criminal trials are directed primarily at non-defendants but there are some limited protections for some defendants.

Related areas

These relate primarily to criminal trials. Chapter 8 covers some procedures regulating the examination and cross examination of witnesses in criminal trials and included a summary of protections afforded certain classes of witness such as complainants in rape trials. The evidential consequences to the defendant of electing not to testify are covered in this chapter and the provisions here are closely related to the drawing of inferences from pre-trial silence covered in Chapter 3 and to the privilege against self-incrimination covered in Chapter 11. Another related area is that of hearsay, covered in Chapter 6, since increasingly witnesses are able to give evidence through written submissions rather than appearing in court. The close relationship between hearsay and compellability is illustrated in *R v L* (2009) (see p 93). A pre-trial statement by a non-compellable spouse was admissible at the trial of her husband under s114(1)(d) CJA 2003.

The assessment: key points

Questions in this area will mostly be on the exceptions to the general rule that all witnesses are competent and compellable. The limited special measures introduced to protect vulnerable defendants are very recent and so may well form part of an assessment question. The controversial area of witness anonymity where the Government hastily introduced a statute to overrule a powerful decision by the House of Lords raises many principled issues concerning fair trial rights which could form the basis of an essay question.

Key features and principles

The key statutes in this area are: Criminal Evidence Act (CEA) 1898, Criminal Justice Act (CJA) 2003, Criminal Justice and Public Order Act 1994, Police and Criminal Evidence Act (PACE) 1984, Youth Justice and Criminal Evidence Act 1999 (YJCEA), and the Police and Justice Act 2006, amending the YJCEA to create a new s33A.

Criminal trials: the general rule on competence

A historically central principle in English trials is that oral evidence given under oath is the superior form of evidence. The reasoning is that this evidence can be subject to cross examination by the opposing side. Given the importance of this principle, known as the **principle of orality** in English trials, the rules regulating the attendance of witnesses assumes special significance. This chapter covers the rules and practices which govern when and how witnesses are eligible to give evidence (ie are competent) and those which govern when they are required, under exercise of penalty for default, to appear (ie are compellable).

This is an area which is now largely covered by statute. The starting point is that all witnesses are competent. Section 53(1) YJCEA reads: 'At every stage in criminal proceedings all persons are (whatever their age) competent to give evidence.' There are exceptions, however, in relation to the defendant who only became competent to testify in his defence in the CEA 1898 in a provision now enshrined in s53(1) YJCEA. Previously, the prevailing belief was that defendant might give perjured evidence. S/he remains incompetent to testify for the prosecution under s53(4) YJCEA. This section also makes incompetent, spouses who are jointly charged. Understandably, under s53(3) 'A person is not competent to give evidence in criminal proceedings if it appears to the court that he is not a person who is able to (a) understand questions put to him as a witness and (b) give answers to them which can be understood.' The former complicated and restrictive rules about child witnesses were liberalised by this provision. Guidance on the application of the provision is given in *R v Sed* [2004]. The witness was a rape victim, 81 years old, who suffered from Alzheimer's disease. Her video-recorded evidence was admitted. Auld LJ stated (at para 46) it was '... for the judge to determine the question of competence almost as a matter of feel'. In effect the section does not require total comprehension by the witness.'

Revision tip

Obviously, a witness who is not competent is not compellable in that it would be contempt of court not to appear, see *R v Yusuf* (2003). There a witness to a murder failed to respond to a summons to testify. He was brought to court and cross examined as a **hostile witness**. He was found to be in contempt. Not all competent witnesses on the other hand are compellable. Although the general rule is that a witness who is competent is also compellable there are a number of exceptions to this based on public policy considerations.

Criminal trials: exceptions to presumption of compellability

The starting point is the presumption of compellability of all witnesses, the three main groups of exceptions applying firstly to defendants, secondly to co-defendants, and thirdly to spouses and civil partners.

Defendants and inferences from failure to testify

Defendants cannot be compelled to testify in their defence under s1(1) CEA 1898 since this would breach the privilege against self-incrimination. There is, however, indirect pressure to do so under **s35 Criminal Justice and Public Order Act (CJPOA) 1994**. This allows the court or jury, in determining whether the accused is guilty of the offence charged, to draw such inferences as appear proper from the failure of the accused to give evidence or his refusal, without good cause, to answer any question. The leading case is *R v Cowan* (1996). The Court of Appeal held that the judge must direct that:

- the burden of proof remained on the prosecution;
- the defendant was entitled to remain silent;
- an inference from failure to testify alone cannot prove guilt;

Key features and principles

****

- the jury must be satisfied that the prosecution have established a case to answer before drawing inferences from silence; and
- if the jury conclude that the silence can only sensibly be attributed to the defendant's having no real answer, or one that would stand up to cross- examination, they may then draw an adverse inference.

The judge must direct the jury carefully on these points see *R v Birchall* (1998). See also *R v Friend* (1997) where even though the defendant had the mental age of a nine-year old, the Court of Appeal held that the judge had been correct to direct that jury could draw adverse inferences.

Co-defendants

The law might appear complicated but bear in mind that under certain conditions, particularly if there is a 'cut-throat' defence put forward, the evidence of a co-defendant may assume the adversarial status of that of the prosecution. See Fig 7.1.

Revision tip

The rules change where the co-defendant becomes an 'ex-co-defendant'. This could happen where the co-defendant pleads guilty and is acquitted or a *nolle prosequi* is entered, see *R v Boal* (1965). In such a situation the ex-co-defendant is indistinguishable from other witnesses.

Figure 7.1 Competence and compellability (1)

Type of trial: two defendants: D1 pleading not guilty D2 pleading not guilty	
Are D1 and D2 competent for the prosecution?	No, see 53(4)YJCEA. **Note**: It follows that since D1 and D2 are not competent they are not compellable.
Are D1 and D2 competent for their own defence?	Yes, see s53(1) YJCEA. **Note**: Same rules would apply if there was only one defendant.
Are D1 and D2 compellable for their own defence	No, see s1(1) CEA 1898. **Note**: See above for evidential consequences to D1 and/or D2 of not testifying.
Is D1 competent for D2's defence (and vice versa)?	Yes, see s1(1) CEA 1898.

Witnesses, spouses, and civil partners

You will need to familiarise yourself with the various technical permutations of compellability which are summarised in the tables below. You will also need to prepare for the possibility of an essay question which will ask you to comment on the theoretical coherence, or lack of it, of the law. The general rule is that witnesses can be compelled to testify for the prosecution. The common law created an exception to this general rule, so that the defendant's spouse could not be compelled to testify. Cohabitees who are not married (and ex-spouses: *R v Cruttenden* (1991)) are compellable under the common law rule, as are persons whose marriage is not recognized in English law: *R v Khan* (1987). The spouse exception was said to protect the sanctity of marriage. Because of concern about domestic violence, the rules were changed in PACE 1984. Where the defendant is charged with assaulting, injuring or threatening to injure his or her spouse or a person under 16, the spouse may be now compelled to testify at trial. Similarly, the spouse may be compelled to testify about an allegation of a sexual offence against a person under 16. Roberts and Zuckerman (2004, p 234) indicate some continuing illogicalities, including the non-recognition of cohabiting partners, the limited range of offences covered and the lack of protection for other potentially vulnerable persons, such as elderly or disabled people, whether members of the household or not. Nowadays, **civil partners** are in the same position as spouses. The term spouse or civil partner does not cover cohabiting partners even in the light of **Art 8 European Convention on Human Rights (ECHR)**. In *R v Pearce* (2002) a long-term unmarried partner was compellable for the prosecution.

Figure 7.2 Competence and compellability (2)

Type of trial: D is on trial for sexually assaulting his 19-year-old daughter. He is legally married to S	
Is S competent and compellable for D's defence?	S is competent under the general rule in s53(1) YJCEA. She is compellable under s80(2) & (4) PACE since she is not charged herself.
Is S competent and compellable for the prosecution?	S is competent to give evidence for the prosecution under s53(1) YJCEA but she is not compellable under s802A(b) & (3) PACE since the offence does not involve an assault on or injury etc to a wife, husband or person under 16, nor is it a sexual offence against a person under 16.

Figure 7.3 Competence and compellability (3)

Type of trial: Husband (H) and wife (W) jointly charged and are both pleading not guilty, whether or not the same offence and whatever the offence	
Are H and W competent for the prosecution?	No, see s53(4) YJCEA. **Note**: It follows that since H and W are not competent they are not compellable. See s80(4) PACE.

Key features and principles

✳✳✳✳✳✳✳✳✳✳

Type of trial: Husband (H) and wife (W) jointly charged and are both pleading not guilty, whether or not the same offence and whatever the offence	
Are H and W competent for their own defence?	Yes, see s53(1) YJCEA.
Are H and W compellable for their own defence?	No, see s1(1) CEA 1898. **Note**: See above (p 110) for evidential consequences to H and/or W of not testifying.
Is H competent for W's defence (and vice versa)?	Yes, see s1(1) CEA 1898.
Is H compellable for W's defence (and vice versa)?	No, see two overlapping provisions, s1(1) CEA 1898 and s80(4).

Figure 7.4 Competence and compellability (4)

Type of trial: Two accused D1 and D2, both pleading not guilty, where the spouses/civil partners are called as witnesses, S1 and S2, and the charge is not covered by s80(3)(a). The general rules on competency apply to S1 and S2 as non-defendants, s 53 YJCE	
Are S1 and S2 compellable to give evidence for the prosecution against D1 and D2 respectively?	No, s80(2A)(b) PACE 1984.
Are S1 and S2 compellable to give evidence in defence of D1 and D2 respectively?	Yes, s80(2) PACE.
Is S1 compellable to give evidence for the defence of D2?	No, s80(2A)(a). **Note**: The same rule applies to S2 giving evidence for the defence of D1. Tapper (2007, p 269) comments, '... these provisions run counter to the general principle of not fettering the defence of a co-accused, and are difficult to justify'. Note also S1's evidence for D2 could incriminate D1.

✅ *Looking for extra marks?*

You will show a good grasp of the law in this area if you point out that there is a ban on the prosecution commenting on the failure of the defendant to call a spouse to give evidence. **Section 80A PACE** states that 'the failure of the spouse or **civil partner** of a person charged in any proceedings to give evidence in the proceedings shall not be made the subject of any comment by the prosecution'. This wording is a wide one and thus prevents comment even if it is based on a logical inference, see *R v Davey* [2006].

Figure 7.5 Competence and compellability (5)

Type of trial: two accused, D1 and D2, both pleading not guilty, where the spouses/civil partners are called as witnesses, S1 and S2, and the charge is a physical attack on S1, spouse of D1. **The general rules on competency apply to S1 and S2 as non-defendants, s53(1) YJCEA** 1999. **The offence is covered by** s80(3)(a) **in that 'In relation to the spouse or civil partner of a person charged … it involves an assault on, or injury, or threat of injury to, the wife or husband'**	
Is S1 compellable to give evidence in defence of D1?	Yes, s80(2A)(a) PACE.
Is S1 compellable to give evidence for the prosecution against D1 and D2?	(S)he is compellable against both as the spousal victim, s80(2A)(b).
Is S1 compellable to give evidence in defence of D2?	Yes, s80(2A)(a) PACE.
Is S2 compellable to give evidence for the defence of D1?	No, s80(2A)(a) PACE.
Is S2 compellable to give evidence for the prosecution of D1 and D2?	(S)he is not compellable for either prosecution case since she is not the spousal victim, s80(2A)(b) PACE.
Is S2 compellable to give evidence for the defence of D2?	Yes, s80(2) PACE – general rules of spousal compellability apply.

Revision tip

Be careful in answering questions about spousal compellability that you are alert to the type of offence which is specified. In the example in Fig 7.5, S2 would have been compellable to have given evidence for the prosecution against both D1 and D2 if the offence had involved a sexual or physical attack on a person, not necessarily in the household of D1 or D2, who at the material time was under 16 years.

Criminal trials: sworn evidence

A witness under 14 years cannot give sworn evidence, s55(2)(a) YJCEA 1999. A witness who has attained the age of 14 can be sworn if he has '… sufficient appreciation of the solemnity of the occasion and of the particular responsibility to tell the truth which is involved in taking the oath', s55(2). Otherwise, the witness may give unsworn evidence, s56. False unsworn evidence may still give rise to a perjury charge, s57.

Criminal trials: protective measures for vulnerable witnesses

In line with its policy of re-balancing the criminal justice system to give more protection to victims and witnesses other than the defendant the Government introduced a number of measures protecting witnesses in the YJCEA 1999.

Who is eligible for special measures?

The most extensive of these measures apply to four groups of witnesses whose quality of evidence may be diminished which is defined as 'its quality in terms of completeness, coherence and accuracy', s16(5). The groups are:

(i) those under 17 years old;

(ii) those where the quality of the evidence is likely to be impaired by or mental disorder;

(iii) those where the witness has a physical disability or disorder; and

(iv) witnesses in fear or distress.

This final category automatically includes complainants in sexual cases, unless they elect otherwise. Factors to be taken into account by the court in assessing the last category include the social and cultural background and ethnic origins of the witness, the domestic and employment circumstances of the witness, and any religious beliefs or political opinions of the witness. In addition, the court may pay attention to the behaviour to the witness of the accused and his family and any other person who is likely to be an accused or a witness in the proceedings. See ss16–18 YJCEA 1999.

A further set of provisions in s21 apply to child witnesses, other than the defendant. These are witnesses who are under 17 at the time of the hearing (or the making of the video-recording if relevant) and cover:

• a witness in a case concerning one of the sexual offences in s35(3)(s), namely those in the Protection of Children Act 1978 or Part 1 Sexual Offences Act 2003;

• a witness in a case concerning one of the offences in s35(3)(b), (c) or (d) which include kidnapping, false imprisonment, abduction, cruelty, or violence; and

• a witness in a case concerning any other offence.

The first two categories cover child witnesses 'in need of special protection' under s21(1)(b) who get a higher level of protection than the third category of child witnesses in general. Special measures including video and live link outlined below are available to all child witnesses under what is called the 'primary rule' in s21(3). However, child witnesses 'in need of special protection' are not covered by s21(4)(c) which provides that the 'primary rule' does not apply 'to the extent that the court is satisfied that compliance with it would not be likely to maximise the quality of the witness's evidence so far as practicable' for any reason.

Section 22 makes provision for child witnesses who were under 17 at the time of the video-recording but over 17 at the time of the hearing.

In *R (on the application of D) v Camberwell Green Youth Court* (2005) the House of Lords held the fact that this meant there was no need for individual consideration of the necessity for the special measures in those instances was not a violation of **Art 6(1)** or **(3)(d)**. Baroness Hale referred (at para 53) to '... the use of modern equipment to put the best evidence before the court while preserving the essential rights of the accused to know and to challenge all the evidence against him'.

What are the measures?

They include screening witnesses from accused (**s23**), live-links (**s24**), evidence given in private (**s25**), removal of wigs or gowns (**s26**), video-recorded evidence in chief (**s27**), examination of witnesses through an intermediary (**s29**), and various aids to communication (**s30**).

Section 28 is as yet unimplemented. It specifies that a video recording to be admitted as evidence in chief may also provide for any cross examination and re-examination to be video-recorded and for the recording to be admitted as the witness's evidence under cross examination or re-examination. There is particular concern that this will not overcome the problem of the traumatic nature of cross-examining children. (See Choo (2009, p398)).

Note that live links are also available under **s51 CJA 2003** (but not to defendants) if the court considers it is in the interests of the efficient or effective administration of justice and where relevant factors include the availability of a witness and the need for the witness to attend in person. However, unlike the provisions in the **YJCEA** in those instances a witness may be seen and heard by the defendant.

What safeguards are there?

Judge must give jury a warning to ensure that the fact a special measures direction was given in relation to a witness does not prejudice the accused (**s32 YJCEA 1999**).

✅ *Looking for extra marks?*

As well as the scholarly text books you should read academic articles such as: D Birch, 'A Better Deal for Vulnerable Witnesses?' [2002] Crim LR 223 and LCH Hoyano, 'Variations on a Theme by Pigot: Special Measures Directions for Child Witnesses' [2000] *Crim LR* 250.

Note also the review of the operation of the Special Measures in B Hamlyn, A Phelps, J Turtle, and G Sattar, *Are Special Measures Working? Evidence from Surveys of Vulnerable and Intimidated Witnesses* (Home Office Research Study 283 (2004) 80–81 available at http://www.homeoffice.gov.uk/rds/pdfs04/hors283.pdf).

- The Strasbourg Court has found breaches of **Art 6** in the UK's treatment of child defendants, see *T v UK* (2000). However, the non-availability of special measures to the defendant is not a breach of **Art 6** as there are other safeguards for vulnerable defendants. See *R (on the application of S) v Waltham Forest Youth Court* (2004) where a special measures direction was not available for a 13-year-old defendant.

- Some limited changes were introduced for vulnerable defendants in the Police and Justice Act 2006 creating a new s33A YJCEA 1999. The accused may give oral evidence through a live link if the court is satisfied that it is in the interests of justice and one of the following apply:

  ○ the accused is under 18 years and his ability to participate effectively in the proceedings as a witness giving oral evidence is compromised by his level of intellectual ability or social functioning, or

  ○ the accused is over 18 years and suffers from a mental disorder or otherwise has a significant impairment of intelligence and social function that he is unable to participate effectively in the proceedings as a witness giving oral evidence in court.

These limited statutory provisions should be set alongside the common law power for a defendant to be absent from the trial and other technical means such as a video link found to ensure participation. See *R v Ukpabio* (2008).

Witness anonymity

The Criminal Evidence (Witness Anonymity) Act 2008 became law in July 2008. The Act was Parliament's extremely speedy reversal of *R v Davis* (2008), a powerful House of Lords' judgment delivered on June 18, 2008. There the Lords had held that a murder trial was unfair and a violation of Art 6(3)(d) where an order preserved the anonymity of a civilian witness. That evidence was in Lord Mance's words (at para 96) 'the sole or decisive basis on which alone the defendant could have been convicted'. The court held that that the particular combination of protective measures violated Art 6 and observed, in addition, that it departed from common law principles. On the facts the measures adopted to protect witnesses, which included full anonymity, screens, voice distortion, and the use of pseudonyms, rendered the trial unfair. The cumulative effect of these measures meant that the defendant could not test the witness's **credibility**.

The Act allows various measures to be taken to protect the identity of a witness such as the use of a pseudonym and screening and voice modulation. In order for this to apply the following conditions must be satisfied (see ss1–4):

- the measures must be necessary, for example, to protect the safety of the witness having regard to reasonable fear on his part if he were identified or to protect the carrying on of activities in the public interest;

- the taking of the measures would be consistent with the defendant receiving a fair trial; and

- the interests of justice require the order, since it appears to the court that it is important the witness should testify and the witness would not testify if the order were not made.

Section 3 of the Act sets out relevant matters the court must consider which include whether evidence given by the witness might be the sole or decisive evidence implicating the defendant. Section 7(2) provides that 'The judge must give the jury such a warning as the judge considers appropriate to ensure that the fact that [a witness anonymity] order was made in relation to the witness does not prejudice the defendant.' Section 11 provides that the Court of Appeal has to consider an appeal on this issue as if the Act were in force even if the trial ended before the statute was implemented.

The Act has a **sunset clause**. The statutory regime applies to undercover police as well as other witnesses whereas critics have pointed out the superiority of the New Zealand scheme which provides for separate regimes for civilians and police.

The Act was applied in a series of conjoined *R v Mayers; R v Glasgow; R v Costelloe; R v Bahmanzadeh; R v P and others* (2008). The Court of Appeal allowed the appeal in *Mayers* because the court could not be confident that everything relating to the witness's **credibility**, motivation, and integrity had been revealed. The convictions in *Glasgow, Costelloe and Bahmanzadeh* were safe since knowledge of the true identities of undercover police officers was rarely of importance to the defendant. *R v P* involved the application of s116 CJA 2003 which required **disclosure** of the witness's name to the defence and the prosecution's challenge to the trial judge's ruling on this was dismissed. The s114 inclusionary discretion could not be applied since that would involve rewriting the 2008 Act.

Civil cases

All witnesses are presumed to be competent and compellable. The major exception is that of child witnesses. Section 96 Children Act 1989 provides that where a child under 18 years does not, in the opinion of the court, understand the nature of an oath, he or she may give unsworn evidence in civil proceedings provided he or she understands the duty to speak the truth and he or she has sufficient understanding to justify the evidence being heard. Thus, the test for competency for unsworn evidence, in referring to the duty to speak the truth, is stricter than under criminal law. Note, however, that a child's evidence may be more readily admissible by hearsay in civil cases.

① Conclusion

Traditionally, questions on competence and compellability form part of larger questions containing a number of other issues. However, the overlap of this area with the much broader question of policy towards victims as witnesses means it is subject to topical debate and therefore assumes larger importance. Compellability, and the consequential finding of contempt for failure to appear as a witness, is a reduced deterrent now that there are increased opportunities to appear as an anonymous witness or give evidence through special measures or by exceptions to the rule against hearsay. In spite of all these apparent concessions to the understandable reluctance of some witnesses to appear in court, you should not lose sight of the importance attached to the public duty of giving evidence in open court.

Key cases

✶✶✶✶✶✶✶✶✶✶

In *R v Yusuf* (2003) Rose LJ stated (at para 16), 'The role of the courts, in seeking to provide the public with protection against criminal conduct, can only properly be performed if members of the public co-operate with the courts. That co-operation includes participation in the trial process.'

(✶) *Key cases*

Case	Facts	Principle
R v Boal [1965] QB 402	B, one of the Great Train Robbers, sought in his appeal against conviction **to adduce** the evidence of an ex-co-defendant, C, who had pleaded guilty. B was not allowed to adduce this new evidence but the court held that C would have been a competent and compellable witness.	The general presumption of competence and compellability applies to a former co-defendant subsequently pleading guilty.
R v Pitt [1983] QB 25	Wife gave evidence as a prosecution witness at husband's trial without sufficiently appreciating her right to refuse to testify against him.	Once a spouse elects to give evidence, provided he or she has had the right of refusal clearly explained by the trial judge, he or she is to be treated as any other witness. Here the conviction was overturned.
R v Khan (1987) 84 Cr App R 44	The appeal turned on whether the second wife of a Moslem defendant whose first wife was alive at the time of marriage was both competent and compellable as a witness against him.	The position of a woman who had gone through a valid form of marriage which was of no effect in English law was no different from that of a woman who had not been through a ceremony at all or whose marriage was void because it was bigamous.
R v Cruttenden [1991] 2 QB 66	The former wife of a council planning officer testified at his trial that he had corruptly received free petrol in return for favours. At the time of the alleged offences the two were married and she would have been incompetent as a witness against him. The law had been changed in 1986 so as to make a former spouse competent as a witness against his or her ex-spouse. The court held that the provision should not have been applied retrospectively.	Once a marriage is legally terminated a former spouse or **civil partner** is competent to testify about matters which occurred while the marriage existed.

Case	Facts	Principle
R v Cowan and others [1996] QB 373	The appellants who had not testified at trial appealed on the grounds that the trial judge had not given a proper direction on the application of s35 CJPOA 1994. They argued that the discretion to draw adverse inferences should only apply in exceptional cases.	The Court of Appeal rejected the arguments put. It specified, however, that the jury should be carefully directed on the uses to be made of the defendant's failure to testify.
R v Pearce [2002] 1 WLR 1553	The defendant's long-term unmarried partner made statements which were prejudicial to him. At trial she gave answers which were inconsistent with her statements and was cross-examined by the prosecutor as a **hostile witness**. His appeal on the grounds that the ECHR required his partner be treated as if she were his wife was dismissed.	A long-term unmarried partner is both competent and compellable.
R (on the application of S) v Waltham Forest Youth Court [2004] 2 Cr App R 21	The defendant was aged 13 years and had serious learning difficulties. She was jointly charged and, despite her vulnerability and alleged fear of her co-defendants, she was refused permission to give evidence by video link. She appealed against conviction.	The Administrative Court held that there was no breach of Art 6 since there were other protections available to defendants.
R (on the application of D) v Camberwell Green Youth Court [2005] 1 All ER 999	Two under-17-year-old victims were allowed to give evidence against two under-16-year-old defendants by a video-link.	The House of Lords expressed the opinion that courts have wide and flexible powers to protect defendants and ensure a fair trial.

⑨⑨ Key debates

Topic	**Do the special measures for witnesses undermine the defendant's rights by limiting the right to confrontation and to cross examination?**
Author	M Burton, R Evans, and A Sanders
Viewpoint	The authors examine recent Home Office-funded empirical research
Source	'Vulnerable and Intimidated Witnesses and the Adversarial Process in England and Wales' (2007) 11(1) E&P 1

Exam questions

✱✱✱✱✱✱✱✱✱✱

Topic	The law on competence and compellability for spouses and civil partners
Authors	J Roberts and A Zuckerman
Viewpoint	The spousal privilege rests on unconvincing rationales and flawed reasoning
Source	*Criminal Evidence* (OUP, 2004) pp230–235

⑦ Exam questions

Essay question

Have the special measures provisions now available to witnesses undermined the protection of the defendant?

An outline answer is available online at http://www.oxfordtextbooks.co.uk/orc/concentrate/

Problem question

Janet and John, who are married, are jointly charged with an assault on their child, Tim, who at the time of the alleged offence was twelve. The alleged incident took place in the back garden of their home and was witnessed through the back window of the neighbouring house by Agnes who is in her nineties and is suffering from early stages of dementia. Janet is considering pleading guilty but John wishes to plead not guilty. John is also charged in the same indictment with cruelty to the family pet, a Labrador called Ron. The prosecution case is that John threw a garden spade at Ron as the dog tried to protect Tim.

    Advise on evidence.

An outline answer is available at the end of the book.

#8
Issues in the course of trial

Suspect evidence

- The general rule is that one piece of evidence is sufficient to convict but there are statutory exceptions to this where there is a need for **corroboration** eg s13 Perjury Act 1911.
- The common law obligatory requirement for **corroboration** warnings in the case of certain categories of witnesses such as children was repealed in the Criminal Justice and Public Order Act (CJPOA) 1994. The emphasis now in looking for supportive evidence is more on the strength or otherwise of the evidence rather than the intrinsic nature of the witness.
- There is a requirement for the judge to give a direction (a *Turnbull* direction) of the need for care in cases of disputed identification.
- In cases where lies (in or out of court) told by the accused are presented as suggestive of guilt, the judge should give a care warning (a *Lucas* direction).
- The judge has discretion to issue a care warning if there is reason to believe the witness might be unreliable.
- The Police and Criminal Evidence Act 1984 (PACE) Code D sets out the procedures for identification parades and for video identification.

Examination in chief

- The witness is allowed to refresh his memory from documents under ss120 and 139 Criminal Justice Act (CJA) 2003.
- Previous consistent statements are inadmissible unless there is a statutory or common law exception.

Key facts

****

- Parties are not allowed to cross examine their own witnesses except with leave of the judge under s3 Criminal Procedure Act 1865 in cases where the witness changes their evidence from pre-trial.

Cross examination

- There are statutory limits on the questions that may be asked of complainants in cases involving sexual offences, see ss41–43 Youth Justice and Criminal Evidence Act (YJCEA) 1999.
- Previous inconsistent statements of the witness may be admissible under ss4 and 5 Criminal Procedure Act 1865.
- A witness's answers to a collateral question should be treated as final. This rule of finality on collateral questions has a number of exceptions.

Related areas

This area is concerned with some procedural matters, particularly concerning examining of witnesses, which arise during a trial. It is closely related to hearsay since much of it touches on the admissibility of out of court statements. Cross examination on previous sexual behaviour of complainants overlaps with character evidence and also with Chapter 8 which includes a discussion on vulnerable witnesses. Indirectly, the discussion on **corroboration** concerns inferences from silence since that is one area where a single piece of evidence, the inference of guilt, is not enough to found a conviction. Periodically there are arguments put that corroborative evidence ought to be sought before convicting on a confession alone (see Chapter 3).

The assessment: key points

Since this area contains a disparate range of predominantly procedural issues it is more likely to form the basis of a problem question along with some other issues. You may have to discuss alternative ways of considering admitting evidence. Thus, for example, evidence of previous discreditable behaviour of a complainant in a sexual case may raise issues about bad character (see Chapter 5) as well as cross examination under s41 CJA 2003. The controversial question of the relative rights of defendants and witnesses is also covered in Chapter 8 on Special Measures and might well form the subject of an essay question particularly concerning the vexed question of the treatment of complainants in sexual cases.

You need to be clear about the difference between evidence of consistency and evidence of truth. Under the common law non-hearsay out of court statements admitted at trial could be evidence that the witness was telling the same account at trial. Under the CJA 2003 such statements are largely, but not entirely, evidence of the truth of their contents, thus creating an exception to the rule against hearsay.

This area forms a somewhat eclectic mix of evidential and procedural issues. The relative incoherence of the law is highlighted by the fact that it is to be found in a disparate set of statutes and case law precedents. The key statutory sections are:

- **Criminal Procedure Act 1865 ss 4 and 5** on the admissibility of previous inconsistent statements;
- **Criminal Procedure Act 1865 s3** on a party's questioning of their own witness whose evidence at trial differs from that pre-trial;
- the **PACE 1984 Code D** on the procedure for identification parades;
- **YJCEA 1999 ss41–43** on cross examination of victims in sexual cases;
- **CJA 2003 ss120 and 139** on a witness's use of memory refreshing documents at trial;
- **CJA 2003 s120(4) and (5)** on the admissibility and evidential status of identification evidence; and
- **CJA 2003 ss119 and 120** on the evidential status of some previous consistent statements (others are covered by the common law).

Key features and principles
Suspect evidence

In English law a verdict can be based on evidence of a single witness or a confession. There were two exceptions to this. Firstly, a very small number of statutes provide that a conviction must be supported, or **corroborated**, by more than one piece of evidence. Secondly, under the common law there were some categories of witnesses whose evidence was thought to be potentially unreliable. Again, confirming evidence, known as '**corroboration**' was required. There *were* three main categories of cases:

(i) those where **corroboration** of an item of evidence is required as a matter of law. Their absence means no conviction;

(ii) those cases where the judge must warn of the dangers of convicting in the absence of **corroboration** where the prosecution witness was a child, a complainant in a sexual offence, or an accomplice; and

(iii) identification cases where there was a need for a 'care' warning'.

Statutory erosion of category (ii) led to the removal of the need for **corroboration** warnings in s32 CJPOA 1994. Subsequently, the case of *R v Makanjuola* (1995) held that any warnings on the dangers of convicting on certain pieces of evidence should be decided on a case-by-case basis. A further change was that any supporting evidence need not amount to **corroboration** in the very technical sense which formerly prevailed, see *R v Baskerville* (1916). In essence, the supporting evidence had to be relevant, admissible, credible, and independent of the witness who needed to be corroborated and implicate the defendant in the commission of the offence.

Figure 8.1 Situations where corroboration/warning may be required

Nature of corroboration/warning	Provision/comment
Judge must give a mandatory warning where identification evidence is disputed.	*R v Turnbull* (1976): Failure to give the warning will lead to an appeal. Elements of the warning are specified in the case.
Judge may exercise discretion to issue a care warning.	*R v Makanjuola* (1995): The judge has discretion whether to issue a warning and the nature of the warning. There are no categories of witness where a warning is necessarily required.
Corroboration required by statute.	Examples are s1 Treason Act 1795, s13 Perjury Act 1911, and s89(2) Road Traffic Regulation Act 1984. Under the latter a defendant cannot be convicted of speeding '…on the evidence of one witness to the effect that, in the opinion of the witness the person prosecuted was driving the vehicle at a speed exceeding a specified limit'.

Nature of corroboration/warning	Provision/comment
Lies told by the defendant as evidence of guilt or as supportive of other evidence.	A judicial direction should be given to the jury when the prosecution proposes to rely on the defendant's lie or lies. The content of the direction is set out in *R v Lucas* (1981) (see also JSB Specimen Direction No 27) and the occasions when the direction is necessary are set out in *R v Burge* (1996).

Identification evidence

One of the most notorious cases of multiple mistaken identity was that of Adolf Beck in 1896. The scandal of his wrongful conviction was instrumental is the establishment of the Court of Criminal Appeal. In the 1970s, a spate of miscarriages of justice led to the setting up of the Devlin Committee to review procedures for identification evidence. It made some radical proposals for legislation but before these could be implemented the Court of Appeal decided the landmark case, *R v Turnbull* (1977). Emson writes (2008, p 265), 'Cynics might suggest that the speed with which the Court of Appeal acted demonstrated its fear of Devlin-inspired legislation and its desire to introduce a watered down version in its place.' The current safeguards cover two areas. Firstly, **Code D** issued under **PACE 1984** specifies how police identification procedures should be organised. The Code is regularly revised. Secondly, the leading case *R v Turnbull* sets out mandatory directions which should be given to juries in cases of disputed identification.

Pre-trial procedures

Code D-3 came into force in February 2008. It provides that the suspect will normally be offered a video **identification parade** (VIPER). The **Code** sets out procedures for three situations:

- when the suspect's identity is not known;
- when the suspect is known and available; and
- when the suspect is known but not available.

Revision tip

You may need to comment on other possible forms of identification which the police or prosecution may set up. Dock identifications, for obvious reasons, are not desirable. See *R v Conway* (1990), where such an identification at the committal hearing should have been excluded. However, they are admissible at the discretion of the judge and are not uncommon in magistrates courts.

Code D does allow for group identifications and, as last resort, confrontations particularly where the suspect will not attend a parade.

Key features and principles

Further provisions in relation to identification evidence are summarised in Fig 8.2.

Figure 8.2 Identification evidence: pre-trial provisions under PACE 1984 Code D

Situation	Provision
When should the police show a witness photographs?	When there is no suspect available to attend an identification. If there is to be a video identification or parade, the witness should not see photographs.
Can witnesses communicate before an identification?	No, there should be no risk of collusion. Code D Annex A para 10 and Annex B para 14
Can the officer involved in the investigation take part in the procedures for the identification under Code D?	No – Code D para 3.11
What is the role of the defence lawyer in video identifications or parades.	She has a right to view the film and be present at the showing to witnesses and at a parade. If the accused does not have a representative present the parade should be videoed or a colour photograph taken.
When might Code D not apply?	The identification procedure might not apply if the witness continually observed the suspect during the offence – see *R v Byron* (1999).

In *R v Forbes* (2001) the House of Lords held that identification parades should always be held where the identification is disputed. As a result of this decision **Code D** was amended to allow more discretion on the holding of a parade. Thus, failure to hold a parade will not now be necessarily fatal to the prosecution case.

Procedures at trial

The lengthy *Turnbull* guidelines which must be given by the judge in all cases of disputed identification include the following provisions:

- the judge must warn the jury of the special need for caution if the case depends wholly or partly on one or more identification and should remind them that honest witnesses may be mistaken;
- the jury must look closely at the circumstances of the identification such as the light or any impediment to the witness's view;
- if the identification is of good quality it can be left to the jury; and
- the judge may withdraw the case if the witness had only a fleeting glance or longer observation in difficult circumstances and there is no other evidence.

It was decided in *Daley v R* (1994) that such a case could be withdrawn even if it did not meet the high standards of no case to answer set out in *R v Galbraith* (1981). In determining whether there is a case to answer the judge should have regard not only to the circumstances of the original identification but also subsequent factors such as breaches of Code D-3. The authorities' cases suggest that recognition cases are less likely to fall in this category than identification of strangers (see *R v Ryan* (1990)).

In *R v Nash* (2004) the Court of Appeal stated that the judge should include in the *Turnbull* direction reference to miscarriages of justice arising out of mistaken identification. The judge may invite the jury to look for supporting evidence and this might be the identification evidence from two different witnesses. In *R v Weeder* (1980), the Court held that the judge must warn the jury in such cases that several honest witnesses may be mistaken.

Specific cases where Turnbull *warning is required*

If it is a 'recognition case':

In *R v Bentley* (1994) the defendant and victim knew one another. After a dispute the victim was wounded by having glass driven into his face, He identified the defendant who was convicted. His appeal was allowed since the judge had not given the *Turnbull* warning and it was possible the victim made a mistake even though recognition identifications were more reliable than those of strangers. See also *Shand v R* (1966).

If the accused admits his presence at the scene but denies participation and the scene is crowded:

In *R v Thornton* (1995) a man was attacked by a group at a wedding reception. T admitted being there but denied participation. Two witnesses identified him and he was convicted. The appeal was allowed since the judge should have given a *Turnbull* warning particularly because several others at the wedding had been dressed like the accused.

If the witness is a police officer a Turnbull *direction may still be required:*

In *R v Moore* (2004) a police officer gave evidence of recognition of the offenders at a fight at a football match. The judge had failed to give a *Turnbull* warning about the difficulties of the sighting such as the risk that the officer was distracted by his other duties.

Specific cases where a Turnbull *warning is not required*

Where accused claims witness is trying to 'frame' him:

In *R v Cape* [1996] the testimony of a publican who had witnessed a fracas was the main evidence. The defendants, who were known to him, claimed he was motivated by a grudge against them. Since the sole issue was truthfulness there was no need for a *Turnbull* direction.

Where the accused who admits his presence at the scene of the crime has unusual features:

In *R v Slater* (1995) a victim of a night-club assault identified his attacker, an unusually heavily built man who admitted being present but denied participation. No **identification parade** was held and no *Turnbull* guidelines given. The appeal against conviction failed since there was no evidence to suggest anyone like him was also present. In *R v Oakwell* [1978] the Court of Appeal stated that *Turnbull* was 'intended primarily to deal with the ghastly risk run in cases of fleeting encounters'. No warning was required in this case where the defendant agreed he was at scene of crime but denied he was the assailant.

Key features and principles

✳✳✳✳✳✳✳✳✳✳

Where the identification concerns a vehicle:

In *R v Browning* (1991) the Court of Appeal observed that there were important differences between cars and people and a *Turnbull* direction was not needed when the contested identification related to car.

✅ Looking for extra marks?

Increasingly, police surveillance may produce evidence of voice recordings as identification. In *R v Hersey* (1998) the Court of Appeal held that *Turnbull* guidelines should be given if the evidence is presented at trial. In *R v Roberts* [2000] the Court of Appeal referred to the need for a modified *Turnbull* warning in the case of 'ear-witnesses'. Ormerod (2001) deplores the lack of statutory control in an area which may lead to miscarriages of justice.

See also *R v Flynn and St John* (2008) for the court's approach to expert evidence in such cases.

The overlap between this area and hearsay is shown by the variety of ways in which identification evidence may be admissible at trial as an exception to the hearsay rule as Fig 8.3 illustrates.

Figure 8.3 Admissibility of out of court indentifications

Admissibility	Authority
Declarant's performance of a relevant act	*R v MacCay* (1990). In this case a witness who had identified the suspect at a parade could not remember the number she had stated. The police officer was permitted to state the number. The Court held that the evidence was correctly admitted either as the common law hearsay exception based on a statement accompanying an act or as a statutory exception for identification evidence under PACE.
As exception to the inadmissibility of previous consistent statements	Identification evidence was routinely admissible before the CJA 2003 as an exception to this common law rule. The courts took a creative approach since this was likely to be cogent evidence.
As statutory exception	Section 120 CJA 2003 specifically renders statements of identification admissible as evidence of their truth.

Defendant's lies as evidence

R v Lucas (1981), a case decided under the common law **corroboration** rules, set out the conditions under which lies by a defendant could amount to supporting evidence. The case is still good law in those situations where the prosecution seeks to rely on the defendant's lie or lies, either at interview or at trial, as evidence of guilt in the instant case. Such lies must be distinguished from other situations where untruthfulness is indirect evidence of lack of **credibility** (see Chapter 5). The *Lucas* direction must tell the jury to consider that the lie must be proved to be so beyond reasonable doubt and that a lie in itself is not evidence of guilt since people may lie for other reasons such as wanting to hide embarrassment. In short, to be evidence of guilt the lie must:

- be deliberate;
- relate to a material issue; and
- be prompted by a realisation of guilt and fear of the truth as opposed to an innocent reason.

R v Burge (1996) sets out the occasions on which a *Lucas* direction should be given. See Fig 8.4.

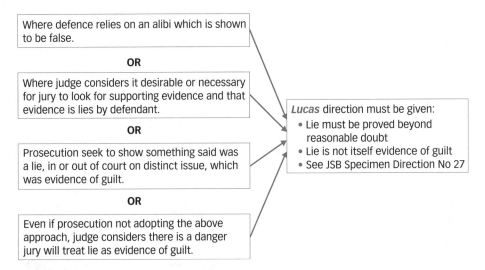

Figure 8.4 Lies (non-hearsay) by defendant - see *R v Burge* (1996)

There is no need to give a *Lucas* direction if the lies told by the defendant relate to a central issue in the case. In *R v Middleton* (2001) the accused had an elaborate set of alibis to explain his non-involvement in a robbery. The prosecution alleged he was lying. It would confuse the jury to give a *Lucas* warning since there was no distinction between the issue of guilt and that of the lie. If they disbelieved him it followed that they must find him guilty.

Exam tip

You will have to take care that you distinguish the elements of hearsay from that of lies. Note the case of *Mawaz Khan v R* (1966) where a statement concerning an alibi was admissible as non-hearsay since the purpose of adducing it was to show its falsity, not its truth.

Examination in chief

Refreshing memory

Under **s139 CJA 2003** a witness may refresh his memory from documents while giving evidence if:

- he states in his oral evidence that the document records his recollection of the matter at that earlier time; *and*
- his recollection of the matter is likely to have been better at that time than it is at the time of his oral evidence.

Under **s120(3)** such a statement may be received in evidence and is evidence of the truth of its contents, thus creating a new statutory exception to the rule against hearsay.

Previous consistent statements

The general rule is that a previous out of court statement cannot be admitted to support a statement made from the witness box. There are a number of exceptions to this common law rule. Three are now contained in **s120 CJA 2003** and two governed by the common law:

CJA 2003

Such statements are admissible if the witness admits that to the best of his belief, firstly, that he made the statement and, secondly, that it is true and, thirdly, that *any* of the following three conditions apply, namely identification evidence, **res gestae** statement, and 'recent complaints':

- the statement identifies or describes a person, object, or place (**s120(5)**);
- the statement was made when the matters stated were fresh in his memory and he cannot reasonably be expected to remember them well enough to give oral evidence (**s120(6)**); or
- the statement is a complaint made by the witness (**s120(7)**).

The 'recent complaint' exception to the inadmissibility of previous consistent statements is a major development from the common law which limited admissibility to complainants in sexual cases and then only as evidence of consistency. The main elements of the statutory provision are:

- the witness claims to be the person against whom an offence was committed;
- the offence is the subject matter of the proceedings;
- the complaint was made as soon as could reasonably be expected after the alleged conduct;

- the complaint was not made as a result of a threat or a promise (but may be made as a result of a leading question (**s120(8)**)); and

- before the statement is **adduced** the witness gives oral evidence in connection with its subject matter.

All three of the above categories of statements are admissible as evidence of any matter, thus creating another exception to the rule against hearsay (**s120(4)**).

Common law

Previous out of court **exculpatory statements** giving the accused's reaction to an accusation may be admissible but only as evidence of consistency and thus to support the witness's creditworthiness. See *R v Storey* (1968), where the accused explained to police when they found illegal drugs on her premises that she had been forced against her will to keep them. The statement was admissible as relevant to the consistency of the accused's explanation. The statement does not have to be made immediately on first accusation but the length of time which has elapsed is a factor in admissibility, see *R v Pearce* (1979). Admissibility depends on the weight of the evidence and *R v Tooke* (1990) establishes that a statement will not be admitted if the evidence of the reaction on accusation is given adequately in alternative evidence.

Previous statements made to rebut an allegation of fabrication are admissible under the common law, see *R v Oyesiku* (1971), but their new status as an exception to the rule against hearsay is found in **s120(2) CJA 2003**.

Revision tip

An example of the overlap of hearsay and previous consistent statements is provided in the case of *R v Xabri* (2005) (for facts, see p 100). The complainant alleged she had been raped and forced to work as a prostitute. She had made a number of telephone calls to her parents and others about her situation and the admissibility of these messages was at issue.

The trial judge allowed them in under **s120(5)** (previous identification) and **s120(6)** (a statement the witness could not be expected to recall) and **s120(7)** (a recent complaint). It was held that **s120(7)** was rightly applied but not the others. Alternatively, **s114(1)(d)** was appropriate (inclusionary discretion of hearsay). This was in compliance with **Art 6**.

Unfavourable and hostile witnesses

If a party's witness does not '**come up to proof**', meaning that his answers to questions in examination in chief contradict his pre-trial statements, the following approaches are possible. The witness can be declared either 'unfavourable' or 'hostile', which are terms of art.

Unfavourable witnesses act in good faith and the effect of their unhelpful testimony can be nullified to some extent through other evidence. Such a witness cannot be cross-examined, unlike a hostile witness. A **hostile witness** is one who shows no inclination to tell the truth. The party has to seek leave of court to declare the witness hostile and if that is granted the witness can be contradicted through other evidence or cross-examined on a previous inconsistent statement. The procedure is governed by s3 Criminal Procedure Act 1865. An important recent change is that if a previous inconsistent statement is admitted in that way, then under s119 CJA 2003 it 'is admissible as evidence of any matter stated in it of which oral evidence by the person would be admissible'.

Cross examination
Previous inconsistent statements

If a witness makes statements which are inconsistent with out of court statement he can be cross examined on them under ss4 and 5 Criminal Procedure Act 1865. Section 119 CJA 2003 makes such statements also an exception to the rule against hearsay. Under s124(2)(c), an out of court statement that is inconsistent with a hearsay statement that is admitted in evidence may be used to discredit the hearsay statement and is evidence of its contents.

The rule of finality on collateral questions

The general common law rule is that collateral questions may be asked of a witness but the answer must be treated as final. A collateral question is one which is relevant but does not relate directly to a fact in issue but is specific to the witness such as a question on **credibility**. There are three exceptions to this rule:

(i) If a witness is asked if they have any criminal convictions and they deny it, the conviction can be proved under s6 Criminal Procedure Act 1865.

(ii) If a witness is accused of bias they may be further questioned on their response. In *R v Mendy* (1976) a man was spotted taking notes in the public gallery while a prosecution witness was giving evidence and then describing the evidence to the accused's husband. When the husband denied this in cross examination the prosecution was allowed to call evidence in rebuttal. The scope of the concept of bias is illustrated in *R v Busby* (1981) which concerned the evidence of police officers who it was alleged had threatened a potential witness. The police denied this and the Court of Appeal held that the witness should have been allowed to give evidence of the threat by analogy with *Mendy*. It went on, however, to state that the issue of alleged impropriety was a fact in issue in the trial, not simply a collateral one.

(iii) A witness can be further questioned about any medical evidence of a disability which might have affected their evidence. In *Toohey v MPC* (1965) medical evidence of the liability of the witness to hysteria was called.

Cross examining complainants in sexual cases on previous sexual history

The difficulty of successfully prosecuting rape is well documented. It has been argued that complainants may not come forward because they fear hostile questions from defence counsel. Special measure protection is afforded to such witnesses (see Chapter 7) and in addition there are restrictions on cross examination. The key section is s41 YJCEA 1999 which repealed the controversial s2 Sexual Offences Amendment Act 1976. The complex s41 will be summarised and then the relevant case law examined.

(1) The section relates to trials where a person is charged with a sexual offence, defined as any offence under Part 1 Sexual Offences Act 2003. The Secretary of State has power to add or subtract from this listing.

(2) Except with the leave of the court no evidence may be given or no question asked in cross examination by or on behalf of the accused at the trial about the sexual behaviour of the complainant. Sexual behaviour means any behaviour or other sexual experience, whether or not involving any accused or other person but excluding (except as specified in point (3) below) anything alleged to have taken place as part of the event which is the subject matter of the current charge.

(3) The court may give the defence leave if one of the following four situations applies (Note that the section does not apply to prosecution applications):

(a) The question or evidence relates to a relevant issue which is *not an issue of consent* (s41(3)(a)). This applies to situations where the defence is either the offence did not take place or that the defendant reasonably believed the victim had consented. This is so since 'issue of consent' is defined in s42(b) as:

any issue whether the complainant in fact consented to the conduct constituting the offence with which the accused is charged (and accordingly does not include any issue as to the *belief* of the accused that the complainant so consented).

OR

(b) The question or evidence relates to a relevant issue which is an issue of consent and the complainant's sexual behaviour is alleged to have taken place *at or about the same time* as the subject matter of the charge (s41(3)(b)).

OR

(c) The question or evidence relates to a relevant issue which is an issue of consent. The complainant's sexual behaviour is alleged to have been *so similar* to the alleged sexual behaviour of the complainant *during* the event, which is the subject matter of the charge or to any other sexual behaviour that took place *at or about the same time as* that event, that the similarity cannot reasonably be explained as coincidence (s41(3)(c)(i) and (ii)).

OR

(d) The question or evidence relates to any question **adduced** by the prosecution about any sexual behaviour of the complainant and in the opinion of the court would go no further than is necessary to enable the evidence to be rebutted or explained by or on behalf of the accused (s41(5)).

Cross examination

The general effect is that the complainant can only be questioned about other sexual behaviour with anybody, including that with the alleged offender, if one or more of the following apply:

- if it is not an issue of consent;
- if it is an issue of consent and the relevant sexual behaviour took place at or about the same time as the alleged offence; or
- if it is an issue of consent and the sexual behaviour was so similar to behaviour which took place during the offence *or* at or about the same time as the alleged offence that the similarity cannot be a coincidence.

It is necessary to rebut the prosecution evidence.

In addition, even if one of the above situations applies, before the court can give leave for cross examining the complainant it has to consider the following:

- leave can only be granted if a refusal 'might have the result of rendering unsafe a conclusion of the jury or (as the case may be) the court on any relevant issue in the case' (s41(2)(b)). This in effect means danger of a miscarriage of justice;
- leave for questioning should not be granted even if the above conditions apply 'if it appears to the court to be reasonable to assume that the purpose (or main purpose) for which it would be **adduced** or asked is to establish or elicit material for impugning the **credibility** of the complainant as a witness' (s41(4)); and
- the evidence or question must relate to a specific instance or instances of the complainant's sexual behaviour.

Protection of witnesses from cross examination by accused in person

Sections 34–39 YJCEA 1999 set out restrictions against the accused cross examining certain categories of witnesses in person. Section 34 covers complainants in sexual offences. Section 35 covers complainants and child witnesses who may not be complainants for specified offences. Section 36 gives the court a discretion to extend such protection to other witnesses who may not be covered by these two sections but does not cover a witness who is a co-defendant. Section 38 allows for defence representation for the purposes of cross examination in the situations covered by these sections and s39 specifies that if a defendant in a trial on indictment is prevented from cross examining a witness in person under ss34, 35, or 36 the judge must give such a warning to the jury as he or she 'considers necessary to ensure that the accused is not prejudiced' by any inferences that might be drawn from the fact that the cross examination is not permitted or that it has been carried out by a legal representative.

Cross examination

Exam tip

In answering essay questions on **s41** you need to be familiar with the fertile academic debate in this area. Birch and Temkin have taken respectively a critical and a supportive stance on **s41** and you should familiarise yourself with their debate in the pages of the *Criminal Law Review* in 2002–3, see References on p 172.

The following questions have arisen in the application of **s41 YJCEA 1999**:

Does s41 breach a defendant's right to a fair trial?

In *R v A* (2001) the House of Lords considered whether **s41** could be operated in compliance with the **Human Rights Act 1998** and in particular **Art 6**. The appellant had been convicted of rape. His defence was consent or in the alternative belief in consent and claimed that he had an earlier continuing and consensual relationship with the complainant. Questioning of the complainant on this was excluded at trial. Before the Court of Appeal, the prosecution accepted that evidence of the earlier relationship was admissible under **s41(3)(a)** in relation to the issue of belief in consent but the Court of Appeal held that it was inadmissible in relation to the issue of consent. It stated that directing the jury that the evidence was solely relevant to belief in consent might result in an unfair trial since the sexual relationship might be relevant to consent as well. The House held that it was possible to read **s41**, particularly **s41(3)(c)**, as implying that evidence would not be inadmissible if it was needed to comply with **Art 6 European Convention on Human Rights (ECHR)**. Thus, logically relevant evidence could be admitted. The case was referred back to the trial judge to determine admissibility on that basis.

In relation to this important case, Emson (2008, p495) comments:

> Section 41(3)(c) has therefore been judicially rewritten to represent the general common law position that the accused may **adduce** or elicit any evidence which is relevant to his defence of consent unless its probative value is insufficiently high when weighed against competing considerations, the most important of which in this context are the importance of protecting the complainant from vexation and preventing the accused from misleading the jury.

Is the allegation of making of a false complaint in the past 'sexual behaviour' for the purposes of cross examination under s41(1)?

In *R v MH* (2002) the Court of Appeal established that making a false allegation is not 'sexual behaviour' under **s41(1)**. However, the section may apply if the evidence relates to actual sexual behaviour as well as the content of the false allegation, see *R v H* (2003).

Is the allegation of making of a false complaint 'impugning the credibility of the complainant' under s41(4)?

In two conjoined appeals, *R v T*; *R v H* (2001) the complainants had allegedly made false allegations of sexual assaults in the past but this evidence was ruled inadmissible at trial since the purpose was to impugn the witness's **credibility**. The appeals were allowed since the questions in both were relevant in the normal non-statutory sense. They were not automatically excluded under s41 even if they went principally to credibility. There must, however, be a proper evidential basis for asserting that the complainant made the statement and that it was untrue.

In *R v Martin* [2004] the Court of Appeal held that s41 did not preclude questions which did not solely go to **credibility** but which supported the defendant's contention that the allegations against him were false.

Note also that the requirements of s100 CJA 2003, see *R v Voller* [2006]. It may be necessary for the defence to seek leave under s100(4) CJA 2003.

✔ Looking for extra marks?

Consider whether the case of *R v Edwards* (1991) would be decided in the same way today. The case involved the complex question of the cross examination of police officers by defence counsel and the application of the principle of the rule of finality to collateral questions. It illustrates the close connection of this with character evidence. In this case, evidence could not be called in rebuttal of a denial by officers of the West Midlands Crime Squad, who were giving evidence that they were not involved in an earlier case where perjury had been alleged, and which had resulted in an acquittal. This was an issue of credit only and was collateral.

It is arguable there will be greater scope for such cross examination under s100(1)(b) CJA 2003, as important explanatory evidence. Emson (2008, p460) calls this 'reverse similar facts'.

✶ Key cases

Case	Facts	Principle and comment
R v Turnbull [1977] QB 224	Police, as a result of information, had kept watch at the site of a planned robbery. A man was recognised by police as Turnbull. He appealed on conviction. The appeal was dismissed.	Other evidence supported the identification and, although the officer had only caught a fleeting glimpse of the defendant, the conviction was safe. Guidelines were set out for judicial directions in cases which depended wholly or substantially on disputed identification evidence.
R v Weeder (1980) 71 Cr App R 228	The victim of an assault had caught sight of his attacker and identified him at a parade. An onlooker also identified two assailants whom she recognised. The judge directed that the jury could take into account each witness's evidence as mutually supportive. The defendant was convicted and appealed. His appeal was dismissed.	One identification can support another as long as the judge warns that even honest witnesses may be mistaken.

Case	Facts	Principle and comment
R v Makanjuola [1995] 1 WLR 1348	The appellant had been convicted of an indecent assault. He had denied the charge at the pre-trial interview and did not testify. His counsel cross examined the complainant to the effect that she had a grudge against the defendant. There was no judicial direction on her testimony. The appeal failed since there was no basis for regarding the complainant as unreliable.	The Court stated that where a witness was demonstrably unreliable the judge might consider whether or not to give a warning. Whether a warning should be issued and in what form was a matter for judicial discretion. Such discretionary warnings decided on a case-by-case basis replace the mandatory warnings removed by statute.
R v Slater [1995] 1 Cr App 584	The defendant had been arrested after his alleged victim had described his unusual build to police. He admitted being present at the scene of the attack but denied participation. There was no **identification parade** and no *Turnbull* warning. He appealed and his appeal was dismissed.	There is not necessarily a need for a *Turnbull* warning when the defendant admits being present at the scene but denies the offence. Rose LJ stated that whether a *Turnbull* direction is required or not depends on the circumstances of the case. Here one factor was the unusual build of the defendant.
R v Burge [1996] 1 Cr App R 163	Two defendants lied about the circumstances of their murder of an elderly man in the course of a robbery. They claimed he had been alive when they left the scene and that the neighbour who was known to them had killed him. The judge gave the jury a warning about the lies told to the police. The defence appealed on the grounds that the warning also ought to have been given in relation to lies told in court. Appeal dismissed since the directions had been adequate.	The Court of Appeal held that a *Lucas* direction should be given: • if accused relies on evidence of alibi; *or* • where the judge directs the jury that the lies may be supporting evidence; *or* • where the prosecution rely on a lie as evidence of guilt; *or* • there is a real danger the jury may treat the lie as evidence of guilt.
R v A [2001] UKHL 25	The appellant had been charged with rape. His defence was consent or in the alternative belief in consent and claimed that he had an earlier continuing and consensual relationship with the complainant. Questioning of the complainant on this was excluded at trial. Before the Court of Appeal the prosecution accepted that evidence of the earlier relationship was admissible under s41(3)(a) in relation to the issue	The House of Lords considered whether s41 could be operated in compliance with the Human Rights Act 1998 and in particular Art 6. The House held that it was possible to read s41, particularly s41(3)(c), as implying that evidence would not be inadmissible if it was needed to comply with Art 6 ECHR. Thus, logically relevant evidence could be admitted.

Key debates

✳✳✳✳✳✳✳✳✳✳

Case	Facts	Principle and comment
continued	of belief in consent but the Court of Appeal held that it was inadmissible in relation to the issue of consent. The House of Lords held that it was admissible. The case was referred back to the trial judge to determine admissibility on that basis.	
R v Forbes [2001] 1 AC 473	The victim of an attempted robbery made a street identification of the defendant. A request for an **identification parade** was refused. The defendant was convicted. The House of Lords rejected his appeal. There should have been an identification parade but in this case the conviction was safe.	A procedure under Code D is mandatory unless the suspect is well known to the witness or there are exceptional circumstances. Note that the wording of Code D now contains the words '...an identification procedure shall be held unless it is not practicable or would serve no useful purpose in proving or disproving whether the suspect was involved in committing the offence. For example, when it is not disputed that the suspect is already well known to the witness who claims to have seen them commit the crime.'
R v Flynn and St John [2008] 2 Cr App R 266	The defendants were convicted of conspiracy to rob. The evidence against them included covert recordings from a probe placed in the van used in the robbery. Police officers claimed the voices on the recording matched those of the defendants which they had heard following arrest. The defendants successfully appealed to the Court of Appeal.	Although it was highly desirable, it was not mandatory, that voice recognition be carried out by experts. Minimum standards had not been observed in this case. Where voice recognition was properly admitted the jury should be permitted to compare the recorded voices with the voices of the defendants if they heard them giving evidence.

⟨99⟩ Key debates

Topic	**Sexual history of complainant in rape trials**
Authors	L Kelly, J Temkin, S Griffiths
Viewpoint	Defence lawyers use a number of methods to try and contravene s41(4) YJCEA 1999. Report recommends (at p76) 'A new exception to the rule of exclusion should be inserted into section 41, allowing for evidence of previous or subsequent sexual behaviour with the accused. This exception could have a time limitation'.
Source	'Section 41: an evaluation of new legislation limiting sexual history evidence in rape trials' Home Office Online Report 2006, London available at http://www.homeoffice.gov.uk/rds/pdfs06/rdsoln2000

Topic	Identification and miscarriages of justice
Author	P Roberts
Viewpoint	Draws on recent psychological research to highlight the continuing dangers of mistakes in identification.
Source	'The Problem of Mistaken Identification'(2004) *International Journal of Evidence and Proof* 100

⑦ Exam questions

Essay question

'It is well known that identification evidence, like confession evidence, has contributed to a significant number of miscarriages of justice.' (A Choo, *Evidence* (OUP, 2009) p153)

Examine whether the current rules and procedures governing the use of identification evidence in criminal trials ensures fairness.

An outline answer is available online at http://www.oxfordtextbooks.co.uk/orc/concentrate/

Problem question

Rory is charged with the attempted rape of Gloria. She reported the incident which, she says took place at a pop festival, to the police several days after it allegedly occurred and there is no forensic evidence. Rory denies the offence. Gloria went home the day after the festival and her mother asked her why she was looking so depressed and whether 'anything had happened at the festival?' She then told her mother that she had been assaulted. When first arrested Rory denied the offence and two days later in an interview with police said that Gloria and he were in her tent chatting and listening to music on their ipods. The defence wish to call evidence that Gloria had made false allegations of rape before.

Advise Rory on evidence.

An outline answer is available at the end of the book.

#9
Opinion evidence

Key Facts

Criminal and civil cases

- The general rule is that courts can hear evidence of fact not opinion but there are a number of exceptions.
- Under the common law expert opinion is admissible where the matter is outside the experience of judge or jury.
- The judge decides on admissibility both if court should be assisted and if expert has the required expertise.
- Expertise is decided on a case by case basis.
- The expert gives opinion on basis of facts which must be proved by admissible evidence.

Criminal cases only

- The common law principle is that an expert cannot give an opinion on the very fact the tribunal has to decide (the ultimate issue rule) but in practice this is often ignored.
- The **Criminal Procedure Rules (CPR) 2005** contain guidance on notice and **disclosure** which is particularly relevant in this area.

Civil cases only

- The **CPR** set out details of how expert evidence is to be presented including the use of court appointed experts.
- The ultimate issue rule has been abolished by **s33(1) Civil Evidence Act 1972**.

Related areas

There is some overlap with the rule against hearsay since it is usually the case that the expert has to base his opinion on material generated out of court which is produced to establish the truth of its contents. In civil cases the rule against hearsay itself has been abolished by Civil Evidence Act 1995. In criminal cases also the rule has been affected by statute. Under s127 Criminal Justice Act (CJA) 2003 the expert may rely at trial on statements prepared by other persons at the judge's discretion. Under s30 CJA 1988 expert reports are admissible with leave if the witness is not attending court. Note also the link with confessions as far as evidence from psychiatrists is concerned.

The assessment: key points

The rule on opinion evidence is historically one of the major exclusionary rules in evidence but it has been much eroded. Expert opinion evidence is the major exception and expert scientific evidence particularly is of significant topical interest. Questions may centre on how misuse of medical evidence in particular has led to miscarriages of justice. It is particularly important here to approach problem questions logically and examine to what extent the opinion evidence is based on general scientific knowledge and to what extent it is eyewitness testimony or hearsay testimony based on what a bystander has said. Even experts may also be acting as ordinary witnesses. You should bear in mind that expert opinion is only that and may be rejected by the jury or the trier of fact in a civil court. This is an area where there is considerable mixture of case law and statute which you should draw on for your authorities. As a result English law has been accused of an overly piecemeal and incoherent approach. This controversy is covered in an outline answer to an essay question below.

Key features and principles

The increasing role of science in criminal and civil investigation has transformed the trial process and the admission of expert evidence is now commonplace. **DNA** in particular plays a key part in criminal appeals, sometimes exonerating those convicted of crimes many years before. This area of evidence law is very topical since flawed evidence by experts is one of the major causes of miscarriages of justice. In other words what happens when experts make mistakes is very serious. It is an area where you need to keep clear in your mind the difference between civil and criminal procedures. It is still dominated by case law and English law has been criticised as being pragmatic as a result and to some extent incoherent by comparison with arguably the more fully reasoned United States' approach. Your answers will also be improved in this area perhaps more than any other by an intelligent reading of serious newspapers as well as academic journals. For example, official or parliamentary reports, such as that by the House of Commons Science and Technology Committee, may well be reviewed in *The Times* or *Guardian* before they reach the scholarly press and your answers to an essay question will benefit by knowledge of their findings.

Although the subject is taught in evidence courses as predominantly on opinion evidence and expert evidence as an exception to that it is arguable that expert evidence forms a field in its own right. Roberts and Zuckerman (2004, p290) point out, 'It is more illuminating to see expert evidence as a topic organised around issues of forensic authority, the transparency of the inferential process, and the durability of trust in the legitimacy of criminal verdicts.' In other words, it is a matter of knowledge as much as opinion, although the fallibility of the knowledge may be an issue. Many of the areas of expertise relevant to trials are in the scientific and medical fields and some understanding of statistics in particular would be useful. Finally, there are a number of areas of current controversy such as the survival of the ultimate issue rule in criminal cases and whether new areas of expertise such as **facial mapping** or **psychological profiling** are appropriate for expert testimony. These will be outlined in this chapter.

Criminal cases
Opinion evidence: the exclusionary rule and exceptions

The rule against the admissibility of opinion is simply stated and based in part on the ideal of appreciation of facts in a judgment by a lay and impartial jury who should not be exposed to a witness who is possibly subjectively biased or afforded too high a status as a specialist. Thus, for example, witnesses should not be asked to give opinions on other witnesses's testimony. The two exceptions to the rule relate to the admissibility of the evidence of experts who will be unlikely to have perceived events at first hand and of lay opinion evidence for certain restricted areas from witnesses who are likely to have first hand knowledge of the circumstances giving rise to the proceedings.

Who is an expert and what areas are appropriate for expert evidence?
Does an expert need formal qualifications?

R v Silverlock (1984): An expert does not need to have professional qualifications. Here a solicitor was allowed to give expert evidence on handwriting which was a hobby he had pursued for a number of years.

R v Stockwell (1993): An expert in facial mapping gave evidence in a trial involving disputed identification evidence on videos of the defendant. It was no bar to admissibility that he did not have any formal qualifications.

How competent does an expert have to be and does he, for example, have to have respect from his peers?

R v Robb (1991): Judicial control of the assessment of whether an expert witness is eligible is apparent in this judgment. An expert on voice recognition, a lecturer in phonetics, gave evidence relying on his own methodology which was not generally approved of by other experts in the field since it did not include a procedure called acoustic analysis. The Court of Appeal held, however, that his opinion was admissible although his methods did not have majority approval in the relevant scientific community. The Court attached importance to judicial directions that the jury were entitled to reject the evidence. This remains a controversial decision in particular since the jury were not made aware that the expert's methodology was not widely accepted.

What areas are appropriate for expert testimony?

The following cases give an indication of the sort of considerations which the court will address:

R v Turner (1975): T was charged with murder of his girlfriend. He claimed the killing was a reaction to hearing the news that she had been unfaithful and that her child was not fathered by him. H wished to call expert evidence as to his mental state. This was rightly denied since the question of provocation came within ordinary human experience on which the jury could come to a decision without expert help.

R v Stockwell (1993): This case in contrast to *Turner* shows the sort of situation where expert evidence is admitted. It was held that the evidence was properly admitted since it covered an area that was relevant evidence outside the experience of the court.

Revision tip

It is a good strategy to be familiar with the tests set out in the leading cases. *Stockwell* (for facts see p 138) is authority for the following additional propositions which are covered below:

- an expert may be competent if he possesses the necessary expertise even if he does not possess formal qualifications in the specific area;
- expert evidence may be admissible on new areas of knowledge if it does include relevant material that is beyond the jury's experience; and
- evidence may be admissible on the ultimate issue as long as it is made clear to the jury that they can reject the evidence.

Is expert evidence admissible as to the **credibility** of a witness?

The general rule is that expert evidence on **credibility** is not admissible since the jury can come to a decision. However, this is subject to two somewhat overlapping exceptions. Exceptionally, psychiatric evidence may be admissible to help the jury decide which of two defendants is more likely to be telling the truth.

Criminal cases

✳✳✳✳✳✳✳✳✳✳

First exception: who to believe

R v Lowery (1975): Two men were accused of murdering a girl. Each maintained that the other had done the killing. L's co-defendant called a psychiatrist to give evidence that L's personality made it more likely he was the killer. The Privy Council held the evidence had been rightly admitted. The psychiatrist's evidence was relevant to show that the co-defendant's version of the facts was more likely than L's and to negative L's case. This is an exception to the usual rule that expert evidence is not admissible on matters for which the jury requires no assistance.

You must be careful how you cite this Privy Council case since it is of limited authority. Note that the Court of Appeal in *Turner* (1975) (at p 842) was of the view that this case had 'been decided on its special facts. We do not consider that it is an authority for the proposition that in all cases psychologists and psychiatrists can be called to prove the probability of the accused's veracity. If any such rule was applied in our courts, trial by psychiatrists would be likely to take the place of trial by jury and magistrates. We do not find that prospect attractive and the law does not at present provide for it.'

Second exception: mental disability

Toohey v MPC (1965): T was allegedly the victim of an assault. He had been found by police in a hysterical state. The House of Lords held that expert medical evidence as to his mental state was admissible and was relevant to his **credibility** and to the fact in issue, whether the assault had happened. The House stated, '... when a witness through physical (in which I include mental) disease or abnormality is not capable of giving a true or reliable account to the jury, it must surely be allowable for medical science to reveal this vital hidden fact to them ...'

The difference here amounted to what was considered to be whether an objective reason existed for the difficulty the witness had in telling the truth.

✅ *Looking for extra marks?*

You will impress the examiners if you link your knowledge of confessions to that of expert evidence. A key question is the extent of deviation from the norm. A related area to that of expert evidence and witness **credibility** is whether expert evidence is admissible in a *voir dire* on the question of whether a confession should be admitted or not, or at full trial as to whether a confession is likely to be reliable or not. Again the key question is whether there is evidence suggesting mental impairment, in which case expert evidence may be allowed. This was held to be so in one of the most notorious miscarriages of justice in recent years, that involving Judith Ward whose suggestible personality had led her to confess to IRA terrorist acts she had not committed (*R v Ward* (1993)). By contrast in *R v Everett* (1988) expert evidence was not admissible because there was no evidence of mental handicap or retardation so as to put the defendant outside the normal range of intelligence.

Can an expert give evidence on the very issue on which that the jury/ court must pronounce?

The ultimate issue rule at common law prevented all witnesses from testifying on matters that should properly belong to the trier of fact. In practice it is often applied flexibly as the case of *Stockwell* (see above) illustrates. There the expert gave evidence on disputed identification.

DPP v A&B Chewing Gum Ltd (1968): The defendants were charged under the Obscene Publications Act 1959 with publishing so-called battle cards. The magistrates refused to allow the prosecution to call experts in child psychology to show that the cards would have a tendency to deprave or corrupt children. The Court of Appeal held that the evidence was admissible. Lord Parker CJ observed (p 164):

> ... with the advance of science more and more inroads have been made into the old common law principles. Those who practise in the criminal courts see every day cases of experts being called on the question of diminished responsibility, and although technically the final question, 'Do you think he was suffering from diminished responsibility?' is strictly inadmissible, it is allowed time and time again without any objection.

Note, however, the limitations of this decision since the Court was of the view that if the case had only concerned adults, expert evidence should not have been admitted.

How does the court approach new areas of knowledge and expertise?

In essence the list of areas for which expert evidence is admissible is not closed. The test remains whether it is within the general experience of the trier of facts. There is however not surprisingly somewhat of a conservative view as to what are valid areas of new knowledge. On this view, some of the hesitation about admitting evidence of psychiatrists is not only about encroaching on the proper province of the jury but also scepticism about the validity of this relatively new science. Thus, for example, in *R v Weightman* (1991) at para 297 the court referred to the undesirability of admitting such evidence to help the jury decide on the reliability of a confession. The jury did not need to hear a 'psychiatrist talking about "emotional superficiality" and "impaired capacity to develop and sustain deep or enduring relationships"'.

Consider the following contrasting examples to see how the courts approach this:

R v Luttrell and others (2004): The Court of Appeal was prepared to accept evidence from a lip-reading expert since the tests for admissibility had been satisfied. They were that:

- the evidence was relevant and outside of the jury's experience;
- study or experience gave the opinion of the witness an authority that those not so qualified did not have;
- the witness was qualified to express an opinion;
- the judge gave the appropriate warnings; and
- it was not necessary that the results should be verifiable under cross examination.

By contrast, other areas are not appropriate for expert evidence. *R v Gilfoyle* (2001) is a controversial case which at the time of writing is being remitted to the Criminal Cases Review Commission. One issue which the Court of Appeal had earlier addressed was whether evidence of a 'psychological autopsy' was admissible. This would have been given in relation to the victim's mental state to help the court decide if she had taken her own life. The Court of Appeal agreed with the trial judge that this evidence should not be admitted. The court commented that '... unstructured and speculative conclusions are not the stuff of which admissible expert evidence is made'. There were no acceptable standards by which to assess the work. The question is, therefore, how reliable is the evidence? Here it was so unreliable as to have no probative value. In *Luttrell* (2004) it was probative enough to be admitted and then the weight to be attached to it was a question for the jury.

Revision Tip

This is clearly an area which is rapidly changing as formerly novel areas of expertise become mainstream. You should read as widely as you can to keep an eye on new fields of potential expertise. It is helpful to have an awareness of the way science progresses generally. No procedure is infallible. One key question is that the expert must be able to demonstrate the reproducibility of the experimental results. However, there is always the proviso that later research may prove the method wrong. *R v Dallagher* (2003) is a useful case where the Court of Appeal implicitly accepted that **ear-printing** was a possible field of expertise even though the method used was questionable.

How is expert evidence given?

Criminal cases

Two statutory sections cover the presentation of expert evidence. **Section 30(1) CJA 1988** essentially provides an exception to the rule against hearsay for expert reports. It defines an expert report as 'evidence of any fact or opinion of which the person making it could have given oral evidence'. It provides that an 'expert report shall be admissible as evidence in criminal proceedings, whether or not the person making it attends to give oral evidence in the proceedings'. If the person making the report is not giving oral evidence the written report is only admissible with the leave of the court. In giving leave the court has to have regard:

- to the contents of the report;
- the reasons the person making the report is not giving oral evidence;
- any risk of unfairness to the accused caused by the admission or the exclusion of the report; and
- any other relevant circumstances.

The **CJA 2003** includes sections relevant to expert evidence. **Section 118(8)** preserves the common law rules under which, in criminal proceedings, an expert witness may draw on the body of expertise relevant to his field. In **R v Abadom** (1983) the Court of Appeal held that expert opinion was admissible although the expert had relied on statistics supplied by the Home Office. The expert was entitled to rely on his research in forming his opinion and such evidence did not violate the rule against hearsay.

Section 127 CJA 2003 allows an expert to base an opinion on a statement prepared by another who had personal knowledge of the matters stated and which was prepared for the purposes of criminal proceedings. The accompanying Explanatory Note makes it clear that the provision is designed to address the problem which arises where information that the expert relies upon is outside his or her personal experience and cannot be proved by other admissible evidence. Thus, the rules about advance notice are amended so as to require advance notice of the name of any person who has prepared information on which the expert has relied. In summary, an expert's opinion may be based on statements he or she has not prepared if the following conditions are met:

- the statement was prepared for the purposes of criminal proceedings; and
- any person who prepared the statement had, or may reasonably be supposed to have had, personal knowledge of the matters stated.

You will see that the provisions are not dissimilar to those relating to the admissibility of business documents.

The **Criminal Procedure Rules** have introduced new measures based on those in civil cases (see below). According to Tapper (2007, p 578) the main differences are:

- not the same emphasis on restricting expert evidence;
- clear requirement to furnish details of facts upon which evidence is based; and
- joint expert applies only in case of co-defendants.

✅ Looking for extra marks?

Handwriting as a form of identification makes a not infrequent appearance in problem questions. Your answer will be improved if you are able to distinguish between three types of situation in relation to disputed handwriting: eyewitness testimony, opinion evidence, and comparison of handwriting.

1. It is relatively uncontroversial that, for example, a witness may testify that he saw someone sign a document.

2. A lay witness may testify to an opinion that a piece of writing is that of a specific person. He might do that on the basis of letters received for example. In the words of a nineteenth century case, *Doe d Mudd v Suckermore* (1837), 'The servant who has habitually carried letters addressed by me to others has an opportunity of obtaining knowledge of my writing though he never saw me write or received a letter from me.'

3. The final question of comparison of handwriting is more complex. Under **s8 Criminal Procedure Act 1865** (which applies to civil and criminal trials) where there is a dispute over authorship, a document proved to have been written by the person in question may be

compared with the disputed piece. Although evidence on the comparison may be given by an expert or a lay person, case law has established that in criminal trials a judge should not invite the jury to make a comparison without expert guidance. See *R v Tilley* [1961]. (For a full discussion on this, see Tapper (2007, pp720–721.)

Civil cases

This is covered extensively by statute. Key sections are as follows under the **Civil Procedure Rules (CPR) 1998, Civil Evidence Act (CEA) 1972,** and **Civil Evidence Act (CEA) 1995.** Significant changes were made to the **CPR** as a result of the Woolf Report which were aimed at reducing the numbers and consequential expense of expert reports. The test for admissibility is set out in **CPR 1998 1–6** (see below). In essence the admissibility of evidence is more strictly controlled by the court than is the case in criminal proceedings. The presumption also is that evidence will be given by written report.

Figure 9.1 Civil proceedings: procedure for admissibility of expert evidence

Provision	Overview of the provisions relating to civil proceedings only
s 2 CEA 1972	Rules of court may be made to regulate the admissibility and presentation of expert reports.
s3(2) CEA 1972	Where a person is called as a witness his opinion on any relevant matter on which he is not qualified to give expert evidence is admissible if that statement is made by way of conveying relevant facts.
	[Note that this provision in effect abolishes the 'ultimate issue rule' in civil proceedings.]
rr35.1–6 CPR 1998	Expert evidence is restricted to that which is reasonably required to resolve the proceedings and the court has power to restrict expert evidence and require that it be given in a written report. No party may call an expert as a witness without the court's permission. A party may put written questions to an expert instructed by another party.
	The expert has an overriding duty to the court.
rr35.7–14 CPR 1998	The court has power to direct that evidence is to be given by a single joint expert. If the parties cannot agree who should be the expert the court may appoint one.
	Each party may give instructions to the single joint expert.
	A party who fails to disclose an expert's report may not use the report at trial or call the expert to give evidence orally unless the court gives permission.
CPR 1998 Practice Direction 35	The expert has a paramount duty to the court.

Lay opinion evidence

Civil proceedings

This area is dealt with under s392 CEA 1972. Where a person is called as a witness in any civil proceedings a statement or opinion by him on any relevant matter on which he is not qualified to give expert evidence, if made by way of conveying relevant facts personally perceived by him, is admissible as evidence of what he perceived.

This has replaced the common law, making it possible for non-expert opinion evidence to be given on any issue.

Criminal proceedings

In practice it is often impossible for a witness's testimony to avoid making inferences from facts which may take the form of opinions. The common sense practice is therefore that witnesses can give opinions when this is the accepted way of relaying information on what had been observed. Such matters include most frequently identification evidence, and the speed of vehicles. The fine dividing line between fact and opinion is illustrated in the following case.

R v Davies (1962): In this case, which involved driving while unfit through alcohol, the lay witness was allowed to give his opinion as to whether the defendant had been drinking. He could give an account of the primary facts which had formed the basis of the opinion. He was *not* allowed to testify whether the defendant was unfit to drive for two reasons. Firstly, because such an opinion could only be given by an expert and secondly, because this was the very issue the court was to determine (see the ultimate issue, below).

✅ Looking for extra marks?

Your answers to essay questions will as always be improved by wide reading. It helps to have a historical sense by, for example, showing that the search for infallibility in science is a chimera, eg fingerprint evidence is not flawless. Most commentators point to the difficulty of jurors understanding complex science, eg *Adams* (1996) where the court said, in rejecting the admission of Bayes Theorem that trials are about common sense, not mathematical reasoning.

✳ Key cases

Case	Facts	Principle and comment
DPP v A&BC Chewing Gum Ltd [1968] 1 QB 159	The defendants were charged under the Obscene Publications Act 1959 with publishing so-called battle cards. The magistrates refused to allow the prosecution	Lord Parker CJ observed at p 165: 'with the advance of science more and more inroads have been made into the old common law principles. Those who practise in

Key cases

✳✳✳✳✳✳✳✳✳✳

Case	Facts	Principle and comment
continued	to call experts in child psychology to show that the cards would have a tendency to deprave or corrupt children. The Court of Appeal held that the evidence was admissible.	the criminal courts see every day cases of experts being called on the question of diminished responsibility, and although technically the final question "Do you think he was suffering from diminished responsibility?" is strictly inadmissible, it is allowed time and time again without any objection.'
R v Chard (1971) 56 Cr App R 268	At C's trial for murder, his counsel sought to **adduce** the report of a prison doctor to the effect that C had no mental disorder but had had no intention to kill. The judge's decision to exclude the doctor's report was upheld on appeal.	Where there was no evidence of any mental disorder and the defendant was entirely normal, there was no room for expert medical evidence on the defendant's intent. That was a matter for the jury to decide.
R v Lowery [1974] AC 85	Two men were accused of murdering a girl. Each maintained that the other had done the killing. L's co-defendant called a psychiatrist to give evidence that L's personality made it more likely he was the killer. The Privy Council held the evidence had been rightly admitted.	The psychiatrist's evidence was relevant to show that the co-defendant's version of the facts was more likely than L's and to negative L's case. This is an exception to the usual rule that expert evidence is not admissible on matters for which the jury requires no assistance.
R v Turner [1975] QB 834	T admitted having killed his girlfriend, but claimed he had been provoked by her saying he was not the father of her expected child. He sought to call a psychiatrist to say that he was not violent by nature but that his personality was such that he could have been provoked in the circumstances and that he was likely to be telling the truth. The Court of Appeal upheld the exclusion of the psychiatric evidence.	The evidence was irrelevant because T's mental health was not in issue. There was no general rule that psychiatric evidence was admissible to prove that a defendant was likely to be telling the truth. His veracity and the likelihood of his being provoked were matters for the jury.
R v Gilfoyle [2001] 2 Cr App R 57	G's wife was found hanging in the garage of the family home. He maintained she had committed suicide, but was convicted of her murder. On appeal he sought to adduce expert psychiatric evidence to cast light on the deceased's state of mind. The	An expert's opinion was admissible to provide the court with scientific information that was likely to be outside the jury's experience. But the jury could form an opinion unaided on the proven facts. Expert evidence of how someone's mind operated at the time of an

Case	Facts	Principle and comment
continued	court refused to admit the evidence	offence was inadmissible unless there was an issue of insanity or diminished responsibility.
R v Clark [2003] EWCA Crim 1020	Both her children having suffered cot deaths, the defendant was convicted of murder. Evidence suggesting that the deaths were natural was not disclosed and a leading paediatrician testified that the odds of two such deaths by accident was greater than those of tipping the Grand National winner four years in a row. The Court of Appeal overturned the conviction.	Although the appeal turned on non-**disclosure** of prosecution medical evidence the Court of Appeal expressed concern about the use of statistical evidence. Before admitting statistical generalisations in evidence, the court should examine the evidence carefully to make sure the jury are not misled.
R v Hodges [2003] 2 Cr App R 15	At his trial for drug dealing, a police officer was allowed to give evidence that the amount of drugs found was more than would be required for H's own use – allowing the jury to infer that he was a dealer. The admission of the police officer's evidence was upheld on appeal.	An experienced police officer could act as an expert witness, particularly as he could be cross examined and evidence could be called to rebut his evidence.
R v Cannings [2004] EWCA Crim 01	Another case, like Clark, involving multiple sudden infant deaths.	Where expert opinion was seriously divided about the causes of the multiple infant deaths and there was no evidence other than the fact of the deaths to suggest murder, the prosecution should not be brought.
R v Somanathan [2006] 1 WLR 1885	S, a Hindu priest, was convicted on two counts of rape. Two women other than the victim gave evidence of his inappropriate behaviour towards her, and the judge allowed evidence from a professor of Hinduism that it would be very difficult for a Tamil woman to bring a rape charge against her priest. The appeal court said the evidence had been rightly admitted under s101 CJA 2003.	S had put himself forward not only as having no previous convictions but also as having a good reputation as a priest. This had opened the door to evidence of previous misconduct. The evidence went not only to his **credibility** but also to his propensity to commit the offence charged.

⑨ Key debates

Topic	How poor understanding of scientific evidence has caused wrong decisions in criminal proceedings.
Author	Gary Edmond
Viewpoint	Argues that there is an idealised view of scientific evidence particularly by the appeal court which can be addressed by exploring the conceptual disparity between the assessment of scientific evidence used to acquit and that used to convict.
Source	'Constructing Miscarriages of Justice: Misunderstanding Scientific Evidence in High Profile Criminal Appeals'(2002) 22: 1 OJLS 53

Topic	The rules on admissibility and treatment of expert evidence.
Author	Andrew Roberts
Viewpoint	The English approach in this area lacks principle and coherence. More training of court personnel is needed.
Source	'Drawing on Expertise: Legal Decision-making and the Reception of Expert Evidence' [2008] Crim LR 443

⑦ Exam questions

Essay question

'The principal weakness in the English law concerning the reception of expert evidence is that its development has been based on pragmatism rather than principle.' (A Roberts, 'Drawing on Expertise: Legal Decision Making and the Reception of Expert Evidence' [2008] Crim LR 443, p 443)

Assess the validity of this observation in relation to criminal trials.

An outline answer is available at the end of the book.

Problem question

Pat is suing the police for trespass to the person arising out of her treatment when she was arrested at a demonstration. She claims to have suffered serious injuries to her hip. She plans to produce expert medical evidence from Dr Sprog which suggests her injuries were inflicted by deliberate blows. The police plan to produce expert evidence from Mr Clifford that she most likely suffers from brittle bones. Clifford is basing his evidence on experiments conducted by professors at an American University. The police also want to produce evidence from a psychiatrist, Clementine Friend, that Pat is a habitual fantasist and is not likely to be telling the truth. Advise the parties.

An outline answer is available online at http://www.oxfordtextbooks.co.uk/orc/concentrate/.

#10
Public interest immunity

Key Facts

- Public interest immunity (PII) is a doctrine whereby potentially relevant evidence may be excluded at trial.
- Exclusion of evidence on grounds of public interest immunity (PII) is a recognition of the public interest in non-**disclosure** which outweighs that of access to evidence of the parties to the proceedings.
- The principle mainly relates to non-**disclosure** of documents rather than oral testimony.
- A claim for non-**disclosure** may be made by the parties, by the court, or by third parties including the state or a public body.
- In criminal proceedings **disclosure** is governed by the **Criminal Procedure and Investigations Act 1996** and the **Criminal Procedure Rules 2005**.
- Non-disclosure claims may be made for a specific document (contents claim) or a series of documents (a class claim).
- Areas of public interest which are covered by possible PII claims include national security, defence and foreign policy, the identity of police informers, protection of children, and confidential records held by public bodies.
- PII claims primarily occur in civil cases. The main area in criminal cases is the protection of informers.
- The court may scrutinise and in principle reject claims for non-**disclosure**.

Related areas

Since the outcome of a PII claim may be non-**disclosure** of a document it has affinities with legal professional privilege, under which, principle information may not be disclosed at trial in order to protect lawyer–client confidentiality. There are, however, major differences between the two: firstly, legal professional privilege belongs to the parties to the proceedings, it cannot be claimed by the court; and secondly, a claim for privilege may be waived by the individual to whom it belongs.

Public interest immunity forms a part of a wider area which is procedural as well as evidential in scope. That is the question of **disclosure**, or pre-trial exchange of evidence by the parties. Most undergraduate evidence courses do not discuss this in detail since it is very detailed and to an extent is more appropriate for the law professional course. It will not be covered here except in so far as it relates to the specific issue of PII.

A final related area is that of allegedly improperly obtained evidence since in criminal cases, claims for non-**disclosure** are sometimes made in response to allegations that police undercover activities have led to **entrapment**.

The assessment: key points

Your public law course may have included a consideration of PII since it is as much an aspect of administrative law as of the law of evidence. Thus, although it is a fairly technical question of whether certain evidence should be presented at trial, it also raises fundamental human rights' issues about freedom of information and access to justice. You may well then have an essay question on the constitutional issues raised by PII. These may be relevant to both civil and criminal matters. Archival research, for example, has shown that the national security claim in the landmark case of *Duncan v Cammell Laird* (1942) may have had as much to do with bureaucratic considerations of litigation management as protecting the nation in time of war (see Spencer (2004)).

Key features and principles

The common law doctrine of public interest immunity is an attempt to reconcile two interests or rights, namely the right to a fair trial and the public interest in protecting a public good such as the safety of the state or the protection of the identity of those who inform to the authorities about an individual's wrongdoing.

Public interest immunity used to be called **Crown privilege** and the new name indicates that it is open to any body or group to apply for non-disclosure. Until the landmark case of *Conway v Rimmer* (1968) the courts would not challenge a public interest immunity claim which was normally made by a minister. In *Conway*, however, the court inspected the documents and denied the application. It is arguable, however, that the earlier approach as applied in *Duncan v Cammell Laird* (1942) still applies in cases of national security. The European Court of Human Rights (ECtHR) has examined a number of cases where a challenge has been made to an order for non-disclosure on the grounds that there is consequently a threat to the right to a fair trial enshrined in Art 6.

Landmark cases

Most of the landmark cases are in civil law and the current approach in criminal law is very much regulated by statute rather than case law. The civil and criminal law positions therefore have very much diverged in recent years. Nonetheless, leading civil law cases may have an effect in criminal evidential law particularly, for example, in defining the scope of a national security claim. Similarly, the grounds of claims are similar and therefore the categories set out in the civil case of *Duncan v Cammell Laird* (1942) apply also in criminal cases. In essence of course the two areas are very different since it would never be appropriate to deny a defendant in a criminal case information which might raise doubt as to their guilt. On the other hand the balancing act between the public and individual interest does not raise such momentous issues in civil cases. The following chronologies set out the landmarks in civil and criminal evidence separately.

Civil law cases

Year	Event	Comment
1942	*Duncan v Cammell Laird*	Possible grounds of PII claims include 'material injurious to national defence, diplomatic relations, or where the practice of keeping a class of documents secret is necessary for the proper functioning of the public service'. The latter may include the identity of informers both to the police and other public bodies.
1968	*Conway v Rimmer*	Judges should inspect document (s) and make final decision on **disclosure**. *Duncan* was overruled on this point but it is arguable that it still applies in national security cases. The test was set out for decisions on disclosure which is that the judge must weigh up the competing benefits and disadvantages to the public and the litigant.
1947	**Crown Proceedings Act 1947**	Act preserves the right for authorities to claim **crown privilege**.
1979	*D v NSPCC*	Sources that need to be protected include those involving authorised bodies as well as government department.
1980	*Burmah Oil Co Ltd v Bank of England*	There was no class of documents that was totally immune from production.
1983	*Air Canada v Secretary of State for Trade and Industry*	The party seeking disclosure should not embark on a fishing expedition but should demonstrate the potential relevance of the evidence before judge inspects.

Key features and principles

✱✱✱✱✱✱✱✱✱✱✱

Year	Event	Comment
1995	*R v Chief Constable of West Midlands Police ex p Wiley*	Police Complaints Comission (PCC) documents did not belong to an immune class and there had to be compelling evidence before a new class could be identified.
1996	**Lord Chancellor's Announcement**	The Lord Chancellor made a statement that the former division between class and contents would no longer apply to central government bodies. (Other bodies can however continue to make class claims.)

Criminal law cases

Year	Event	Comment
1890	*Marks v Beyfus*	A defendant could not normally require that a police informer's identity be revealed to him. However, if the identity is necessary to establish innocence it will be revealed.
1986	*R v Rankine*	PII may be claimed for police observation points.
1993	*R v Ward*	PII applied in criminal cases applied and the court must make the final decision on the claim to withhold evidence. A failure to do so would jeopardise the right to a fair trial.
1994	*R v Keane*	The case set out the modern test for **disclosure** of identity of informers. If the material may prove that the accused is innocent the court should order disclosure.
1992	**Matrix Churchill trial**	The criminal prosecution of businessmen charged with sending arms to Iraq collapsed after the judge ordered disclosure of government documents for which PII had been claimed.
1996	**Report of Scott Inquiry**	The Report criticised government ministers over the Matrix Churchill PII applications and doubted whether class claims could be made in criminal cases.
1996	**Criminal Procedure and Investigations Act 1996**	The Act set out procedure for PII claims.
2001	**Auld Review of Criminal Courts in England and Wales**	The Review recommended (Recommendation 206) use of special independent counsel in PII cases to protect defendants' interests.
2004	*R v H*	For details see below.

The following key features govern the law on public interest immunity:

- in both criminal and civil cases the courts are the final arbiters on disclosure;
- public interest immunity may be claimed by non-state bodies; and
- class claims should be rarely made in criminal cases but may be appropriate on occasion in civil suits.

The two tables at Fig 10.1 and Fig 10.2 set out the statutory provisions which specify the procedure for making claims in criminal and civil cases.

Figure 10.1 Statutory procedure for claiming PII in criminal cases

Authority	Procedure
s23(1) CPIA 1996 and para 6.12 Code of Practice (2005)	Lists 13 categories of 'sensitive material' which might be appropriate for PII claims.
Criminal Procedure Rules Part 25	Prosecution make an application under ss2(6), 7A(8), or 8(5) CPIA 1996. These require: <ul><li>notification to the defence;</li><li>specification of the nature of the material subject to PII; and</li><li>both parties to make representations to the judge. BUT procedure must be *ex parte* in case of sensitive material and in some extreme cases the defence may not even know of the application.</li></ul>
s15(3) CPIA 1996	Judge must keep any decision for non-**disclosure** under review as trial proceeds.

Fig 10.2 Statutory procedure for claiming PII in civil cases

Authority	Procedure
CPR 31.3	Party to whom a document has been **disclosed** has a right to inspect it unless the disclosing party has a right or duty to withhold inspection.
CPR 31.9	Party can make *ex parte* application to withhold existence of document on grounds of PII.

✔ Looking for extra marks?

Many of the criminal cases are on informers and you should be clear that this relates not only to the police. Whistleblowers can be carrying out a civic duty and they can operate in many areas, not just that of the police. *D v NSPCC* (1978) concerned informers on child abuse and in *Rogers v Home Secretary* (1973) the Gaming Board was informed secretly on the suitability of applicants for Gaming Licences.

Key features and principles

✱✱✱✱✱✱✱✱✱✱

Article 6 and PII

Article 6 European Convention on Human Rights (ECHR) requires **equality of arms** before the parties and so potentially withholding information could jeopardise the defendant. However, since English law requires that a defendant cannot have a fair trial without prosecution disclosure of evidence it has usually been taken to be Convention compliant. The rights under Art 6 are not absolute.

A number of Strasbourg cases have examined English law:

Rowe and Davis v UK (2000): Three men had been convicted of a series of robberies on the basis of information supplied by police informers. On appeal the defendants sought disclosure of the identity of the informers. This was refused but the Court of Appeal did see the documents and still upheld the convictions. An informer had been paid and all had been involved in the offences and granted immunity from prosecution. The ECtHR found a violation of Art 6 in that the principle of equality of arms had been breached. The matter was referred back to the Court of Appeal which quashed the convictions. The ECtHR accepted that it is possible in principle for non-disclosure by the prosecution not to jeopardise a fair trial. The decision on **disclosure** must be made by the judge.

Permitting non-disclosure may not violate Art 6. The decision, however, must be made by the judge, not the prosecution. Here the procedures used when deciding on disclosure did violate Art 6.

Jasper v UK; Fitt v UK (2000): **Ex parte** PII procedure was not here a violation of Art 6 because the defence were able to make representations to the judge outlining the nature of case. In addition, the judge, after the *ex parte* hearing on disclosure, monitored this during the trial. If circumstances changed he could order disclosure at that later stage. Contrast this situation with that in *Edwards*.

Edwards v UK; Lewis v UK (2004): Both E and L in separate proceedings claimed they had been entrapped by the police; in E's case in connection with drug dealing and in L's case in connection with counterfeit money. The prosecution successfully made *ex parte* application to prevent certain evidence from being disclosed. The ECtHR held there had not been a fair trial. The judge was the tribunal of fact on the issue of **entrapment** and the *ex parte* procedure here violated Art 6. The accused were not able to present their case effectively. Undisclosed evidence may have been relevant to a question of fact to be determined by trial judge. The case led to a review by the Court of Appeal in *R v H* (2004), see below.

It seems that any defects in the trial procedure may be remedied by the Court of Appeal, although as Murphy (2008, p 422) comments. 'It may be, however that *ex parte* applications to the Court of Appeal should be even harder to justify than at first instance.'

PII and informers in criminal cases

In *R v H, R v C* (2004) the appellants, who had been convicted of conspiracy to supply heroin, demanded disclosure of details of police undercover surveillance relating to the charges. The judge had ruled in favour of the appointment of a special counsel. The House of Lords dismissed the appeal. On the facts this was not a borderline case where a public interest immunity hearing should be held. The judge had not considered the nature of the material that was the subject matter of the PII claim and so the decision to seek the appointment of special counsel was premature. In this case Lord Bingham set out the test for considering PII claims in criminal cases in the light of the Strasbourg Court's decision in *Edwards*:

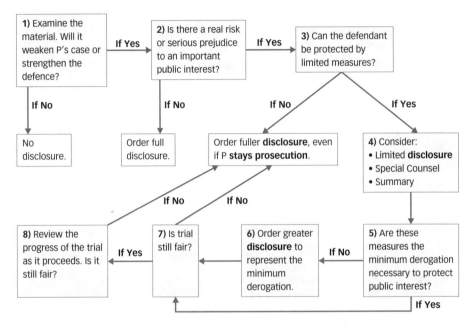

Figure 10.3 Diagramatic representation of test for **disclosure** set out in *R v H; R v C* [2004]

Revision tip

There has been much recent discussion about the future of class claims. You need to distinguish here the approach of the government and the approach of other bodies. You first of all need to examine the nature of the public interest which is at stake. If the claim is potential damage to national security a class claim may well prevail. As far as government documents are concerned the Government has stated it will rarely make class claims.

Two cases, *R v Chief Constable of the West Midland Police ex p Wiley* (1995) and *Taylor v Anderton* (1995) illustrate a more flexible approach in relation to non-central government bodies. They illustrate what Emson (2008, p341) has called a 'wider jurisprudential move away from blanket immunity' while reserving the possibility of class claims in *Taylor* to encourage candour. Even police informer cases are treated on a case-by-case basis.

Key cases
✱✱✱✱✱✱✱✱✱

✅ Looking for extra marks?

In cases involving police informers the examiner may require you to demonstrate your knowledge of waiver in this area. Authority for the proposition that even if a police informer is willing to have his identity revealed the final decision is still a matter for the court is found in the case of *Savage v Chief Constable of Hampshire* [1977]. There might still be wider interest at stake. A first rate answer also would show a refinement of this approach in the case of class-based claims. The court accepted here that, if the claim was in respect of a particular body of people such as the occupants of premises, the willingness of an individual to be identified should be considered in pronouncements on disclosure since the primary aim of the class claim no longer applied.

✳ Key cases

Case	Facts	Principle
Public interest immunity		
CIVIL CASES		
Duncan v Cammell Laird [1942] AC 624	A Royal Navy submarine sank on her maiden voyage in Liverpool Bay with loss of 99 lives. Dependants of the civilian victims requested disclosure of official documents to assist their suit for damages against the shipowners which had been commissioned by the Admiralty. The Government refused and the House of Lords held that the courts could not look behind a properly constituted claim for **Crown privilege**.	Although *Conway v Rimmer* overruled part of this judgment it is arguable that the courts will still not look behind claims made on the specific grounds of national security.
Conway v Rimmer [1968] AC 910	C, a probationer police officer, sued a police superintendent for malicious prosecution. **Crown privilege** was claimed against a demand for the production of probation reports. The House of Lords allowed their production, there being nothing in the documents which was detrimental to the proper functioning of the police force or to the public interest.	Following this case a claim for PII is not conclusive of the issue. The court will inspect the documents and attempt to balance the public interest against **disclosure** with that of the interests of justice in disclosure.
D v NSPCC [1978] AC 171	A mother requested the identity of the person who had made a complaint to the NSPCC about her cruelty to her child. The allegation turned out to be baseless. The House of Lords stated that the public interest in the need for a flow of informers meant the disclosure should not be granted.	This case is an important illustration of the principle that authorised bodies as well as central government departments may claim PII.
Burmah Oil v Bank of England [1980] AC 1090	In challenging a transfer of shares to the Bank after a rescue operation, the oil company's request for disclosure of documents was opposed by the government. The House of Lords held that the documents, which concerned high policy, were not relevant to the case. The House	This decision makes it clear that even high level policy documents might not be immune from **disclosure**.

Case	Facts	Principle
continued	however firmly rejected the argument based on candour as a reason for non-disclosure.	
Air Canada v Secretary of State for Trade (No 2) [1983] 2 AC 394	The airline claimed **disclosure** of ministerial documents relating to increases in charges which it was alleged were *ultra vires*. The House of Lords held that the party seeking disclosure must present a convincing case for it. This had not been made here. The fact that the documents were Cabinet minutes did not mean they were immune from disclosure.	The effect of this case is to put more obstacles in the way of the litigant who wants to secure **disclosure**.
R v Chief Constable of West Midlands Police ex p Wiley [1995] 1 AC 274	The question arose in relation to potential proceedings against two Chief Constables whether their documents created for the purpose of an investigation into the police under Part IX PACE were covered by class immunity. The House held there was here no compelling reason to create such a class immunity. There could however be a contents claim.	In *Taylor v Anderton* [1995] in another claim against the police the Court of Appeal accepted that there may be a class claim for a subset of documents dealing with police reports on professional colleagues or members of the public.

CRIMINAL CASES

Case	Facts	Principle
Marks v Beyfus (1890) 25 QBD 494	M sued for malicious prosecution and sought discovery from the DPP of the identity of the person who had informed against him. The DPP's refusal to disclose was upheld.	Most of the criminal cases involving PII concern police informers. The court recognised, however, that if disclosure was necessary to ensure a fair trial it should prevail.
R v Rankine (1986) 83 Cr App R 18	An alleged drug dealer was watched from an observation point by police. At his trial he requested details of the post. The Court of Appeal refused.	The reasoning is analogous to that dealing with police informers and the same test for disclosure applied.
R v Ward [1993] 1 WLR 619	A mentally disturbed woman who fantasised about associating with the IRA had confessed to bombings she did not commit. Government scientists had withheld material on the basis that it might damage the prosecution case. The Court of Appeal held that this was an improper ground of PII.	This notorious miscarriage of justice case led to a change in the procedures for claiming PII in criminal cases.
R v Keane [1994] 1 WLR 746	K was charged with counterfeiting notes. He argued he had been tricked. The Court of Appeal upheld the decision to refuse to disclose the identity of the informant. The court set out the procedure for deciding on disclosure. It must examine the material and balance the public interest for and against disclosure. If the material may establish innocence it must order disclosure.	In the subsequent case of *R v Turner* [1995] the Court of Appeal discussed the potential problem of defences being fabricated in order to obtain disclosure. Thus, the judge is required to hear details of the defence in any application.

Key debate

****

(99) Key debate

Topic	**What is the role for Special Advocates?**
Author	John Ip
Viewpoint	Argues that the role of **special advocate** effects a compromise between the need to ensure a fair trial and the need to protect the public interest. They are most appropriate in cases involving national security.
Source	'The Rise of the Special Advocate' [2008] PL 717

(?) Exam question

Problem question

James is charged with unlawful possession of controlled drugs. They were found in his front garden after a legally conducted raid on his house. He had never been convicted of drugs offences before. His defence is that someone had deliberately placed them in his garden without his knowledge. He wants to know who informed on him so that the police carried out the raid. He suspects that his neighbour Joan, who is a known drug user, told the police. She had borne him a grudge since he had refused to buy heroin from her. Advise him on whether he is likely to succeed in an application to have the informer identified.

An outline answer is available at the end of the book.

#11
Privilege

- Both legal professional privilege and the privilege against self incrimination are doctrines whereby potentially relevant evidence may be excluded at trial. The rules relating to both differ.

Legal professional privilege

- Legal professional privilege is the only privilege which applies by rule to communications between a professional advisor and his client, its purpose being to ensure the parties to legal action proceedings are not constrained in preparing their action. It applies in civil and criminal proceedings.

- Legal professional privilege is a common law principle which is acknowledged in **s10 Police and Criminal Evidence Act (PACE) 1984**.

- Legal professional privilege is implicitly but not explicitly contained within **Art 6**.

- This privilege covers: (1) **advice privilege**: communications conveying legal advice between a lawyer and his client; there does not have to be litigation in mind; (2) **litigation privilege**: communications between lawyer, client and third parties (eg other professionals) for the purpose of pending or contemplated litigation.

- The privilege does not protect communications covering fraud.

- The privilege remains even if the party to whom it attached could gain no further benefit from it.

- The privilege prevents facts from being disclosed but does not prevent facts in the documents from being proved by other means.

- The privilege may be lost by waiver, deliberate or accidental.

Key facts

✳✳✳✳✳✳✳✳✳✳

The privilege against self-incrimination

- The principle is protected by common law, by statute and Art 6.
- The privilege is based on the concept that an individual should not be expected to offer evidence to the state or answer questions which might lead to his conviction.
- The privilege is enshrined in the s14(1) Civil Evidence Act 1968.

Related areas
Legal professional privilege

It is helpful also in revising this area to recall the work you have done on discretionary exclusion of evidence under s78 PACE or the procedure to stay a prosecution, see Chapter 4. If the prosecution improperly use material which is subject to legal professional privilege these procedures may be applied. The privilege is at issue in relation to the erosion of the right to silence under the Criminal Justice and Public Order Act. If a suspect claims legal advice as a reason for refusing to respond to police questions he may have to disclose details of communications with his solicitor. He cannot be asked, however, to waive the privilege. Finally, consider what you have learnt about competence and compellability and the application of the well known maxim 'there is no property in a witness'. The fact that communications with a witness may be privileged does not preclude the opposing party's right to call the witness to testify.

Privilege against self–incrimination

Clearly, this area also overlaps with that of the right to silence covered in Chapter 3. The common law privilege is of course much wider and applies particularly in civil law. Another related area is that of witness compellability and the position of spouses and civil partners in criminal proceedings.

The assessment: key points
Legal professional privilege

You are most likely to be asked about legal professional privilege in a civil context although in the light of the controversial decision in *R v Derby Magistates' Court, ex p B* (1996) you may be asked an essay question examining the justifications for this absolutist approach to the privilege. Although you must keep clear the distinction between the civil and criminal case law the key principles are common to both and they will be treated together in this chapter.

Note that the privilege does not cover objects or documents which are pre-existing in that they did not come into existence for the purpose of obtaining legal advice. The test for objects or documents which are pre-existing is whether or not to make them available to the other side would have the effect of revealing the content of the legal advice that was subsequently given, in which case they would be privileged. Thus, if a problem question concerns a document that may have passed through several hands be careful to look at its origins. *R v King* (1983) is a useful case.

Privilege against self–incrimination

It is helpful in this area to have some knowledge of the history of evidence in order to appreciate how the law on the privilege against self-incrimination evolved. In an essay question on this area you should demonstrate how the law has gradually been eroded over the centuries in part because it is arguable that the defendant in a criminal trial has sufficient protection from abuse of state power by the stricter controls that have been put on the police.

A key question here is distinguishing essay questions on the right to silence which may simply require an analysis of the provisions in **Criminal Justice and Public Order Act (CJPOA) 1994** from the larger question of the privilege against self-incrimination. You will need also to distinguish the principles in **Art 6** from those derived from the common law which are broader.

Key features and principles

Legal professional privilege

Protected by statute

The current definition is to be found in **s10 PACE**. The purpose of this section is to specify which items are protected from the entry search and seizure provisions of the Act.

Section 10 PACE gives the meaning of 'items subject to legal privilege':

(1) Subject to subsection (2) below, in this Act, 'items subject to legal privilege' means –

   (a) communications between a professional legal adviser and his client or any person representing his client made in connection with the giving of legal advice to the client;

   (b) communications between a professional legal adviser and his client or any person representing his client or between such an adviser or his client and any other person made in connection with or in contemplation of legal proceedings and for the purposes of such proceedings; and

   (c) items enclosed with or referred to in such communications and made –

      (i) in connection with the giving of legal advice; or

      (ii) in connection with or in contemplation of legal proceedings and for the purposes of such proceedings,

   when they are in the possession of a person who is entitled to possession of them.

(2) Items held with the intention of furthering a criminal purpose are not items subject to legal privilege.

Case law has amplified the definition here and *R v R* (1994) provides some useful guidelines. In that case the Court of Appeal held that the reference in s10(1)(c) to 'made' was wide enough to include a sample of blood obtained and held in a particular container.

The courts take an absolutist approach

The courts have adopted what some would call an overly principled approach to the privilege. In criminal cases some commentators argue that this has disadvantaged defendants on occasion. The leading case is:

R v Derby Magistrates' Court ex p B (1996): B confessed to his solicitor to the murder of a 16-year-old girl. He retracted his confession before trial and blamed his stepfather. He was acquitted and his stepfather subsequently charged and convicted. He had failed to secure **disclosure** of B's confession. The House of Lords held that the communication was protected by legal professional privilege. Note, however, the statutory curtailment of the privilege in *Re McE and Others* (2009), see p 58.

The European Court of Justice has set out a detailed and rational test for disclosure of legally privileged material taking into account the public as well as client interest, see *Kingdom of Sweden v Council of the European Union* (2009).

Legal advice includes advice given in a relevant legal context

In *Three Rivers* (No 6) [2004] the claimants sought disclosure of further documents (which had not been the subject of the court order in the case above). The newly requested documents concerned communications with solicitors about the presentation of the Bank's evidence to the official inquiry. The House of Lords held that these were covered by legal **advice privilege**. The decision leaves some doubt as to whether a '**dominant purpose test**' has to be applied to legal advice privilege as to **litigation privilege**. In that case Lord Scott framed the relevant test to be first to establish that the advice 'relates to the rights, liabilities, obligations, or remedies of the client either under private law or under public law'. Then the question to be asked (at para 84), is 'Is the occasion on which the communication takes place and is the purpose for which it takes place such as to make it reasonable to expect the privilege to apply.'

Advice privilege only applies to two-way communications between client and legal adviser

Note that the main distinction between **advice privilege** and litigation privilege is that the former only covers such direct communications. Note that in *Three Rivers DC v Bank of England* (No 5) (2003) the House of Lords took a narrow view of who was a client. The effect of this decision for large corporations is that they must be careful to specify who among their employees constitutes the client in order to be covered by legal professional privilege. Those outside this group constitute third parties.

A 'legal adviser' is not necessarily a lawyer in private practice

The definition includes in-house lawyers and even non-legally qualified staff such as legal executives who may attend suspects at police stations. Statutes have extended the privilege to communications with others such as licensed conveyancers and trade mark agents.

Key features and principles

✻✻✻✻✻✻✻✻✻✻

Litigation privilege does not cover inquisitorial proceedings

In *Re L (a minor) (police investigation)* (1997), during care proceedings concerning a child whose parents were drug addicts, an expert's report on the mother's explanation of certain events was passed to her solicitors. She appealed the disclosure of the report. The appeal was dismissed by the House of Lords since litigation privilege did not arise in relation to non-adversarial proceedings.

The privilege may be waived deliberately or accidentally

At a trial the plaintiff's counsel read out an account of an unprivileged conversation from a document which also contained privileged information. The counsel had not been aware that the additional material was privileged and had not intended to waive privilege. It was held that the whole memorandum was privileged and the waiver therefore applied to its entirety.

The privilege will not be lost if fraud or deceit is involved in obtaining documents from the other party

In *Guinness Peat Properties Ltd v Fitzroy Robinson Partnership* (1987) the solicitors of the plaintiff were sent privileged documents by mistake. The solicitor copied them before returning them. The owner sought an injunction to prevent the plaintiff using them. The injunction was granted. The privilege is not lost if disclosure is obtained by fraud or by means of making use of an obvious mistake.

In such instances the injunction to halt **disclosure**, a discretionary remedy, to be made promptly. CPR 31.20 provides that a party who is allowed to inspect a privileged document by inadvertence may only make use of it with permission of the court.

Contrast this case with that of the criminal case of *R v Tompkins* (1977) where the privilege was lost. The prosecution was allowed to cross examine the defendant on the contents of a note which had been found on the floor of the court. The evidence had come into the prosecution's hands innocently.

The privilege will not protect fraud or criminal activity

In *R v Central Criminal Court ex p Francis and Francis* [1989], in a police investigation into drug trafficking, a judge ordered disclosure of a document held by the solicitors of a member of the suspect's family, G. The solicitors applied for judicial review to have the order quashed citing s10(2) PACE whereby 'Items held with the intention of furthering a criminal purpose are not items subject to legal privilege.' The House of Lords held that even if G was an unknowing benefactor of the proceeds of drugs that s10(2) applied. The statute reflected the common law principle that communications furthering crime or fraud are not covered (*see R v Cox and Railton* (1884)). Note that fraudulent activity does not have to be necessarily criminal.

The 'dominant purpose' test must be applied in applications for litigation privilege

The leading case is *Waugh v BRB* (1980). W was the widow of a man killed in a railway accident. She sued the BRB and sought **disclosure** of an internal accident report made two days after the accident by engineers and sent to the BRB solicitors. The House of Lords ordered disclosure since in order to be covered by litigation privilege the dominant, if not the sole, purpose of the submission of the document had to be pending litigation. This was not the case here. Note also the definition in **s10(1)(b) PACE** above. Although other professionals and experts will often be the **third party** in questions involving litigation privilege this is not always the case. Other prospective witnesses, including lay ones, may be covered including their identities.

Revision tip

Be very careful that you make it clear you are aware of the different procedures for remedying the situation where privileged documents are obtained by the opposing party in civil and in criminal proceedings. In civil procedures application would be for an injunction, a discretionary remedy. In a criminal case consideration should be given to stay or prosecution or discretionary exclusion of evidence by **s78 PACE**.

✔ Looking for extra marks?

Ex p B (1996) is clearly a case where arguably a defendant was denied access to evidence which might have raised a reasonable doubt about his guilt. You will gain extra credit if you refer also to the absolutist nature of the privilege as demonstrated by the case of *R v Grant* (2005). The difference is that the defendant here benefited from the Court of Appeal's decision. By secretly recording conversations between a suspect and his solicitor the police had violated the principle of legal professional privilege. In this instance no evidence had been obtained against G as a result of this impropriety. Nonetheless, the Court of Appeal quashed the conviction since the trial should have been abandoned as an abuse of process.

Privilege against self-incrimination

The privilege against self-incrimination has in various ways been observed in English law for several centuries. In *R v Director of Serious Fraud Office ex parte Smith* (1993), Lord Mustill in the House of Lords' judgment stated that the privilege was part of a disparate group of immunities, which differ in nature, origin, incidence and importance, and as to the extent to which they have been encroached upon by statute. Note that the privilege does not apply to administrative proceedings.

In *R v Hertfordshire CC ex parte Green Environmental Industries Ltd* (2000) the privilege did not protect against the use of compelled questions in an administrative enquiry. It does

Conclusion

****

not cover material having an existence independent of the will of the suspect. According to *Saunders v UK* (1997) this included '*documents* acquired pursuant to a warrant, breath, blood and urine samples and bodily tissue for the purpose of **DNA** testing'. The principle was made clear also in *C plc and another v P* (2007). In this case the claimant did not succeed in preventing the submission of pornographic images on a computer to the prosecuting authorities. These had been discovered as a result of an official search on another matter. Another limitation of the privilege is that it may be limited in its application if that limitation pursues a legitimate objective and is proportionate.

In *Brown v Stott* (2003) the Privy Council accepted such a limitation. **Section 172(2)(a) Road Traffic Act 1988** required the occupants of a car that was speeding to identify who was driving. Criminal penalties could be imposed for non-responses. B responded and was convicted of speeding. The conviction was upheld.

In *Luckhof v Austria* (2008) the Strasbourg court found no violation of **Art 6(1)** on similar facts. There was a legitimate public interest in road safety.

Revision tip

Contrast the case of **Brown v Stott** (2003) with that of **Heaney v Ireland** (2001). There, degree of compulsion to respond to questions effectively abolished the privilege against self-incrimination. The applicants faced charges under anti-terrorist legislation which made it an offence not to give an account. The Strasbourg Court could not justify 'a provision which extinguishes the very essence of the applicant's rights to silence and against self-incrimination guaranteed by Article 6(1) of the Convention'.

✅ Looking for extra marks?

You need to be on the lookout for questions on compellability which may be inserted in questions on the privilege against self-incrimination. Examiners may, for example, refer to spouses in a problem in civil proceedings concerned with the privilege. Note that **s80 PACE** has been amended by the **CJA 2003** extending the privilege to questions tending to incriminate a witness's spouse or **civil partner**.

① Conclusion

The connecting thread between public interest immunity and privilege is that they both deal with ways potentially relevant evidence may be excluded at trial for extrinsic policy rather than intrinsic fair trial procedural reasons. The doctrines have quite distinct rules and you should study them separately. However, it is helpful to keep in mind the main differences, particularly between legal professional privilege and public interest immunity. They are set out in the table in Fig 11.1.

The privilege against self-incrimination is a more diffuse concept and it has been subject to continuing statutory encroachment such as **s31(1) Theft Act 1968**. The case of *Saunders v UK* (1997) shows that statutory encroachments have to be Convention compliant.

Figure 11.1 Differences between PII and legal professional privilege

PII	Legal professional privilege
Non-disclosure is a duty	Non-disclosure is a right
PII may be claimed by the court or by a **third party**.	Privilege can only be claimed by parties to the proceedings.
Cannot be waived by the party claiming it (possible exception if informer non-disclosure of identity).	Can be purposefully or accidentally waived by party claiming it.
In civil proceedings, party may apply to court *ex parte* that even the existence of the document should not be disclosed to the other side (CPR 31.19(1)). (In very exceptional cases such *ex parte* applications may be made in criminal proceedings.)	Existence of disputed document must be revealed to other side during 'discovery'.
Secondary evidence of the relevant document cannot be **adduced**.	The privilege attaches to the original document and secondary evidence may be **adduced**.
Disclosure or stay of prosecution may be ordered if establishing innocence is threatened by non-disclosure.	**Disclosure** will not necessarily be ordered even if necessary to establish innocence.

(✱) Key cases

Case	Facts	Principle and comment
Legal professional privilege		
Waugh v BRB [1980] AC 521	W was the widow of a man killed in a railway accident. She sued the BRB and sought disclosure of an internal accident report made two days after the accident by engineers and sent to the BRB solicitors. The House of Lords ordered disclosure since in order to be covered by **litigation privilege** the dominant, if not the sole, purpose of the submission of the document had to be pending litigation. This was not the case here.	The public interest in **disclosure** here prevailed over an extension of **litigation privilege**.

Key cases

****

Case	Facts	Principle and comment
Great Atlantic Insurance v Home Insurance [1981] 1 WLR 529	At a trial the plaintiff's counsel read out an account of an unprivileged conversation from a document which also contained privileged information. The counsel had not been aware that the additional material was privileged and had not intended to waive privilege. It was held that the whole memorandum was privilege and the waiver therefore applied to its entirety.	Here counsel was acting as the client's agent and thus waived privilege on his behalf.
Guinness Peat Properties Ltd v Fitzroy Robinson Partnership [1987] 1 WLR 1027	The solicitors of the plaintiff were sent privileged documents by mistake. The solicitor copied them before returning them. The owner sought an injunction to prevent the plaintiff using them. The injunction was granted. The privilege is not lost if disclosure is obtained by fraud or by means of making use of an obvious mistake.	In such instances the injunction to halt **disclosure**, a discretionary remedy, to be made promptly. CPR 31.20 provides that a party who is allowed to inspect a privileged document by inadvertence may only make us of it with permission of the court.
R v Central Criminal Court ex p Francis and Francis [1989] AC 346	In a police investigation into drug trafficking a judge ordered **disclosure** of a document held by the solicitor of a member of the suspect's family, G. The solicitor applied for judicial review to have the order quashed citing s10(2) PACE whereby 'Items held with the intention of furthering a criminal purpose are not items subject to legal privilege.' The House of Lords held that even if G was an unknowing benefactor of the proceeds of drugs s10(2) applied.	The principle here is the common law one that communications furthering crime or fraud are not covered, see *R v Cox and Railton* (1884). The fraudulent activity does not have to be necessarily criminal.
R v Derby Magistrates' Court ex p B [1996] 1 AC 487	B confessed to his solicitor to the murder of a 16-year-old girl. He retracted his confession before trial and blamed his stepfather. He was acquitted and his stepfather subsequently charged and convicted. He had failed to secure disclosure of B's confession. The House of Lords held, overruling earlier authorities, that the communication was protected by legal professional privilege.	Lord Taylor CJ said (at p507) '... a man must be able to consult his lawyer in confidence, since otherwise he might hold back half the truth. The client must be sure that what he tells his lawyer in confidence will never be revealed without his consent. Legal professional privilege is thus much more than an ordinary rule of evidence ... It is ... fundamental condition on which the administration of justice as a whole rests ...'.
Re L (a minor) (police investigation) [1997] AC 16	During care proceedings concerning a child whose parents were drug addicts an expert's report on the mother's explanation of certain events, was passed	Note, however, that the *Three Rivers* series of cases establishes that legal advice privilege may be

Case	Facts	Principle and comment
continued	to her solicitors. She appealed the disclosure of the report. The appeal was dismissed by the House of Lords since **litigation privilege** did not arise in relation to non-adversarial proceedings.	available in non-adversarial proceedings.
Three Rivers DC v Bank of England (No 5) [2003] QB 1556	Facing an action for misfeasance in public office the Bank of England claim legal **advice privilege** in relation to documentary evidence produced for an official inquiry into the collapse of the BCCI. The documents had been generated some time before the current action. The Court held that the **advice privilege** only attached to a small group of individuals in the Bank.	The controversial decision in this case had the effect of narrowing the group of people who could be called 'clients'. In effect, corporate bodies must now take care who they nominate as the 'client' if they wish to protect confidential documents. Employees who are outside this nominated group will be third parties.
Three Rivers (No 6) [2004] QB 916	The claimants sought **disclosure** of further documents (which had not been the subject of the court order in the case above). The newly requested documents concerned communications with solicitors about the presentation of the Bank's evidence to the official inquiry. The House of Lords held that these were covered by legal **advice privilege**.	The House extended the scope of legal advice privilege to cover documents generated in a relevant legal context even if they were not specifically directed to legal matters.

Privilege against self-incrimination

Case	Facts	Principle and comment
Blunt v Park Lane Ltd [1942] 2 KB 253	In an action for slander the plaintiff challenged the requirement to respond to interrogatories on her alleged promiscuity on the grounds that her responses might lead to penalty or censure by an ecclesiastical court for adultery. The court held that answering did not infringe her privilege against self-incrimination.	In this case the only likely penalty was to have the sacraments refused and this did not constitute a penalty within the scope of the rule.
Saunders v UK (1997) 23 EHRR 313	In a criminal trial for false accounting and theft, evidence was produced from S's responses to questions from DTI inspectors. They had powers under the Companies Act to compel responses.	Article 6 was breached by the use in a criminal trial of answers which were obtained under compulsion.
R v Hertfordshire CC ex p Green Environmental Industries Ltd [2000] AC 412	The Environmental Protection Act made it an offence for local authorities not to give information about their waste management. It was held that this did not breach Art 6.	The outcome shows how the courts will distinguish responses which might be used in criminal proceedings and those used for administrative inquiries.

Key debates

✱✱✱✱✱✱✱✱✱✱

⑨ Key debates

Topic	The rationale behind the decision to exclude legal professional privilege from inquisitorial proceedings.
Author	AAS Zuckerman
Viewpoint	Discusses the relationship between the decision in *Re L* and that in *ex p B* and suggests that an alternative and fairer approach would have been to declare *ex p B* wrongly decided.
Source	'Legal Professional Privilege: The Cost of Absolutism' (1996) 112 LQR 535.

Topic	The reasons for protecting the privilege against self-incrimination.
Author:	M Redmayne
Viewpoint:	Discusses the reasons for protecting the privilege one of which is the need for distance from a powerful state.
Source:	'Rethinking the Privilege against Self-Incrimination' (2007) 27: 2 OJLS 209

⑦ Exam questions

Essay question 1

Does the current law on legal professional privilege undermine or ensure the right to a fair trial? Answer, giving reasons, in relation to legal professional privilege in civil and criminal proceedings.

An outline answer is available at http://www.oxfordtextbooks.co.uk/orc/concentrate.

Essay question 2

'To exclude otherwise relevant and admissible evidence from civil or criminal proceedings may undermine the right to a fair trial.'

Discuss in relation to legal professional privilege in civil and criminal proceedings.

An outline answer is available online at http://www.oxfordtextbooks.co.uk/orc/concentrate.

Problem question

Freda is suing the Pets Holiday Camp (PHC) for negligently causing the death of her pet dog by leaving it in a van without water on a hot summer day. She had paid to have the dog in the kennels for a week. Martin is a member of a charity organization called Keep Pets Safe. He works as a clerk with Fixit, the lawyers acting for PHC. He sends to Freda anonymously a copy of an email PHC's insurers have sent to Fixit which refers to poor staffing levels in PHC. Advise Freda whether she can adduce the text of this email at trial.

An outline answer is available at the end of the book.

References

Ashworth, A, 'Criminal Proceedings after the Human Rights Act; The First Year' [2001] Crim LR 855

Birch, D, 'Rethinking Sexual History Evidence: Proposals for Fairer Trials' [2002] Crim LR 531

Birch, D, 'Untangling Sexual History Evidence: A Rejoinder to Professor Temkin' [2003] Crim LR 370

Burton, M, Evans, R, and Sanders, A, 'Vulnerable and Intimidated Witnesses and the Adversarial Process in England and Wales' (2007) 11(1) E&P, 1

Choo, A L-T, *Evidence* (OUP, 2009)

Dennis, I, 'Reverse Onuses and the Presumption of Innocence' [2005] Crim LR 901

Dennis, I H, *The Law of Evidence* (Sweet and Maxwell, 3rd edn, 2007)

Edmond, G, 'Constructing Miscarriages of Justice: Misunderstanding Scientific Evidence in High Profile Criminal Appeals' (2002) 22: 1 OJLS 53

Emson, R, *Evidence* (Palgrave Macmillan, 4th edn, 2008)

Hoyano, LCH, 'Variations on a Theme by Pigot: Special Measures Directions for Child Witnesses' [2000] Crim LR 250

Laudan, L, *Truth, Error and Criminal Law: An Essay in Legal Epistemology* (CUP, 2008)

Lloyd Bostock, S, 'The Effect on Juries of Hearing about the Defendant's Previous Criminal Record: A Simulation Study' [1973] Crim LR 734

Lloyd Bostock, S, 'The Effect on Lay Magistrates of Hearing that the Defendant is of 'Good Character', Being Left to Speculate, or Hearing that he Has a Previous Conviction' [2006] Crim LR 189

Mirfield, P, 'The Argument from Consistency for Overruling *Selvey*' [1991] CLJ 490

Munday, C, 'Privilege, Policy and Principle' [2005] LQR 181

Murphy, P, *Murphy on Evidence* (OUP, 2008)

Ormerod, D, 'Sounds Familiar? – Voice Identification Evidence' [2001] Crim LR 595

Pattenden, P, 'Should Confessions be Corroborated?' (1991) 107 LQR 317

Roberts, A, 'Drawing on Expertise: Legal Decision-making and the Reception of Expert Evidence' [2008] Crim LR 443

Roberts, P, and Zuckerman, A, *Criminal Evidence* (OUP, 2004)

Spencer, M, 'Bureaucracy, National Security and Access to Justice: New Light on *Duncan v Cammell Laird*' (2004) 55(3) *Northern Ireland Legal Quarterly* 277

Spencer, M, and Spencer, J, *Questions and Answers on Evidence* (OUP, 6th edn, 2009)

Tapper, C, *Cross and Tapper on Evidence* (OUP, 11th edn, 2007)

Tapper, C, 'The Law of Evidence and the Rule of Law' [2009] Cambridge Law Journal 67

Temkin, J, 'Sexual History Evidence – Beware the Backlash' [2003] Crim LR 217

Tribe, L, 'Triangulating Hearsay' [1974] 87 Harr LR 957

Twining, W, *Rethinking Evidence: Exploratory Essays* (Blackwell, 1990)

Witting, C, 'Res Ipsa Loquitur: Some Last Words' (2001) 117 LQR 392

Worthen, T, 'The Hearsay Provisions of the Criminal Justice Act 2003: So Far Not So Good?' [2008] Crim LR 431

Zuckerman, A, *Principles of Criminal Evidence* (Clarendon Press, OUP, 1989)

Outline answers

Chapter 2

Problem answer plan a)

First list the elements of the offence and any statutory defences. The offence consists of setting traps to kill rats. It is assumed this is an offence requiring **mens rea**.

The elements of the offence/statutory defences are:

- knowingly setting traps to kill rats,
- where there is a risk that humans will be harmed.

You should then state the general rule which is that the burden of proof lies on the prosecution subject to any statutory or common law exceptions, see **Woolmington v DPP** [1935] and **Art 6 ECHR**. There is little doubt that the task of proving **mens rea** in relation to the setting of the traps lies on the prosecution.

The court will address the question of who has the legal burden of establishing that humans were unlikely to be harmed. On the basis of the statutory construction it is not clear if the question of the likely harm to humans is an element of the offence or a defence which takes the form of an 'exception, etc, following s101 Magistrates Courts Act'. According to **Edwards** (1974), confirmed in **Hunt** (1986), the burden could impliedly shift to the defence. This applied whether the offence was tried summarily or on indictment.

If on its construction the burden is shifted to the defence the question is whether this is a proportionate response in the light of the **HRA 1998**. Applying **Lambert** (2002) and **Sheldrake** (2004) factors to consider are:

- the moral blameworthiness of the offence;
- the size of the penalty; and
- the ease of production of the proof.

Here the offence appears to be a regulatory one. It has some similarities with **Johnstone** [2003] in that it is imprisonable. It could be argued that this is the sort of situation Dennis (2005) refers to as 'a voluntary assumption of risk'. It is likely that the legal burden will be on the defendant.

It is arguable in particular that he would find it easier to prove the actual situation in his yard.

Problem answer plan b)

First list the elements of the offence:

- knowingly possessing material and that material could be used by terrorists,
- it is a defence to prove he did not know material was of the nature as could be used by terrorists.

It seems clear that the prosecution should prove the **actus reus** and the **means rea** of possessing the offending material. The statute is unclear on whom the burden of the defence should lie.

The court therefore will assess whether in the light of the requirements of **Art 6** it will be a proportionate response to place the burden on Jane.

Bearing in mind the moral dimension of the offence and the size of the penalty it seems likely that **Lambert** (2002) will be followed and the evidential burden only placed on Jane.

Note that the **A-G's Ref (No 4 of 2002)** [2005] discussed the importance of Parliament's intention and held that in grave situations this might be disregarded.

It is likely therefore that the statute will be 'read down' to impose the lesser burden on Jane.

Chapter 3

Essay answer

The scope of the question:

The question does not specify what are the ingredients of a fair trial and so you would be entitled to draw on **Art 6 ECHR** as offering one possible set of guidelines but you should make it clear in your answer that the Article is a minimum rather than a maximum list of essential features. You could in your introduction point out that fairness is a contested concept and that, as **s78 PACE** demonstrates, may include fairness to the trial ie is not narrowed to fairness to the defendant. Thus any meaningful

Outline answers

✳✳✳✳✳✳✳✳✳✳

answer would have to include your own evaluation of what is a fair trial. You should have read some of the academic literature on this – a very powerful analysis is for example included in Roberts and Zuckerman (2004). They suggest (pp 19–20) that the foundational principles of criminal evidence should be: promoting factual accuracy, protecting the innocent from wrongful conviction, minimum state intervention, humane treatment, and maintaining high standards of propriety in the criminal process. Such a framework might provide a conceptual framework for your essay, alongside more specific references to **Art 6**. Your introduction should then outline the current state of the law and the changes brought about in **YJCEA 1994**.

A possible plan is:

Arguments to support the view that **ss34–38 CJPOA** violate fair trial rights:

• Privilege against self-incrimination is an ancient common law value which upholds the principle of minimum state intervention, ie it is connected to the presumption of innocence.

• Inferences from silence are ambiguous, since people can be silent for reasons other than guilt and therefore factual accuracy may not be maintained and the innocent be convicted.

• The effect of the changes to the law is that the defendant, if explaining that he was silent on legal advice, may be held to have waived his right to legal professional privilege.

• The law has generated excessive case law and is difficult to apply, particularly in relation to silence on legal advice – see the conflict between *R v Betts and Hall* [2001] and *R v Howell* [2003].

Arguments to support the view that **ss34–38** do not violate fair trial rights:

• The Strasbourg court has held that the right to silence is not an absolute right under **Art 6**.

• There are safeguards eg the defendant cannot be convicted on silence alone and has to have access to legal advice before the provisions apply.

• Fair trial rights apply to victims as well as defendants and the law increases the chance of conviction of the guilty.

• The law has been interpreted in favour of the defendant in a number of cases eg *R v Knight* [2003] in relation to written statement

being accepted as responding to police questions.

Conclusion:

You might here refer to current academic debate and alternative proposals to deal with ambush defences. This might include full disclosure of the case by the police to the suspect. See Dennis (2007, pp 148–206) for a critique of the law in this area.

Chapter 4

Essay answer

The scope of the question:

The comment invites you to review the case law under **s78 PACE** and analyse the judgments to see if you derive a coherent set of principles. You should initially contrast the pre-**PACE** position, exemplified by *Sang* [1980], where the very existence of a discretion to exclude was left unclear.

You will need to be familiar with the leading cases and also with academic comment, most of which has been critical of an overly cautious stance of the judiciary.

Your introduction should stress the importance of the **HRA 1998** and the subsequent more jurisprudential approach.

Arguments to suggest the statement is still valid:

Apart from confessions, there are few cases where **s78** has been applied to exclude evidence and thus, although the courts accept the principle that **s78** may exclude entrapment evidence, for example, it is rarely applied. Also the test set out eg in *Smurthwaite* [1994], are based on practical considerations rather than principle.

Academic commentary has identified a possible structured approach to exclusion as being based on reliability, deterrence, compensating the defendant, providing a fairer balance between the state and defendant, and upholding the integrity of the criminal justice process.

Reliability of evidence does provide a coherent thread in the cases- usually ensuring admissibility not exclusion – see *Chalkley* [1998],

Khan [1997] – but this is a pragmatic not a principled stance.

The case law suggests deterrence is not a recognised principle – see **Mason** (1988) – although it may have that indirect effect. It is difficult to argue that police behaviour will be affected by an exclusion of evidence at a trial some time away.

Public opinion would arguably not countenance acquittal of the obviously guilty to compensate for earlier police transgressions. The evidence exists and it might defy common sense to exclude it.

The doctrine of abuse of process (see **Looseley** [2001]) has operated more robustly to safeguard a principled approach than has **s78**.

Arguments to suggest the statement is no longer valid:

On the other hand there is evidence to suggest that the courts have increasingly adopted a principled stance on **s78**.

In **Shannon** [2001] the court applied the test of the violation of a Convention right as one of the criteria for exclusion.

In **Looseley** [2001] the House of Lords acknowledged the importance of both the protective principle and the need to uphold the integrity of the criminal justice process.

The **ECHR** and the **HRA 1998** have led to an increasingly principled approach eg *Allan v UK* (2002), *Texheira v Portugal* (1998).

Looseley [2001] has demonstrated the close link between abuse of process and **s78** grounds of exclusion.

Conclusion:

Some academic commentators acknowledge that a blanket exclusionary practice would not be appropriate. (See Roberts and Zuckerman (2004).)

Ashworth stresses the importance of protecting constitutional rights – see for example, the Canadian Charter of Rights and Freedom.

The legitimacy of the proceedings appears to be an increasingly important factor in deciding on admissibility.

Judicial discretion cannot override parliamentary provisions which give increased powers to investigative authorities.

A v Secretary of State for Home Department (2006) is a landmark principled stance although not on **s78**, it does illustrate the increasingly jurisprudential reasoning of the House of Lords also shown in **Looseley** [2001].

Chapter 5

Essay answer

Introduction

To answer this question properly requires at least an outline knowledge of the earlier law. The concept behind the question is that a defendant cannot only refer to parts of their character which might be favourable to them and expect that other less favourable parts will be ignored. Your introduction should set out the definition of character in legal terms and compare that with some of the evidence from psychological science. You should make the point that only 'bad character' is defined in the statute (**s101**) and that good character is defined by the common law still. The question is really about whether, if the defendant claims to be of good character, his 'bad character' will also be admitted. Refer to the particular problems of character evidence identified by the Law Commission, namely moral and reasoning prejudice and the difficulties since the 1898 statute of achieving a fair balance between the interests of the defendant and the public interests in prosecuting crime successfully. This is an area where relevance may have to give way to other considerations. Refer to Lloyd-Bostock (2006) and the empirical support her research gives to the possibility of prejudice in a jury. The approach of the courts has been, even before the defendant was allowed to testify, that the jury on the other hand must not be misled and that a defendant could not claim to be of good character without having his bad character admitted. A possible outline for your essay is:

1. Pre-2003 position under common law (non-testifying defendant) and under **CEA 1898**. If the defendant claimed to be of good character his bad character would be admitted. See *Rowton* (1865). Three problems arose from this.

2. Firstly, the different definitions of good and bad character – the former in terms of general reputation, the second in terms of criminal record.

Outline answers

✱✱✱✱✱✱✱✱✱✱

3. Secondly, see *R v Winfield* (1939) where Humphreys J stated, 'there is no such thing known to our procedure as putting half a prisoner's character in issue and leaving out the other half'.

4. What Mirfield (1991) has called the 'no-stymie principle' was not accepted. If the accused made an imputation against a prosecution witness that was necessary for his defence, he risked having his criminal record put in see *DPP v Selvey* [1970].

5. *Winfield* but not *Selvey* has been effectively overruled by the **CJA 2003**. As regards the former, retaliatory evidence of an accused's bad character under **s101(1)(f)** if he claims to be of good character is admissible 'only if it goes no further than is necessary to correct the false impression'. See *Weir* [2006]. However, it is arguable that *R v Somanathan* [2006] shows how difficult it is to keep to such a restriction. In that case a Hindu priest accused of rape claimed he enjoyed a good reputation and had not behaved inappropriately to women. The court then allowed evidence from women who claimed to have been assaulted by him.

6. Despite contrary recommendations by the Law Commission the defendant has no immunity from his bad character being admitted because he makes imputations which relate to the facts of the defence or the conduct of the investigation.

Conclusion:

The comment is correct in relation to the approach on admissibility in relation to good character. But the 'tit for tat' principle remains in relation to imputations against prosecution witnesses and co-defendants. Thus, there is a limited prosecutorial advantage in relation to this aspect of **CJA 2003**.

Chapter 6

· ·

Problem answer

i) John's statement fulfils the definition of hearsay to be found in CJA 2003, ss114, 115, 121. It is being tendered to suggest that it is true, namely that Anna killed John. It may be admissible under **s116** as oral first-hand hearsay where the reason for not calling John is

that he is dead. Alternatively, it may be admitted under the common law exception *res gestae*, see *Andrews* [1987].

ii) The email is a document not covered **s117**, see *Taylor* [2006], since it is multiple hearsay and is not received in the course of trade etc. It is, therefore, only admissible by exercise of the discretion under **s121(1)(c)** considered in conjunction with the factors in **s114(1)(d)** – see *Maher*, where the court considered that the trial judge should have considered this section as well as **s114(1)(d)**. However, the court took a liberal view on inclusion in that the statement could be considered to be properly admitted. Alternative route to admissibility is **s76(A) PACE**, confession by a co-accused.

Chapter 7

· ·

Problem answer

You should take each witness in turn:

- Can John testify against Janet and Janet against John?
- Is the compellability of spouses dependent on the nature of the offence?
- Does the situation change if either plead guilty?
- Is Tim eligible as a witness and will his age affect how he gives evidence?
- Is Agnes competent to give evidence?
- What are the evidential consequences if the defendants choose not to testify? (It is easy to overlook this last point since it strictly goes beyond the rules on competence and compellability but you will gain extra marks if you show you know the difference between compellability and evidential consequences.)
- What sanctions are available if a non-defendant compellable witness fails to testify?

The general rule in criminal proceedings is that all witnesses are competent and compellable (**s53(1) YJCEA**). We are not given any details of the age or mental state of Janet and John but it is obvious they are adults and it is assumed that they do not suffer from mental or physical incapacity. If they are jointly charged then neither are competent or compellable to give evidence for the prosecution, see **s53(4) YJCEA** and **s80(4) PACE**. Both are competent to give evidence for their own and the other's defence (**s53(1) YJCEA**) but neither is compellable (**s80(4) PACE**). The situation will change if Janet pleads guilty since she will no longer be a co-defendant. She will be competent to give evidence for the prosecution but only compellable for the assault on Tim (**s80(3) PACE**). She will not be compellable for the attack on the dog since it is not a specified offence. She will be competent and compellable to give evidence on behalf of John (**s53(1) YJCEA and s80(2) PACE**).

If Janet and John plead not guilty and chose not to give evidence in their own defence they run the risk of the jury drawing an adverse inference, **s35 CJPOA 1994**. See *R v Cowan* [1996].

Tim is the alleged victim and the presumption is that he is competent and compellable to give evidence for the defence or prosecution (**s53(1) YJCEA**). As he is under 17 years of age he will be eligible for Special Measures (**ss16–17 and 23–30 YJCEA**). He will give evidence unsworn, **s55(2) YJCEA**. In the unlikely event that there is a challenge to his competence he may have to satisfy the test in **s53(3) YJCEA**. That test may also be applied to Agnes in view of her alleged mental condition, but see *R v Sed* [2004] for the willingness of the courts to apply the provision generously. If Agnes is judged to be competent to give evidence but does not satisfy the tests for **sworn evidence (s55(2)(b)YJCEA)** she may give evidence unsworn (**s56 YJCEA**). It is for the party wishing to have the witness sworn to satisfy the court on the balance of probabilities that the test is satisfied (**s55(4)**).

If a witness is held to be compellable but fails to testify (s)he will be subject to a finding of contempt (*R v Yusuf* (2003)).

Chapter 8

Problem answer

The following issues are raised all requiring knowledge of **s41 YJCEA 1999**, the new provisions in the **CJA 2003**, and of the common law rule on previous consistent statements.

- Can Rory's initial denial to police be admitted?
- Can Gloria's statement to her mother be admitted?
- Are Gloria's allegedly previous false allegations admissible?

Rory's denial

Although previous consistent statements are not admissible at trial this denial may be admissible as an exception to this rule under the common law (*R v Storey* (1968)) Previous out of court exculpatory statements giving the accused's reaction to an accusation are admissible as evidence of consistency and thus to support the witness's creditworthiness. The statement does not have to be made immediately on first accusation but the length of time which has elapsed is a factor in admissibility (*R v Pearce* (1979)). Whether the statement is admissible will in part depend on whether there is other adequate evidence of Rory's reaction (*R v Tooke* (1990)). It is admissible only of consistency. Alternatively, the statement may be admissible as an exception to the rule against hearsay if it satisfies the 'interests of justice' test in **s114(1)(d) CJA**. Then it would be evidence of the truth of its contents.

Gloria's statement to mother

This is arguably a 'recent complaint' which forms an exception to the inadmissibility of previous consistent statements in **s120(7) CJA 2003**. The following statutory conditions appear to apply:

- Gloria claims to be the person against whom an offence was committed;
- the alleged attempted is the subject matter of the trial;
- Gloria made the complaint as soon as could reasonably be expected after the alleged conduct;
- her complaint was not made as a result of a threat or a promise. It does appear to have been prompted by a leading question from the mother but this is not fatal to admissibility (**s120(8)**); and
- before the statement is **adduced**, Gloria must give oral evidence in connection with its subject matter.

If it is admitted the statement is evidence of its truth (**s120(4)**).

Gloria's previous allegations

The defence will wish to bring these in. The question is whether leave is required under **s41**.

The question is whether this is evidence of previous sexual behaviour which is inadmissible

Outline answers

✳✳✳✳✳✳✳✳✳✳

under **s41 YJCEA 1999** without leave of the court. In *R v MH* (2002) the Court of Appeal held that making false allegations was not 'sexual behaviour' under **s41** but if proof of the falsity of the allegations involves questions on sexual behaviour then **s41** would apply (see *R v H* [2003]) If the judge were required to grant leave then since the case does not turn on consent the conditions under **s41(2)(b)** apply which sets a high test.

The prosecution may argue that this raises a question also of **credibility** under **s41(4)**. The defence may rely on *R v T; R v H* (2001) where the complainants had allegedly made false allegations of sexual assaults in the past and the Court of Appeal held they were admissible as relevant in the normal non-statutory sense. They were not 'sexual behaviour' under **s41** and were not automatically excluded under the section even if they went principally to credibility. There must, however, be a proper evidential basis for asserting that Gloria made the allegations and that they were untrue. See also *R v Martin* [2004] where the Court of Appeal held that **s41** did not preclude questions which did not solely go to credibility but which supported the defendant's contention that the allegations against him were false.

The defence should be reminded that the requirements of **s100 CJA 2003** in such a situation must be satisfied, see *R v Voller* [2006] and it may be necessary for the defence to seek leave under **s100(4) CJA 2003** to admit the evidence since Gloria is a non-defendant witness.

Proferred defence evidence cannot be excluded under **s78 PACE**.

Chapter 9

· ·

Essay answer

Introduction

Your answer to this question would be improved if you were able to refer to a number of recent miscarriages of justice which have been based on flawed expert evidence. These indeed demonstrate 'weakness'. You should refer, as does Roberts (2008) to cases such as *R v Cannings* (2004) and the comments made in *R v Kai-Whitewind* (2005), para 85, that, 'In *Cannings* there was essentially no evidence beyond the inferences based on coincidence

which the experts for the Crown were prepared to draw.' You should set out arguments which criticise the current approach and those which point to its effectiveness. Note that the quotation refers to 'reception' of expert evidence so you should cover both admissibility and the treatment of evidence once it is admitted. It is important in essays of this sort that you adopt a critical approach and do not simply give a narrative account. You should try to give evidence of having read widely – see also the comments by Choo (2009, p 309) referring to the twin arguments of 'necessity and reliability' which underlie considerations of the admissibility of expert evidence. This could provide a framework for your essay.

Arguments critical of the present approach

The distinction between acceptable areas of expertise and 'quack' areas is unclear – see *Robb* (1991). Roberts (2008) is critical of the judgment in accepting voice identification evidence and suggests that the 'relevance' test is too vague. See also *Luttrell* [2004] on questionable expertise of the expert. It is arguable that necessity and reliability are not sufficiently distinguished and that the vaguer concept of relevance prevails.

Gilfoyle [2001] – evidence helpful to the defence was excluded and subsequent investigations have shown this is a possible miscarriage of justice.

Expert evidence is given too much weight by judge and jury who cannot assess it because it is beyond their competence – see *Clark* [2003] and *Cannings* [2004].

The position on psychiatrists' evidence is confusing – compare *Turner* [1975] and *Lowery* [1975].

The cases are also incoherent on the ultimate issue rule eg *DPP v A&BC Chewing Gum Ltd* (1968) and also the question of diminished responsibility.

The law on reception of evidence on credibility is unclear – see *Somanathan* (2006).

Arguments to support current approach

The courts are adopting a liberal approach eg *Stockwell* [1993] and allowing more evidence. This accords with the principle of full proof and the judge can direct on weight and improper treatment if corrected on appeal eg *Tilly* [1981] where the Court of Appeal held the judge was wrong to invite the jury to make comparisons of handwriting without the guidance of an expert.

The flexible approach in criminal law is fairer to defendants rather than the more structured cost-aware civil approach.

The main problem is inequality of arms and resources not the law.

The current approach reflects popular values – eg scepticism about new sciences.

The much praised US approach is still led by case law and pragmatism prevails – eg *Daubert* (1993) replacing *Frye* (1923).

Conclusion

You should suggest some areas for reform and comment on Roberts' (2008) argument that more education is needed. See also House of Commons Science and Technology Committee Report, 'The complexity and role of forensic evidence are ever increasing and we have not seen evidence to reassure us that the criminal justice system has kept pace with these developments.' Arguably, the current position aids the prosecution; see Edmond (2002, p58) 'Scientific evidence is an important component of most high profile miscarriage of justice cases.' Note that the most elementary mistakes seem to have been made by the greatest legal brains. Consider how bench, counsel, and jury all were taken in by the elementary flaws in the statistics presented in the case of *(Sally) Clark* [2003]. Common sense and a healthy scepticism about received truths is an asset in the court room and the examination room.

Chapter 10

Problem answer

English law protects the identity of informants in matters concerned with public prosecutions. Public Interest Immunity certificates are issued in order to protect the public interest in keeping such flows of information. See *Marks v Beyfus* (1890).

There is a presumption of non-disclosure here and it will be for James to convince the court of the need for disclosure.

On the other hand, *R v Ward* (1993) established that the prosecution is obliged to disclose to the defence all material on which the prosecution is based.

Section 21(2) CPIA 1996 states that the common law rule on non-disclosure in the public interest is preserved.

Under **s3 CPIA** (as amended by the **CJA 2003**) the procedure for the judge to hear argument in cases about contested disclosure is set out. On the facts this would not appear to be a situation in which an *ex parte* hearing was appropriate.

James may rely on *R v Agar* (1989) where it was held on appeal that disclosure of the name of an informer in a drugs case was necessary where the defendant claimed to have been set up by the informer and police acting together.

In reaching a decision on whether to allow disclosure, the court can take into account the alleged informer's willingness to be named but this is not conclusive (*Savage v Chief Constable of Hampshire* (1997)).

Here James is claiming that he was framed, not just informed upon and he must put up some evidence to convince the court that it is necessary to name Joan.

James may find some support in the robust approach to PII claims taken in *Rowe and Davis v UK* (2000).

If the prosecution wish to protect their sources in the face of a disclosure order they may apply to stay the proceedings.

Chapter 11

Problem answer

The question is asking you to analyse the arguments for and against the protection of the common law rule on legal professional privilege. You should not consider such a question unless you are familiar with some of the controversial case law such as *ex p B*.

Introduction

Explain the history and general rationale of the principle. You could point that the doctrine has evolved through the common law in response to new situations. It is generally assumed to have its origins in the seventeenth century fight against monarchical absolutism in particular

Outline answers

✳✳✳✳✳✳✳✳✳✳

the use of the inquisitorial Star Chamber. Defendants need protection from the state so that they could prepare their case with their lawyers without fear of state intrusion and therefore get the best advice. The growth of the adversarial system in the eighteenth and nineteenth centuries and the increased use of lawyers gave the doctrine more prominence and this led to the extension of the privilege to litigation. The following are arguments both supportive and critical of the current application of the doctrine.

Arguments in favour of the current approach

- Legal professional privilege is a fundamental right and deserves a very high standard of protection – see *Derby Magistrates Court ex p B* The House of Lords courts held that the privilege was absolute and permanent.

- The current approach is flexible and it is open to a witness to waive the privilege

- The scope of the privilege has been made clearer by statutory intervention as in **PACE s10**

Arguments critical of the current approach

- Changes in the criminal law of evidence have not taken sufficient account of the need to protect the privilege. *R v Bowden* [1999] 1 WLR 823 the accused had no choice but to waive the privilege in order to resist the drawing of inferences of guilt under CJPOA s34.

- Defining some civil trials as inquisitorial e.g. *Re L* is an incoherent way of dealing with the need to make inroads into legal professional privilege to protect vulnerable groups such as children.

- *Ex p B* is a controversial decision and arguably weakened the defence Emson for example (p 365) comments '… there can be little doubt that to deny the accused access

to cogent (and otherwise admissible) evidence of his innocence on the ground that it is privileged material will on occasion result in a violation of **Article 6(1)**…there is nothing in the Strasbourg jurisprudence to suggest that the privilege can be allowed to override all other considerations whatever the circumstances.'

- The concentration on legal professional privilege ignores other areas that may require privilege such as doctor/patient, compare the Canadian system where there is limited privilege for medical/psychiatric details for rape victims. The protection for journalists sources under **PACE** and **Contempt of Court Act 1981** is weak.

Conclusion

There are strong fair trial rights for upholding the privilege but arguably it is now somewhat archaic in the face of development of multi-professional firms. This applies particularly to civil suits. The privilege can be a means of preserving corporate secrecy which may be against the public interest as in the BCCI litigation. Note by contrast the more structured approach of the European Court of Justice in *Kingdom of Sweden v Council of the European Union* (2009), taking into account public interest in disclosure as well as client interest in non-disclosure. A further argument is that public policy such as protection against terrorism may require limiting the privilege, see the recent case *in Re McE* (2009). Tapper (2005, p 184) writes that the privilege 'hardly accords with current espousal of the principle of freedom of information…it is not over cynical to suppose that the privilege is often invoked to keep secret information about the substance of the case which will assist the other party, and to which he is entitled, then to preserve confidence in the advice which has been requested or received.'

Glossary

actus reus the criminal act, contrasted with 'mens rea' the guilty mind

adduce evidence putting evidence before the court either at trial or in preliminary proceedings

advice privilege a sub-species of legal professional privilege which protects from disclosure communications made with the **dominant purpose** of seeking or obtaining legal advice

agent provocateur a person acting for the authorities who sets out to provoke others into committing a crime. The use of an *agent provocateur* may make it unfair to prosecute the crime they have provoked

caution must be given by police before questioning to persons whom there are grounds to suspect of an offence. The current words of the caution, to be found in **PACE Code C para 10(a) 10.5(b)**, 'You do not have to say anything. But it may harm your defence if you do not mention when questioned something which you alter rely on in Court. Anything you do say may be given in evidence.'

civil partner relationship analogous to marriage sanctioned by the state for homosexual partnerships

Civil Procedure Rules body of rules by the governing procedure in civil courts

come up to proof used of a witness whose evidence in court matches what was said before the trial

corroboration is additional evidence or evidence of a different kind that supports a proof already offered in a proceeding

Court of Star Chamber this court sat in Westminster until its abolition in 1641 and became a byword for unfairness and a symbol of royal tyranny. The court sat in secret to try state cases with no indictment or right of appeal

credibility the extent to which an assertion or a witness can be believed

Criminal Procedure Rules body of rules governing procedure in criminal courts

Crown privilege (now called public interest immunity) a claim for exemption from disclosure for government documents

disclosure procedure by which a party to litigation gives lists to the opposing party of relevant documents (including privileged documents) which are or were in his possession

discovery procedure by which non-exempt documents previously disclosed by a party to litigation are handed over to the other side

DNA (deoxyribonucleic acid) unique genetic material found in a person's body cells and secretions

dominant purpose documents qualify for legal professional privilege if made for the main reason of giving legal advice or conducting litigation

double jeopardy the principle that once a verdict has been delivered at a defendant's trial, he cannot be tried again for the same offence. In English law it took the form of a procedural defence of *autrefois acquit* (or *autrefois convict*). The principle has the status of a constitutional right in the United States, but was abolished in England in 2003.

ear-printing finding a match for the impression left by a criminal's ear at the scene of a crime

entrapment a procedure whereby a person may be tricked into committing an offence by undercover actions of a state official or non state actors such as journalists It is not recognised as a specific defence in English law, unlike the position in the United States but abuse of the procedure may require stay of prosecution of exclusion of evidence under **s78 PACE**

equality of arms part of the concept of fair trial under **Art 6 European Convention on Human Rights and Fundamental Freedoms**. Each party must have a reasonable opportunity to put his case under conditions which do not place him at a substantial disadvantage compared with his opponent. Includes the

Glossary

✱✱✱✱✱✱✱✱✱✱

requirement that a party should be able to see all the evidence before the court

ex parte used for hearings in which one side appears without notice to the other

exculpatory statement a statement tending to exonerate its maker

facial mapping a technique for matching a suspect or the image of a suspect with a photograph or video image

fact-finder/trier of fact a jury is often referred to loosely as the trier of fact on the basis that the judge decides issues of law and leaves determination of the facts to the jury. A judge or tribunal without a jury acts as fact-finder as well as deciding issues of law.

gravamen of an offence the weighty or serious part of an offence

hostile witness a witness is presumed hostile if he testifies for the opposing party. A party can have one of his own witnesses declared hostile if the witness's evidence turns out to be openly antagonistic or clearly prejudicial. The witness can then be asked leading questions

identification parades (including video) procedure by which a witness chooses from among a number of similar-looking persons, one of whom is the suspect, regulated by PACE Code D

inculpatory statement a statement tending to incriminate its maker

interlocutory appeal an appeal on some point arising before the final determination of the issues at trial. An appeal against the judgment is called a final appeal

litigation privilege a sub-species of legal professional privilege which protects from disclosure communications made with the dominant purpose of use in litigation

mens rea (Latin for 'guilty mind') the state of mind required to commit an offence. Contrasts with the criminal act ('*actus reus*' in Latin). The general principle is that the act does not make a person guilty unless the mind is also guilty

mischief rule a rule of statutory construction requiring the court to interpret a statutory provision by reference to the wrong which the statute was intended to put right

peculiar knowledge by its nature is only available to the individual concerned. A party relying on peculiar knowledge may be put to proof of the fact concerned

principle of orality refers to the oral examination of witnesses as a fundamental feature of the trial in English law. Oral evidence contrasts with evidence given on affidavit

propensity evidence is that which shows a pattern of prior criminal behaviour by the defendant or suspect

proscribed organisations under the Terrorism Act 2000, are officially designated by the authorities as terrorist organisations, making membership or financial support of the proscribed organisation a criminal offence

psychological profiling a method of predicting the psychological make-up of the perpetrator on the basis of the nature of a crime

res gestae a common law exception to the rule against hearsay, making a statement admissible as evidence of any matter stated, if its maker was so emotionally overpowered by an event that the possibility of concoction or distortion can be disregarded

res ipsa loquitur (Latin 'the matter speaks for itself') a plea in the law of negligence signifying that further details are unnecessary, the negligence is self-evident on the facts. The classic case is the scalpel left inside the patient after surgery.

reverse burdens (of proof) the normal rule for allocating the burden of proof is that 'he who asserts must prove'. Where there is a reverse burden the party against whom a fact is asserted must disprove it, which in criminal cases detracts from the presumption of innocence since it places the burden of proof on the defendant right to confrontation the right of a defendant to see, hear, and question his accuser in person

similar fact a rather misleadingly named principle that evidence of the accused's past misconduct may be admissible as evidence of guilt, since the similarity between the earlier behaviour and the current charge if the prosecution is so similar, it is unlikely to be a coincidence. Previously a common law rule now covered by CJA 2003

special advocates appointed by the government and given security clearance to represent the interests of suspects and defendants who cannot be allowed to see the evidence themselves. Primarily but not exclusively used in terrorism cases. The advocate may not reveal to the suspect sensitive materials he has seen

stay of proceedings an order of the court which has the effect of preventing any further moves in the case either indefinitely or for a fixed period

sunset clause a term in a statute which has the effect of of repealing a provision after a certain time unless additional specific legislation extends it

sworn evidence evidence given on oath

third party to a trial used loosely to describe parties who are not directly involved in the primary dispute between defence and prosecution in criminal cases or claimant and defendant in civil suits

voir dire a 'trial with the trial' to determine, for example, the admissibility of evidence or the defendant's fitness to plead. Also describes the process of selecting a jury, especially in the United States

Wednesbury **unreasonableness** conduct so unreasonable that no reasonable person (or body) could do it, after the public law case *Associated Provincial Picture Houses Ltd v Wednesbury Corpn* [1948]

Table of cases

Table of cases

✳✳✳✳✳✳✳✳✳✳

Table of cases

✱✱✱✱✱✱✱✱✱✱✱

Table of statutes

Table of statutes

****

Table of statutes

✳✳✳✳✳✳✳✳✳✳

Table of secondary legislation and codes

Index

Index

****

Index

✻✻✻✻✻✻✻✻✻✻